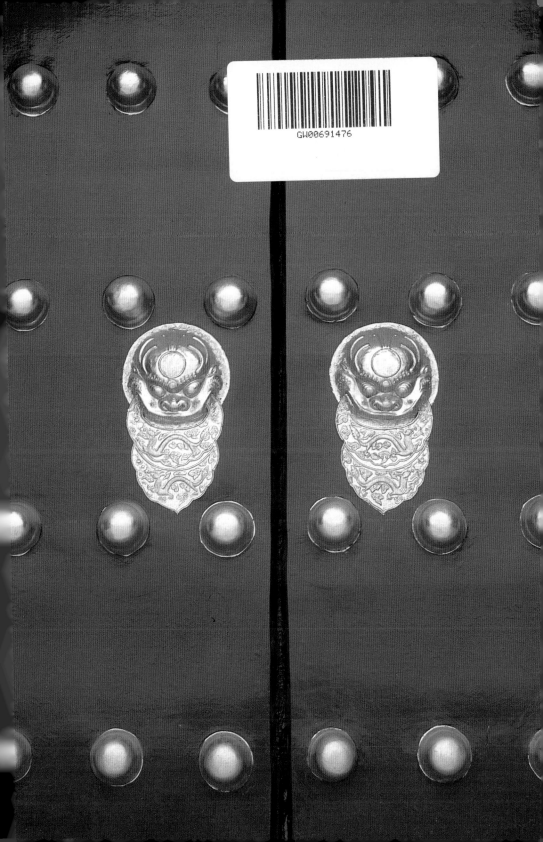

INSIGHT GUIDES

The world's largest collection of visual travel guides

BEIJING

Executive Editor: Scott Rutherford

Editorial Director: Brian Bell

APA PUBLICATIONS

Part of the Langenscheidt Publishing Group

INSIGHT GUIDES
Beijing

CONTACTING THE EDITORS: Although every effort is made to provide accurate information in this publication, we live in a fast-changing world and would appreciate it if readers would call our attention to any errors or outdated information that may occur by writing to us at Apa Publications,
P.O. Box 7910, London SE1 8ZB, England.
Fax: (44) 171-620-1074.
e-mail: insight@apaguide.demon.co.uk.

First Edition 1990
Third Edition (updated) 1999

Distributed in the United States by
Langenscheidt Publishers Inc.
46–35 54th Road
Maspeth
NY 11378
Fax: (718) 784 0640

Distributed in the UK & Ireland by
GeoCenter International Ltd
The Viables Centre, Harrow Way
Basingstoke, Hampshire RG22 4BJ
Fax: (44) 1256-817988

Worldwide distribution enquiries:
APA Publications GmbH & Co. Verlag KG
(Singapore branch)
38 Joo Koon Road
Singapore 628990
Tel: 65-8651600
Fax: 65-8616438

Printed in Singapore by
Insight Print Services (Pte) Ltd
38 Joo Koon Road
Singapore 628990
Fax: 65-8616438

DISCOVERY CHANNEL®

This guidebook combines the interests and enthusiasms of two of the world's best-known information providers: Insight Guides, whose range of titles has set the standard for visual travel guides since 1970, and Discovery Channel, the world's premier source of nonfiction television programming.

The editors of Insight Guides provide both practical advice and general understanding about a destination's history, culture, institutions and people. Discovery Channel and its Web site, www.discovery.com, help millions of viewers explore their world from the comfort of their own home and also encourage them to explore it first-hand.

Morgenstern

The first edition of this book was completed at a turbulent and momentous time in China, when millions of people in Beijing were protesting against the political leadership of the country. Martial law had been declared and thousands of students were on a hunger strike in Tiananmen Square, the Square of Heavenly Peace. Those were dramatic times in the Chinese metropolis, harbingers of tragedy and social upheaval. While the memory of 1989 is still strong, inside and outside of the country, China has nevertheless plowed ahead towards the 21st century, taking its ancient capital of Beijing along with it.

Forster-Latsch

The project editor for the first edition of *Insight Guide: Beijing* was **Manfred Morgenstern**, who fell in love with China during his student years, when he made his first trip that was funded with money earned from holiday jobs. That trip was in 1977, only a short while after the death of the China's Great Chairman and Helmsman, Mao Zedong. Later, he made several trips a year to Beijing as manager of a travel company, tour guide and travel journalist. During his early years in Beijing, he and friends would meet in the lobby of the Hotel Beijing, or in the summer, on the roof terrace of the Friendship Hotel, and exchange information and have discussions while drinking Chinese beer

Pansegrau

Beppler-Lie

Sparling

and Maotai until the lights went out – often much too early, thought many.

One of those in the gatherings was **Helmut Forster-Latsch**. As a Sinologist who spoke Chinese, Forster-Latsch had spent several years in China working as a translator and consultant to Chinese publishers and editors. He is the author of a number of studies on the Chinese economic system, and has also translated numerous Chinese fairy tales and modern literature.

He met his wife **Marie-Luise Forster-Latsch**, an ethnologist and Sinologist working in Beijing, whose special interest is the non-Chinese peoples in China. She contributed to several essays in this book, particularly to the colourful descriptions of Beijing opera.

Marie-Luise Beppler-Lie also decided to spend some time in China after her studies. She taught German to Chinese students from 1979 to 1982 at the Foreign Language Institute in Chongqing, while working to improve her Chinese. Her hobby, well-nurtured during her years in China, is Chinese cooking.

Elke Wandel, who studied English, political sciences and theology, went from Berlin to Taiwan in 1978 as a teacher. Wandel had a desire to study the Chinese way of life. It was this that took her all around Asia, and she was particularly fascinated by her experiences in China, and by the Chinese culture. She later taught at the Foreign Language Institute in Beijing.

Jochen Noth considers Beijing as his second home. He began work in 1979 as a translator for the German language broadcasts of Radio Beijing and later lectured at the Beijing Foreign Language Institute. He then returned to Germany to become a consultant for German businesses trading with China.

Work has taken **Klaus Bodenstein** to Beijing on and off since 1980, and he has been living there since 1985. He married a Chinese and spends half of every year in "Old Beijing". While not a native Chinese, he is certainly privy to the customs and traditions of a fascinating part of Beijing.

More so than most other countries, China – and Beijing – have changed rapidly in the past decade. The Beijing of the first edition is no longer the city of today. Updating the previous edition was **Ron Sparling**, a freelance writer in Beijing. This edition was updated by Beijing-based **Bill Smith**.

T he photographers make an important contribution to the success of each Apa guide. **Erhard Pansegrau** was no doubt right in giving up his profession as an electronic engineer decades ago so that he could explore the world with the camera. He went on his first big photographic safari in 1976, travelling in a minibus to India.

Bodo Bondzio also discovered the camera at a late stage. His earlier profession was that of a typesetter. He first visited China in 1981, and he has made numerous trips there since. **Kosima Weber-Liu** is a Sinologist who went to Beijing for an intensive study course and enrolled at the Central Academy of Arts. Since 1983, she has been living there with her husband, a television producer. She has spent her free time wandering through the hidden alleys of Beijing with her camera.

Pictures in *Insight Guide: Beijing* have also been supplied by Photobank in Singapore, Manfred Morgenstern, Elke Wandel, Colosio, Ulrich Menzel and Peter Schneckmann. The publisher is also grateful to all those German and Chinese friends not mentioned but who contributed to the success of this book with suggestions and support.

CONTENTS

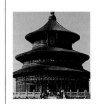

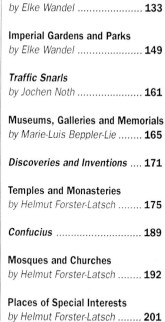

TRAVEL TIPS

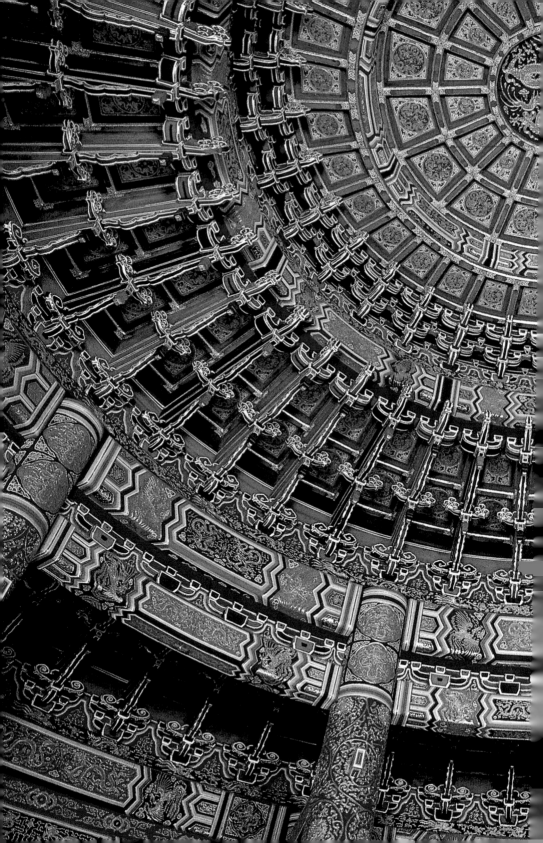

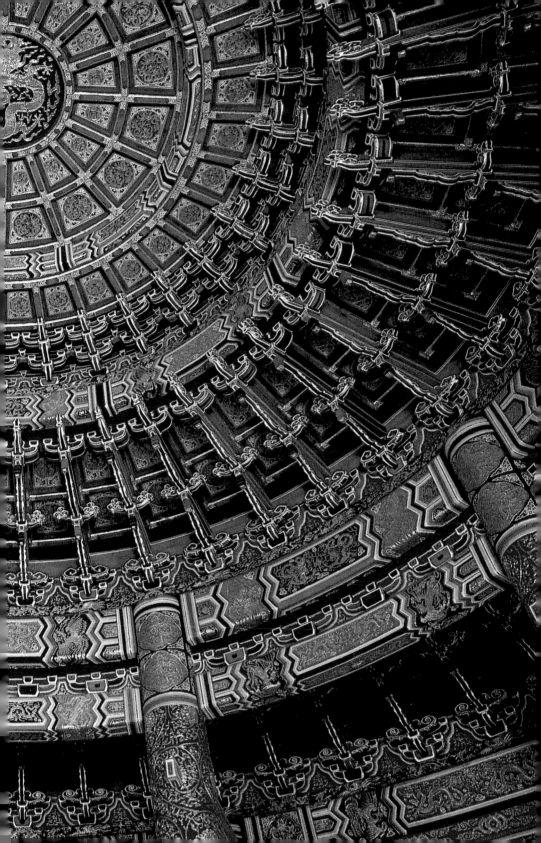

INTRODUCTION

Beijing is, of course, the capital of the People's Republic of China, a relatively young political entity with the foundations of the world's oldest and most continuous civilization.

For 1,100 years, Xi'an and Luoyang were the capitals of the great dynasties, and it wasn't until the arrival of "barbarians" from the north – the Khitan, the Nüzhen, and finally the Mongols – that Beijing was made capital of an empire. Then, from the early 15th century onward, the Chinese Ming emperors and the Manchu emperors of the Qing dynasty lived without interruption in the Forbidden City, in the heart of Beijing.

Early this century, Beijing missed out on the beginnings of the modern age and the transition from the agrarian to the industrial period. The heartbeat of that shifting age was already being felt in Shanghai and Guangzhou (Canton), however, while in Beijing, despite the fall of the emperor, residue of the court continued to define life.

Beijing entered the modern era, finally, on 1 October 1949, when Mao Zedong proclaimed from Tiananmen, the Gate of Heavenly Peace, "China has arisen!" This proclamation symbolized Beijing's moment to shake off the image of feudalism. In the following years of the 1950s, the area just to the south of the Imperial Palace was built up in a monumental attempt – literally – to make socialism manifest through architecture in public buildings.

More recently, Beijing has slowly been setting out on a long march towards a market economy. Although the coastal provinces in the south remain far ahead in economic daring and prosperity, skyscrapers nevertheless are rising into the Beijing sky, and wide ring roads, which meet in monstrous and tangled intersections, mark new boundary lines between the city's expanding districts.

In the midst of modernisation, however, Beijing's ancient city and its significance give the capital a rock-solid – if not celestial – foundation. Old manuscripts show that the city was divided into grid-like sections in such a way that it reflected the harmony of the universe. Walls were the modules of this cosmic order. The empire had long retreated behind the safety of the Great Wall just to the north, while the city itself was protected by massive walls with mighty gate structures that faced the four points of the compass. (None of this, however, did much to block the vicious winters that slipped down from the steppes.) The emperor himself was surrounded by palace walls, and even his subjects hid their daily lives behind the walls of courtyard houses in the *hutong*, the little alleys of the old city.

Visitors to the Temple of Heaven, standing at the Altar of Heaven, will see a round wall covered with blue-glazed tiles, and beyond it, a second square wall. In Chinese cosmology, Heaven is seen as round while Earth is square. Heaven covers the Middle Kingdom

Preceding pages: evening light over the Summer Palace; lofty woodwork in Tiantan, the Temple of Heaven; Beijing centre; schoolchildren on an outing. **Left**, Beijing's people have shed both the emperor's and the revolution's old clothes.

and grants its favour to the Sons of Heaven, the Chinese emperors. The barbarian people, mostly to the north, lived in the dark corners of the Earth, where they apparently thrived and belonged, at least until they started descending upon the Middle Kingdom.

Another element has also contributed to the structure of the city. The strict orientation of the central buildings on a north–south line goes back to the traditional concept of *yin* and *yang*. According to this ideology, *yin*, which represents the north – night, danger, evil, death, coldness and hardness – symbolises the barbarians of the north. Therefore, all buildings open towards the south and the sun. There *yang* rules, providing day, life and warmth. This main axis, which slices through today's Temple of Heaven, Qianmen, Tiananmen Square, the Imperial Palace and right up to the Bell and Drum Towers in the north, is still known by its old name, Hatamen Street. At one time, it was the centre of city life.

Today's Beijing has shifted, however, to a new urban axis: Chang'an Boulevard, the Street of Eternal Peace. Stretching for 40 kilometres (25 mi) from east to west and dividing the city into northern and southern hemispheres, this impressive roadway may be seen as a symbol of China's development. The sun's circle of amber flame – rising above its eastern end, passing high over the old Hatamen Boulevard, and finally sinking behind the hills far past the west end of Chang'an Boulevard – is emblematic of China's movement towards greater interaction (frequently rocky and tumultuous) with the West, and its increasingly active role in the complex sphere of world politics.

Many old structures that were witness to imperial times – gate arches, or *pailou*, erected in all the major streets – have had to make way for the modernisation of Beijing. Innumerable old temples lie in ruins today, diminished by Red Guards in the 1970s, or now used for irreverent purposes. Whole city districts have been demolished, including that part of the city that comprises the enormous Square of Heavenly Peace, Tiananmen. The city wall that ran along what is now the second ring road, passing the Yonghegong Lama Temple in an easterly direction and continuing up to the foreign diplomatic quarter, has been demolished. Camel caravans – which came from out of the desert right up to the walls of the Imperial Palace as late as the 1940s – are over. The rickshaw coolies who once filled the streets have also disappeared.

No-one knows if it will be possible for city planners to save parts of the old city. It is certainly hard to believe when watching the skyscrapers shoot out of the ground like sun-crazed mushrooms. However, in all this nostalgia, we shouldn't forget the fact that the people of Beijing prefer high-rise apartments to their old housing. As is so often the case, those who are directly affected view as backward what outsiders perceive as idyllic.

In any case, Beijing still casts a spell over visitors, who can't help but notice that there is something decidedly special about this city. This is the Beijing, as the German architect Ernst Boerschmann described in 1931, that was, and is, a "crucial place for Chinese history and development."

Flags in front of the Great Hall of the People.

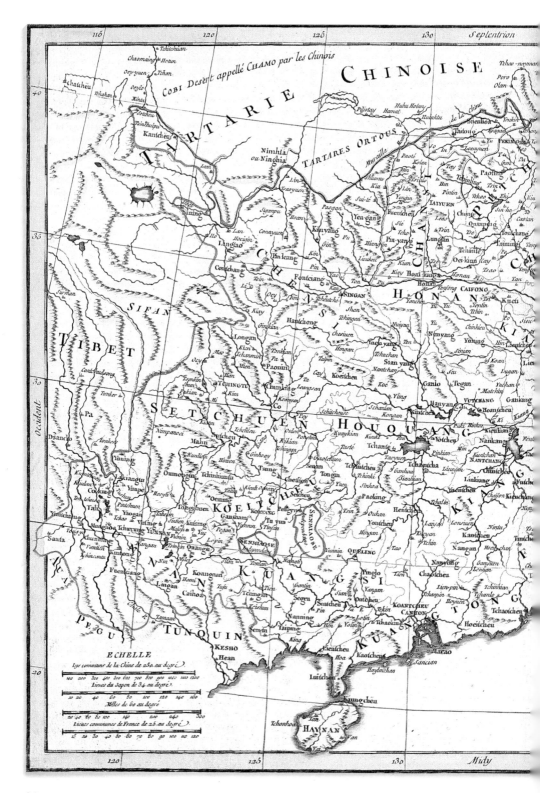

24

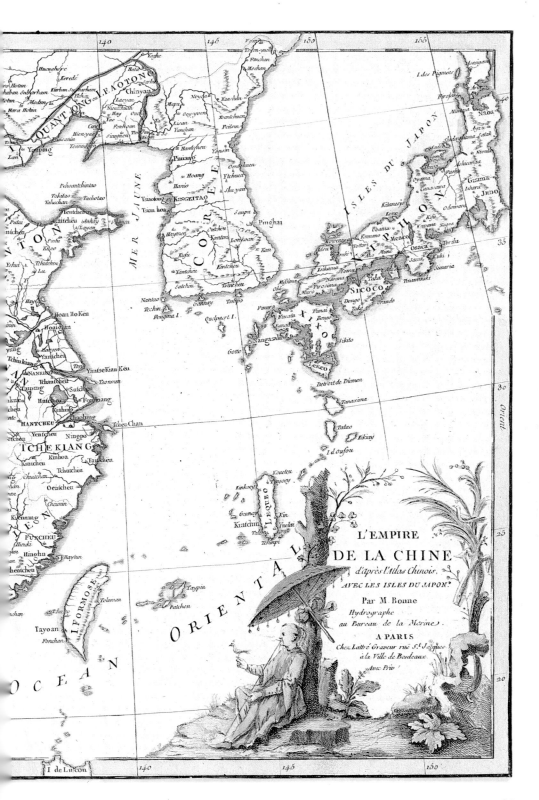

The geographical position of Beijing has been one of the leading causes of the city's eventful history. Lying at the edge of the empire – where the very different cultures of the settled Chinese farmers and the nomads of the northern steppes collided – the city became the prey of each victorious faction in turn, a fact reflected by the many changes to its name throughout the centuries.

The Khitan, who founded the Liao dynasty and only ruled the north of the empire, called their capital Nanjing, which means Southern Capital. The Nüzhen, who succeeded the Khitan, had a different geographic perception and renamed the city Zhongdu, the Central Capital. The Mongols, not a modest people, called the residence of their Great Khan, Dadu, or the Great Capital. The subsequent dynasties knew the city as Beijing, which means the Northern Capital, except for those periods when it was renamed Beiping, Northern Peace.

However, long before the city had a name or was recorded in history, it already had a long-reaching past. Evidence of human settlement goes back half a million years or so with the discovery of the remains of Peking Man (*Sinanthropus pekinensis*). This find in Zhoukoudian, 50 kilometres (30 mi) southwest of Beijing, revealed that the Peking Man belonged to a people who walked upright and were already using stone tools, and who knew how to light fires. Yet Peking Man marks a point when there is a break in developments, and little is known from then on until about 5,000 years ago.

Around 3000 BC, neolithic villages had already been established in the area of modern Beijing, inhabited by people familiar with agriculture and the domestication of animals. There is, to this day, dispute as to the existence of the first dynasty recorded in Chinese historical writings, the Xia dynasty (21st to 16th centuries BC). The dynasty's legendary Yellow Emperor Huangdi (who allegedly ruled between 2490 and 2413 BC)

Preceding pages: silk painting of Ming emperor's procession; map of the ancient Chinese empire. Left, the Emperor Kangxi at his calligraphy. Right, the imperial bodyguard at guard.

is supposed to have fought battles against the tribal leader Chiyo here, in the "Wilderness of the Prefecture of Zhou." It is presumed that Zhuluo, a town to the west of Beijing, was the earliest urban settlement in this area. It was here that Huangdi's successor, Yao, is said to have founded a legendary capital named Youdou, City of Calm.

Throughout Beijing's prehistory, the hills to the north, northeast and northwest served as a natural frontier for the people who settled here and who traded with the nomadic

tribes living beyond the passes of Gubeikou and Naku. These northern hill tribes also had close ties with the people who occupied the Central Plain, which stretched along the Yellow River.

The important role of trading post played by the city for the different regions promoted its rise as the ancient city of Ji. During the period of Imperial Conflict (415–221 BC), the count of the state of Yan annexed this area and made Ji his central city. In those times, the city lay to the north of Guang'anmen Gate near the Baiyuanguan (White Cloud Temple).

In the 3rd century BC, the first emperor of

the Qin dynasty and of China, Qin Shi Huangdi, made the city an administrative centre of the Guangyang Command, one of 36 prefectures of the unified, centrally-organised feudal empire. Thus, the historically documented city of Ji was established. Ji remained a strategically important trade and military centre for about 1,000 years, until the end of the Tang dynasty (AD 618–907). During this time, the city was often the subject of war and conflict.

Beijing, the Imperial City: Beijing became the residence of the Chinese emperors, who ruled over the Middle Kingdom with the Mandate of Heaven, in the 11th century – about the same time that the Normans conquered England.

Beijing's rise as the dominant city and centre of the Chinese empire is due, indirectly, to the work of nomadic tribes, including that of foreign barbarians. At the beginning of the Tang dynasty, Ji was not that different from the other great cities of feudal China. Towards the end of the dynasty, in the 10th century, the city became the second capital of the Khitan. By then, the Great Wall had for a time lost its protective function. In the year 936, the Khitan made Ji their southern capital, now renamed Nanjing, also known as Yanjing. As the southern centre of the nomad empire, this area became a point of support and departure for many expeditions of non-Chinese peoples – Khitan, Nüzhen and Mongols – on their way to the south and the Central Plain.

In relation to today's Beijing, Yanjing lay roughly in the western part of the modern capital. The temple of Fayuansi was in the southeastern corner of the old walls, the Imperial Palace lay to the southwest and the markets were in the northeast corner. Each of the city's four quarters was surrounded by massive walls.

In the early part of the 12th century, the Nüzhen vanquished the Liao dynasty and replaced it with the Jin dynasty. In 1153, they moved their capital from Huiningfu (in the modern province of Liaoning) to Yanjing, and renamed it Zhongdu, Central Capital. New buildings began cropping up in the city, and the Jin moved the centre of their capital – the Imperial Palace – into the area to the south of today's Guang'an Gate. The ground plan of the city remained square, with three gates on each side. In 1215, Mongol cavalry occupied Zhongdu and the city was completely destroyed by fire.

The Great Khan's capital: It was not until 1279 that Kublai Khan – after giving the dynasty the name of Yuan – made Yanjing his capital. He completely rebuilt the city and gave it the Chinese name of Dadu, meaning Great Capital. In the west, it was mostly known by its Mongol name, Khanbaliq or Khambaluk. In the 14th century, Marco Polo waxed enthusiastic about this city of the Great Khan in his journals:

"There are in Khanbaliq unbelievable numbers of people and houses, it is impossible to count them. The houses and villas outside the walls are at least as beautiful as those

within, except, of course, for the imperial buildings. And take note of this: if anyone dies in the city, he may not be buried there… And another thing: no wanton women may live in the city, none who take money for their services. Therefore they live in the suburbs, and indeed in incredible numbers. There are at least twenty thousand women of pleasure and all of them find custom, for daily, countless traders and strangers come. You may work out the size of the city's population from the number of women who sell themselves… Nowhere in the world are such rare and precious goods traded as in Khanbaliq. I will name some of them for you. The most costly things come from India, jewels, pearls and other precious items... Just imagine, every day more than a thousand wagons arrive, fully laden with silk. In these regions cloth is woven of gold and silk. The city draws in wealth from some two hundred towns. From them, people travel to the capital, bringing their wares with them and buying such things as they need themselves," wrote Polo.

The Italian explorer was even more enthusiastic about the grandiose Imperial Palace, the centre of the city, built under the rule of the Great Kublai Khan:

"You must know that this is the greatest palace ever built... The hall of the palace is

In the south, Dadu reached the line of today's Chang'an Boulevard, with the observatory marking the southern corner. In the north, it reached as far as the present Yonghegong Lama Temple, at that time the site of the trade quarters by the bell and drum towers. In 1293, the Tonghua Canal was completed, linking the capital with the Grand Canal and making it possible to bring grain from the south into the city by boat. The circumference of Dadu was, at that time, some 20 kilometres (12 mi). The city population was about 500,000 inhabitants.

Chinese conquest: Beijing's role as capital city continued during the Ming and Qing dynasties. With the conquest of Mongol Dadu

so big that 6,000 people could easily eat therein, and it is truly a wonder how many rooms there are besides. The building is altogether so wide-spreading, so rich, so beautiful that no man on earth could think of anything to outshine it."

The building of Dadu lasted until 1293 while Kublai Khan ruled the empire. The centre of the city at that time was moved to the vicinity of the northeast lakes. The Imperial Palace stood in what is now Beihai Park.

Left, old painting of imperial court ladies-in-waiting. <u>Above</u>, an early view of the Imperial Palace.

by Ming troops in 1368, Beijing became Chinese once more and was renamed Beiping (Northern Peace). Zhu Yuanzhang, founder of the Ming dynasty, at first made the more modern Nanjing his capital and gave Beiping to one of his sons as a fief. When the latter succeeded to the throne in 1403, taking the ruling name of Yongle, he had the country's capital moved back to Beijing.

At first the city was made smaller. The outer city wall was demolished and rebuilt more towards the south, between today's Desheng Gate and Anding Gate. One can still see remains of the demolished northern wall of Dadu outside the Deshengmen. It is known as the Earth Wall by the people of Beijing, since only a broken row of hillocks remains nowadays.

During the period 1406 to 1420, the new Beijing was built, with the Imperial Palace that still exists today as its centre. Most of the Beijing that we see in the Inner City dates back to the Ming dynasty. Like Kublai Khan, the Ming emperors followed the square pattern dictated by the old rules. The main axis ran southwards and the city was completely enclosed by walls with three gates on each side. The ground plan resembled a chessboard, with a network of north–south and east–west streets, with the Imperial Palace nestled in the centre. The Palace stood, sur-

Yongle's decision was, in all probability, an expression of his drive for expansion. Under his rule, the imperial boundaries were pushed as far as the river Amur, and Beijing took on strategic importance for establishing control of eastern Mongolia and the northeastern territories. Moving the capital to the edge of the steppe zone could also be viewed as a sign that the Ming dynasty planned to restore the pre-eminence of the Chinese empire in Asia, the foundations of which had been laid by the Mongols.

This ambition later became the hallmark of the entire Qing dynasty. In 1644, Li Zicheng led a peasants' revolt, conquered the city of Beijing and felled the Ming dynas-

rounded by a red wall in the heart of the city, and to the south of it, starting from today's Qianmen, the Chinese Town was built.

The decision of the Ming emperor Yongle to retain Beijing as capital may seem surprising, as the position of Beijing was not central, and the climatic influence of the steppe was always strongly felt. This position on the borders also brought with it the permanent danger of attack by the Mongols or other nomadic tribes (which did indeed follow in the 16th and 17th centuries). Beijing had become a capital in 1271 under the Mongols, and now, for the first time, it was the capital of a dynasty of Chinese origin.

ty. But a mere 43 days later, Manchu troops marched into Beijing, making it their capital.

The Manchu rulers: The Manchu did not change the orientation of the city. They declared the northern part of the city, also known as the Tatar City, their domain, in which only Manchu could live, while the south was designated as the Chinese City. They left their mark on the architecture of the Imperial Palace, but did not change the basic structure. Outside the city walls, palaces and temples were built – Yuanmingyuan, the Old Summer Palace, to the northwest and, at the end of the 19th century, Yiheyuan, the New Summer Palace.

Around the year 1800, at the time when the Qing empire had reached its greatest power, Beijing had a population of 700,000. A Portuguese priest, Gabriel de Magaillans, described the city during the early years of Emperor Kangxi's rule:

"The city Pe Kim lies on a plain. It forms a great square, and each side measures twelve Chinese stadia... This city is now inhabited by Tatars and their troops divided under eight banners. Under the previous dynasty the people had increased so much that there was no more space in the city and the nine suburbs outside its gates, and so a new city, also square in form, has been built with each side measuring six Chinese stadia, the northern side adjoining the southern side of the old city. The new city has seven gates with seven suburbs, of which the west-facing ones are the most extensive, as travellers by land arrive on this side.

"Both cities are each divided into five quarters. The main streets run sometimes north to south, sometimes east to west. They are all as long, broad and straight as it is possible to be, having been laid out by design and not by accident, as is the case with European roads. The little streets all run from east to west and divide the space between the main roads into islands of equal size. They all have their names.

"There is a book that can be bought that deals only with the names and the situation of the streets and that the servants of the mandarins use when they accompany their masters on visits or on the way to the tribunal or to deliver gifts. The most beautiful street is called Cham gan kiai (Chang'an Boulevard), which is 'Street of Eternal Peace.' It runs from east to west, with the wall of the Imperial Palace to the north, and on its southern side there are various state buildings and the houses of great persons. The buildings are all low, in honour of the palace of the emperor. There are some high and splendid buildings of the great lords, but these lie within. From the outside, only the great gate and to either side the low houses of servants, workers and traders with their shops can be seen. This has the advantage that right at one's front door one can buy all the necessi-

Left, Kublai Khan, and the Ming emperors: Hongwu and Wanli. <u>Above</u>, Johann Adam Schall von Bell.

ties of life. The crowds of people on the streets of the new and of the old city are very great, as is only seen in our cities at market times or during processions."

During the long rule of the Manchu Qing dynasty, the last imperial dynasty, foreigners came to Beijing and settled in the city. In 1601, the Italian Jesuit Matteo Ricci arrived, followed in 1622 by Johann Adam Schall von Bell (1592–1666), who in 1650 received permission to build the first Catholic church in Beijing, the Nantang, or South Church. The dialogue with China begun by the Jesuit missionaries continued throughout the rule of the first two Qing emperors. The missionaries tried to win over the Chinese upper

classes and the imperial court by adapting Christian teaching to Confucian philosophy. They quickly won influence at court because of their excellent astronomical and scientific knowledge. In their reports home, the missionaries supplied Europe with much information about China. By the early 19th century, a small foreign community had already established itself.

Fall from glory: Signs of the decay of the ruling Manchu dynasty became evident during the early 19th century. Revolts increased and secret societies sprang up everywhere, rapidly gaining influence. Xenophobia grew. The first persecutions of Jesuits and the destruction of churches took place. The emperor Qianlong, still self-confident, may have told the ambassador of the British queen that the Middle Kingdom had no need of "barbarian" products, for the Middle Kingdom produced all that it required. And yet, the time of humiliation for Beijing and for all of China was just around the corner, with the advance of foreign colonial powers from the time of the First Opium War (1840–1842) onwards.

By the end of the Second Opium War (1858–1860), the emperor was forced to flee from Western troops, who completely destroyed part of the city, including the Old Summer Palace (the ruins can still be seen today), and plundered Beijing's treasuries.

Just after the First Opium War, the emperor had to make concessions to the foreign powers. Extra territorial areas were granted and the diplomatic quarter in the southeast part of the imperial city was put at the disposal of the foreigners.

Many Chinese, however, were unwilling to accept this humiliation. The hostile attitude towards the foreigners, called "long noses," increased. The Boxer Rebellion in 1900 made the situation even more acute. A moderate programme of reforms, supported by the young but powerless Emperor Guangxu, failed due to the opposition of the imperial court. Extremist groups were

strengthened by the failure. Slogans such as "Drive the barbarians from our country!" were to be heard everywhere.

Two years later, followers of a secret society named Society for Peace and Justice, known in the West as the Boxers, rebelled. For two months, partly supported by imperial troops, they besieged the foreign embassies. Western countries quickly sent forces to Beijing. The real ruler, the Empress Dowager Cixi, fled to Xi'an and the Boxer Rebellion was crushed. A foreign newspaper based in Beijing reported: "The capital of the emperors was partly destroyed, partly burned down. All that was left was a dead city. The streets were choked with the bodies of Chinese, many charred or eaten by stray dogs."

Once again, the increasingly weak Manchu regime had to pay great sums in reparations, while the foreigners received further privileges. As Beijing continued to decay, the imperial court carried on in the same old way, cut off from reality, but also blind to it, bound up as it was in luxury, corruption and intrigue. Neither the Empress Dowager Longyü, nor Prince Chun, regent and father of the child Emperor Puyi, were strong enough to resurrect the shaky throne.

In October of 1910, an advisory council met for the first time in Beijing. By then the middle-class Xinhai revolution, led by Sun Yat-sen, had become a real threat to the Manchu imperial house. The prince regent recalled the Imperial Marshal, Yuan Shikai, the strong man of Cixi, dismissed earlier in 1909. He was appointed supreme commander and head of the government. However, Yuan Shikai wanted to prepare a change of dynasty in the traditional style. He avoided confrontation with the republican forces in the south, elected himself president of the National Assembly in November 1911, and the next month forced the Empress Dowager Cixi and the child Emperor Puyi to abdicate, effectively sealing the fate of the Manchu Qing dynasty.

The long rule of the Sons of Heaven was ended. Chinese men could finally cut off their hated pigtails – the external symbol of servitude imposed by the Manchu. However, the city continued to decay and social problems became more acute.

Above, child emperor Puyi. Right, German troops fight Chinese troops.

The abdication document of Emperor Puyi says: "Yuan Shikai, who some time ago was elected President of the National Assembly in Beijing, now has the opportunity to unite the north and the south. Let him therefore receive all necessary powers to accomplish this and to form a provisional government. Let this be done with the agreement of the representatives of the People's Army, so that peace may be kept and the five races of Chinese, Manchu, Mongols, Muslims and Tibetans may make up one single great state with the name Republic of China."

War and misery: Peace, however, was not something the next few decades was to enjoy. First of all, Yuan Shikai's attempt to defeat the Republicans – who had organised themselves as the Guomindang, the National People's Party, led by Dr Sun Yat-sen – failed. He died in 1916. The dynasty was overthrown, but the social and political problems remained unsolved. Beijing stagnated in a half-feudal state. The Gate of Heavenly Peace, Tiananmen, crumbled and foreigners tied their horses to it; the Gold Water River in front of the Imperial Palace stank because of the build-up of mud and silt; and the square in front of Tiananmen was taken over by food stalls, fortune tellers and boxers.

Instead of unity and peace, China experienced division and battles between the warlords who engaged in rival struggles for the rule of China. The north and Beijing, which remained the nominal capital of the republic after 1911, were affected particularly adversely by these battles. The era of the warlords, which lasted until about 1930, made social and political problems more acute. The misery of the poor was indescribable, further compounded by threats from foreign powers greedy for power and profit in China.

The foreigners brought new ideas into the country, but they also provoked opposition. More than 300,000 young Chinese, mostly students and intellectuals, came together on 4 May 1919 to demand national independ-

ence and territorial integrity, in a demonstration that was noted throughout China. In the Treaty of Versailles of 1919, the former German concessions – Kiautschou, modern Qingdao and the Jiaozhou Bay – were not returned to China but given to Japan. This deeply wounded the national feelings of the young, self-confident Chinese. A manifesto passed at the demonstration ended with the words: "China's territory may be conquered, but it cannot be given to foreign powers. The Chinese people may be slaughtered, but they

will not surrender. Our country is in the process of being destroyed. Brothers, defend yourselves against this!"

As a result of this May Fourth Movement – considered a turning point in modern Chinese history – the Chinese workers' movement grew. Trade unions and the Communist Party came into existence, the latter soon becoming active even in Beijing. At that time, the Party's future leader, Mao Zedong, was a librarian at the University of Beijing, or Beida as it is commonly known. In the 1920s, Guomindang and Chinese Communist Party forces still fought side by side against the warlords in the north. After the

Preceding pages: the Cultural Revolution announces that "the whole country is red". **Left,** peanut seller, old Beijing. **Right,** Dr Sun Yat-sen, the "father" of the Republic.

right wing of the Guomindang had gained the upper hand in 1928, the Communist Party of China was proscribed and Chiang Kai-shek moved his capital to Nanjing.

Beijing of the 1920s was a vibrant city, with a street life of shops, fortune tellers, opera troupes, sing-song girls, foreign businessmen and adventurers. Richard Wilhelm, an expert on China, wrote in 1928:

"For centuries nearly everything was permitted in the streets. You could pour out your dirty wash water, throw away scraps, dogs and cats were allowed to die if there was nothing else for them to do – in short, the street generously took in everything and covered anything unpleasant with its dust…

iang, the rickshaw coolies took to the streets and demonstrated against the new trams that threatened their livelihood. The modern world, though belated, now moved into Beijing. The network of streets was extended, water pipes were laid, hospitals were established and banks opened branches.

The following years, however, were overshadowed by the threat of the Japanese. Already, in 1931, Japan had occupied Manchuria in the northeast of China. In 1935, huge anti-Japanese demonstrations marched through the streets of Beijing. The Guomindang, responding to pressure from the populace, had to make a new alliance with the Communists, this time to fight against Japan.

Of course there are many sick people in Peking, and many die…

"Peking is a city of mysterious freedom. People come and go, and everyone finds a circle of friends who can offer him what he wants. Every person who lives here finds space for whatever work he wants to do. The breeze that blows through Peking is good and free. You can be an eccentric or a sociable person, you can seek to drown your sorrows in the wine of life or you can strive for immortality through ascetic rigour."

In 1928, four years after the "Last Emperor" had finally left the Imperial Palace on the orders of the "Christian" warlord, Feng Yux-

A confrontation choreographed by the Japanese in 1937 on the Marco Polo Bridge, near Beijing, served the Japanese as a pretext for occupying Beijing and then all of China.

Life became worse for the people of Beijing during World War II, a time when the foreigners remained neutral and the Japanese secret police controlled everything. Towards the end of World War II, Communist guerrillas were operating in the hills around Beijing. At first, the Guomindang took control once more after the Japanese surrender, this time supported by the Americans. However, Chiang Kai-shek's Guomindang lost the four-year civil war against the People's Liberation Army, due largely to their inability to solve the pressing problems of hunger, inflation, unemployment and the capricious exercise of power.

Socialist capital: On 31 January 1949, Beijing was taken without a struggle. On 1 October, Mao Zedong proclaimed the foundation of the People's Republic of China in front of Tiananmen, the Gate of Heavenly Peace. Just like the emperors before them, the Communists moved their centre of power into part of the Forbidden City, to Zhongnanhai, west of the Imperial Palace. After 1949, Beijing became, in appearance as well as in fact, the political, cultural and economic centre of China.

Grey and dusty Beijing was supposed to become a green city within the decade. But large-scale demolition and monotony had a negative influence on Beijing instead.

As a centre of political power, Beijing was in the limelight during a number of the campaigns of the 1950s and had to show itself to be particularly enthusiastic. In 1968, the Cultural Revolution began in Tiananmen Square, the Square of Heavenly Peace, with the march of a million Red Guards, to whom Mao Zedong waved encouragingly from Tiananmen Gate. On the one hand, the Cultural Revolution brought chaos, economic stagnation and political repression to Beijing and its people. On the other, it drew attention

All government bodies were based in Beijing. Important schools and colleges moved here, right next to traditional centres of education; the building of numerous factories was a sign of industrialisation. Beijing, which had a mere 1.2 million inhabitants in 1949, grew through the incorporation of eight rural districts of Hebei Province in 1958.

The reshaping of the city began in the 1950s. The slum areas were cleared, new buildings erected and the streets widened.

Left, class enemies are put on trial after the revolution. **Above**, Zhou Enlai, Mao Zedong, and Lin Piao surrounded by Red Guards.

to the "imperialistic" habits of some political leaders. Beihai Park was closed to the public for the duration of the Cultural Revolution, and was used by Mao's wife, Jiang Qing, and other functionaries as a private domain.

During the height of the Cultural Revolution, politics had thickened into a tangle of palace intrigues and countless "campaigns", causing the people to lose comprehension of what was happening. Their earlier support and trust in the leadership turned into silent fury. Dissatisfaction had also increased because of rationing restrictions and the poor quality of goods. This was the 1960s – the time of the new beginning and of change.

In early April of 1976, during the week of the Qingming Festival when the Chinese remember their dead, the silent rage of the people found expression in a massive demonstration. The people of Beijing gathered by the thousands for several days in Tiananmen Square, to pay homage to the dead President Zhou Enlai, and to protest against Mao and the radical leaders of the Cultural Revolution. The first demands for modernisation and democracy were heard, signalling the Cultural Revolution's end.

In response to the unrest, a new face was presented to the Chinese people: Hua Guofeng. He was named the First Vice-Chairman of the Central Committee of the Communist Party (second in position to Mao).

The Chinese, great believers in omens and portents, have always viewed natural disasters as signs from heaven and as forecasts of great changes. In the summer of 1976, a massive earthquake buried the town of Tangshan, to the east of Beijing, and claimed hundreds of thousands of victims. Many Chinese expected far-reaching changes; in imperial times this would definitely have meant a change of dynasty.

The Great Chairman's death: In fact, it was only a few months later that another event shook the Chinese people. Their "Great Helmsman," Mao Zedong, the man who had led China out of feudal servitude, dire poverty and wretchedness, died on 9 September of the same year. The country was shocked. Everywhere machines stood still, shops closed and people gathered on the streets. The television showed pictures of weeping women and men. But an acute observer would have gained the impression that the Chinese were shocked less by the death of their Chairman than by the uncertainty of what the future, after Mao Zedong, would bring.

After the death of Mao came the toppling of the so-called Gang of Four, in October 1976. Hua had the four radical leaders, one of whom was Mao's widow Jiang Qing, overpowered in a meeting, arrested and de-

tained. They were officially blamed for creating and directing the Cultural Revolution, and were tried and convicted.

By the spring of 1977, the new Chairman Hua's portrait was prominently displayed in the central squares of the capital. A more than life-sized poster showed him at the deathbed of the Great Helmsman. Attributed to Mao, the caption read: "You have matters in hand, my heart rests in peace."

Hua, however, remained in power only a short time, though he tried to win power from the reflected glory of the Mao cult. A veteran of the Revolution was waiting in the wings, one who had twice disappeared into obscurity during the intra-party struggles: former Vice-Premier Deng Xiaoping emerged as China's leader in late 1978.

From 1978 to 1980, Beijing was the scene of countless demonstrations by dissatisfied Chinese from all over the country. It was mostly young students who courageously moved to open protest during the spring of 1979, demanding a more democratic society. On the "Democracy Wall" by the Xidan market, the *dazibao* (big character posters) reappeared, familiar from the Cultural Revolution years but with significantly different contents. There were accusations made against officials, exposures of corruption, protests against the caprice of bureaucrats, often just a simple call for justice. One concise wall poster merely asked: "Who knows the representative of my district, who is supposed to represent me in the People's Congress?" Space for name, address and telephone number were left blank, a simple but quite plain pointer to the fact that Congress members in China were chosen by the higher echelons of the party and in practice no elections took place.

Students at the Xidan wall sold journals that they had produced themselves. It was through these journals that many of the people of Beijing now learned for the first time of the mass poverty in the countryside. Delegations of peasants came from all the provinces to complain in the capital of the disastrous situation. Demonstrators marched in front of the seat of the Central Committee of the Communist Party and on Tiananmen

Preceding pages: although the cult of personality for Mao evaporated in the 1970s, Mao's mausoleum still draws visitors. **Left,** young Pioneers.

Square. Countless petitions were handed in daily, putting considerable pressure on the Party. However, while many of the demonstrations' leaders were arrested, some of their ideas have now become part of official government policy.

Building Beijing: During the 1970s, Beijing still seemed very much the Forbidden City to the few foreigners staying there. There was practically no tourism up until 1977. The visitors were almost all guests of the state or of the Party – a handful of business people and a few selected journalists and semi-official delegations. They stayed in the Peking Fandian, now the Beijing Hotel, on the corner of Chang'an Boulevard and Wangfu-

built as refuges after the Tangshan earthquake, using any materials that came to hand. There was no hurry to demolish the huts since they served as additional living space for many. For years, almost no new homes were built, although the population had increased explosively.

The first skyscrapers, however, started to appear as early as 1977. Built in Qianmendajie, the street parallel to, and south of, Chang'an Boulevard, these new buildings had their defects: pressure was insufficient to supply running water to the upper floors; buildings 15 floors high had no lifts, and if they did, the lifts didn't work; and there were no secure places to leave bicycles. But the

jing Street. The eastern, newer part of the building was reserved for Western guests; the western, older part was for guests from other countries and for the Chinese. Some foreign professionals stayed in the Friendship Hotel, Youyibinguan, (built in the 1950s for a colony of Soviet experts) in the Haidian district, in the northwest section of the city.

The most modern and most noticeable buildings were still the so-called 10 great buildings dating from the 1950s, including the Great Hall of the People, the museum buildings along Tiananmen, the Minzu Hotel, and the Radio Beijing building. In stark contrast, unattractive huts lined the streets,

people of Beijing had not really expected anything different. The main thing was that they could move out of their old collapsing huts into a new apartment block.

Awakening of the 1980s: In 1982, a new constitution came into being. An open door policy to foreign countries was one important step in the modernisation programme designed to quadruple China's economic power by the year 2000.

Soon, the first free peasant markets arrived, seen at many major crossroads. In contrast to the state-run shops, these free markets were able to offer fresh vegetables and fruits. For years, independent work and private trade had counted as capitalist sins. Now cobblers, tailors and carpenters simply started to work for themselves and in Tiananmen Square, self-employed photographers were suddenly doing a good trade under their huge sun shades.

Women could now have their hair permed in new salons, and street traders offered all sorts of goods in front of the state-run department stores. The city seemed to have awoken from a sleep, and the pace was hectic.

The people enjoyed the new beginning. The time of forced participation in political events and campaigns was over and interest in politics faded away. It was even considered chic to want nothing more to do with

intentionally or subliminally, the message of the blessings of consumerism. Values previously held firm – a simplistic right-or-wrong view of the world, including indoctrinated slogans – all began to topple once the "imperialist arch-enemies" of previous years became good friends nearly overnight.

The three "luxury goods" – a bicycle, clock and radio – were no longer enough. The department stores filled up with refrigerators, washing machines, television sets and expensive imported goods. Before long, the first fashion shows and fashion magazines, as well as film stars – the new image-makers – awoke the desire of women and men to look attractive and different.

politics. New horizons opened for the youth, and never before had they been known to study so eagerly. Careers as scientists, engineers, and technicians, study trips abroad, and freedom and prosperity beckoned.

In the novels of this new decade, young lovers no longer vowed to fight to the death for the revolution and their homeland. Instead, they would study hard and help with the modernisation of their country. Television showed pictures from abroad and spread,

Left, glass-fronted skyscrapers continue rising in the city. Above, the old-fashion and the simple, and the new fashion.

This process of modernisation and reform, however, was not without controversies. After Deng Xiaoping's protégé Hu Yaobang became general secretary of the party and Zhao Ziyang became prime minister, opposition grew in conservative circles, especially in the army. At the end of 1983, a campaign was set in motion against "spiritual pollution"; many serious criminals were publicly executed as a deterrent, but the fight was mainly against intellectuals and artists, as well as against fashions like long hair and Western music, which were being imported from Hong Kong.

At the end of 1986, students demanded

more democracy; this led to the conservative party leadership pressuring Hu Yaobang to retire as the Party's general secretary, as he had felt sympathetic towards the students and their grievances. Zhao Ziyang, who was regarded as a relative liberal, succeeded Hu, and in 1988 Li Peng took over from him as prime minister.

Tiananmen and after: In April 1989, Tiananmen Square became the focus of the world's media as university students, later joined by workers, aired their grievances against the government at the largest demonstrations since 1949. The protests gained momentum and spread to other cities until, on May 19, martial law was imposed on most of Beijing.

of the two socialist superpowers, Deng Xiaoping and Mikhail Gorbachev, who was pushing reforms in the Soviet Union, met in Beijing in an atmosphere of reconciliation after nearly 30 years of division.

In 1993, Deng Xiaoping officially retired from politics, but remained *de facto* ruler of China. After Deng's death in 1997, the torch of economic reform passed to President Jiang Zemin. In the same year, Hong Kong returned to Chinese sovereignty without incident (although Hong Kong's economy soon dropped into the toilet), and Jiang Zemin visited the United States. Premier Zhu Rongji consolidated his position as China's chief architect of economic reform.

As the movement continued, the army entered the city. In the early hours of June 4, troops moved east along Chang'an Avenue into Tiananmen Square, ordered to put an end to the demonstration. Although versions of what actually happened that morning and over the next few days differ amongst international media, foreign governments, the Chinese government, and other observers, hundreds if not thousands deaths were reported. How many remains a mystery.

Zhao Ziyang, like Hu before him, seemed sympathetic to protesters, and was sacked. Jiang Zemin became Party secretary.

Meanwhile, also in May 1989, the leaders

Despite Western concerns over human rights and China's policy towards Taiwan, China appears poised to play a leading role in world economics and politics in the new century. The West's policy of engagement based, cynics claim, mainly on economic interests led to high-profile state visits to China in 1998 by U.S. President Bill Clinton and British Prime Minister Tony Blair.

The diplomacy seemed to pay off. In a speech at the end of 1998 to mark the 20th anniversary of economic reform, Deng's chosen successor, President Jiang Zemin, promised the reforms begun by Deng Xiaoping would continue.

International companies continue to beat a path to China's door as the 21st century began, drawn by the sometimes misguided idea of the world's "largest market." Most leading multinationals are well-established in Beijing, Shanghai, and Hong Kong.

And as Asia's collective economic troubles continued through the end of the 1990s, China's ability to maintain the value of its currency and the stability of its economy, for the most part, led many other governments to see China, not Japan, as Asia's economic stabilizer in the 21st century.

Today, fashionably dressed people stroll through the city's streets once dominated by dark-blue Mao suits. Even the most daring now have many regular venues, and visiting Western musicians frequently play to full houses. Despite a crackdown by the government, pirated CDs of Western music proliferate on the streets, creating an ongoing international trade issue.

New Asian metropolis: Beijing is well on the way to becoming an international metropolis, though for sheer economic vibrancy it looks increasingly second-best to its great rival Shanghai. (Beijing, however, did not overbuild like Shanghai in the 1990s, leading to empty but gleaming office towers.)

The city is changing fast. Inflation remains high and essential services do not follow urban renewal in some districts. Many prop-

styles – tiny miniskirts, fluorescent hair dye – no longer cause offence or turn heads. Western-style bars and restaurants open almost weekly, especially in the embassy and university districts. Deep in underground shelters that Mao had constructed in the 1960s for fear of a possible Soviet nuclear attack, restaurants, hotels and shops now have sprung up. Karaoke, however, which once swept the capital, is losing its popularity to the delight of many. Chinese bands

Left, student demonstrations in Tiananmen Square, 1989, shook China and the world. Above, karaoke from Japan.

erty developers are unscrupulous and corruption is rife. Bicycles are being banished from some roads by the city government and forced off others by traffic conditions. During the middle of the day, the traffic grinds to a standstill on many main roads, adding to the already heavy air pollution.

Some people now believe the modernisation of the city has run out of control, and recently there have been moves to protect Beijing's heritage and environment, including the old *hutongs*. On the other hand, the government pushed ahead several showpiece projects in the capital to mark the 50th anniversary of communist China in 1999.

LIFE IN THE HUTONG

In a region formerly protected by the Great Wall, Beijing was once hidden behind its own city walls. And within the city walls were its citizens, each with a wall built around their own homes and courtyards, or *siheyuan*. Today, ring roads and walls of high-rise buildings have taken over the function of the city wall, itself a victim of town planning. In the city centre, faceless buildings of the 1950s protect the inner core, a labyrinth of crumbling old grey alleyways, some dating back several centuries. These are the *hutong*.

Once the centre of life for Beijingers living outside the Imperial Palace, hutong still number over a thousand. But these are now being threatened with eradication by progress, and with replacement by the modern high-rise or superhighway.

Hutong history: Beijing is a Mongol city. The conquerors who first made the former city of Yanjing – the name of the city from the 11th to the 3rd centuries BC – their capital brought their customs, way of life and language with them. Originally, the plains around Beijing were intended to be turned into grass-covered steppes. However, the successful cultivation of grass in this harsh region has eluded almost everyone right up to the present day. Nonetheless, wells were dug and horse-troughs, *hut* or *hot* in Mongolian (as in *Hohhot*, the capital of the Province of Inner Mongolia), were set up. The people of Beijing, attempting to assimilate, turned these Mongol wells into Chinese *hutong*.

Mongols or no Mongols, Beijingers could hardly leave their houses and homes lying unprotected amid the horse-troughs. All they had to do was close up the small spaces between the houses with a wall and privacy was restored. It was even simpler to build on to the wall of their neighbours, although no one was allowed to build so as to block another householder's route to water. In this way, the tangle of hutong grew, just wide enough to let a rider through.

The houses and courtyards, hidden away and boxed in, are themselves closed off with

wooden gates, on which one can often see carved characters intended to bring good fortune to the house owner and to his trade. If you try to take a look at such a house – the gates are almost always invitingly open – you will find your view blocked by yet another wall: the ghost wall. Apparently, a Chinese ghost can only move straight ahead, and once it has crossed the wooden threshold between the chiselled stone gateposts, it comes up against the wall that bars any further progress.

Like the main gates, sayings carved into tablets set in the ghost walls may often be found. These carry messages ranging from the philosophical, "Hail jewel in the lotus", to the patriotic, "Long live Chairman Mao".

The spirit of the Great Helmsman, as Mao was often referred, is certainly present in the little lanes of Beijing. In 1949, Beiping or Northern Peace, as the city was known in those days, had just over a million inhabitants, and the population was rising only slightly. This number increased enormously during the Cultural Revolution. The Chinese may seem to have few personal freedoms today, but in 1966 it was quite different. It was one's revolutionary duty to travel about the country, and counter-revolutionary to inform the authorities of one's presence. Suddenly the city had a population of 5 or 6 million, all of whom also wanted to be counted as inhabitants. Where once there were trees and flowers, and spacious courtyards, there were now huts and cooking fires, bicycles and prams.

Idyllic chaos: Is Beijing a city at all? Or is it an immensely overgrown Chinese peasant village that has sprung up around a centre of power? Certainly the recent construction boom has given the city a face lift, with a proliferation of skyscrapers.

However, the heart of Beijing is not to be found in the modern steel and glass monstrosities, but behind them, where buildings are as low as in rural areas and where strangers rarely come. This is where the old Beijingers live, who still add their throaty "rrr" to every word. These are the secret lords of the city, who at five in the morning, before going to work, prefer *taijiquan*, a form of shadow boxing, to jogging, and who fill the parks every evening with their bird cages. These are the old people of Beijing, wrapped in thick blue clothes to protect themselves against the weather, with grey beards and laughter lines framing their last remaining tooth. The women wear black hats like those in the Beijing opera, and can produce a three-minute tirade of curses with ease before they even think of drawing a breath, then fling a convincing "It's all true!" as their opponent withdraws into a courtyard.

Courtyard culture: The visitor who wanders aimlessly through the hutong, and sees, apart from wooden gates, only the numerous public toilets, will be disappointed. You really shouldn't miss visiting one or two of these unique courtyards.

The introverted architecture of these Chinese courtyard tells more about the Chinese family and the psyche of the people of Beijing than any books or lectures. In an ideal situation, you will pass the ghost wall and see a courtyard in which there will be a few trees and many flowers and cacti, in front of which are the family bicycles. Three or four single-storey buildings overlook the courtyard, the lower halves of their windows covered with paper to obstruct the view of nosy passers-by, the upper half glazed.

In the siheyuan of families who are higher in the social order, a second and third court-yard may adjoin the first. There may be two small "ear courtyards" to the sides, which contain the kitchens or serve as storage spaces. But this type of housing has become a rarity, as space is needed for the ever growing population. What were once single family dwellings have now been adapted for four or five families.

Most of these grey brick buildings today are, in fact, hopelessly overcrowded. The courtyard has been turned into somewhat of a pigsty, and is used for storing coal or is filled with the small shacks built to accommodate new residents. Pots and pans and baskets are stacked around. But even in such courtyards, there is always space for a chessboard to be spread out.

The best way to approach the hutong these days is through an organized tour. Starting from the north end of Beihai Park, these tours will expose travellers to the history and culture that lies behind these ancient and curious structures. They also give one a chance

to see past the hutong walls and enter the siheyuan, perhaps even to have a chat, if lucky, with a local inhabitant.

If you want to take a walk through the hutong on your own, it's no problem. In principle, try and find the entrance to the labyrinth anywhere between the houses bordering any street in Beijing.

There are a lot of very typical lanes in the south of the city, where the Chinese were permitted to live (the north was reserved for the Mongol and later for the Manchu conquerors and their allied peoples), around the bird market in the southeast of the city near Longtan Park, directly north of Beihai Park, or to the east of Xidan Street, a well-known

shopping area. Since, like so many visitors, you'll probably end up in Liulichang, a renovated (or, if you like, gentrified) lane of shops with art and antiques for sale, head off south or southeastwards from here into any lane and just walk around. No one gets lost doing this. Another possible starting point is the acrobatics theatre in Dazhalan Street (pronounced Dashalar by *lao* Beijingers). However, you should allow at least half a day before embarking on such an excursion.

What's in a name?: The names of each hutong tell its story by describing the life it contains. Some indicate professions or crafts: Bowstring Makers' Lane, Cloth Lane, Hat

Lane. Some lanes, if mostly populated by a single family, are named after that family: the lane of the Liu family, the front and rear lanes of the Gao family, and even the Village of the Zhuang family, a family name that is also common in the small villages in the surrounding Hebei region. (There may indeed have been a village here at the time of the Mongol Great Khan Timur, 1370–1405.)

Many names are due to the shape of the lane. The Buffalo Horn Curve is, of course, curved, as is the Dog Tail Lane, of which there are at least eight in Beijing. Horse Tail, Goat Tail and Pig Tail Lanes all have similar shapes. Trousers Lane has a "belly" section and two branching "legs", as does East Trou-

Lane, Sausage Lane, Coffin Lane, Mother Sow Lane, Donkey's Hoof Lane and Big Ears Lane get their names?

Summer stories: On a typical summer's evening, young and old sit under the lantern in front of the house entrance, their sleeves rolled up, fanning themselves and chasing the flies off the obligatory chessboard. The husks of melon seeds are piled in little heaps where they've been spit. The housework is done and the children have been sent to bed. The chamber pots have been taken, together with a fly-swatter, to the public toilet (its presence can be sensed from afar). Now is the time for many a story to be told, here in the confusing tangle of grey alleyways.

sers Lane. Sesame Lane (not Sesame Street!) is simply a very small lane.

Sometimes the names still carry echoes of the military organization of the Manchu state. Nearly all the names ending in "camp", such as Mongol Camp, Muslim Camp, or Camp by the Incense Burner, go back to former troop positions. In other lanes it's up to the visitor to find out the origin of the name, if such is possible. How did Chicken Claw Lane, Western Crutch Lane, Heart's Point

Left, idyllic greenery in a courtyard house in the old city. **Above**, relaxing over a game of *xianqi* (Chinese chess).

If one has plenty of time and can speak Chinese, or has a good-natured friend who will interpret, go and join the *lao* Beijingers. Guests are always welcome here. The curious inquiry of "What country do you come from then?" is your ticket of entry to a long conversation.

Everyone in the hutong has a story to tell; no-one will admit to being the one who doesn't know why this particular hutong is called what it's called. You are certainly not going to leave without hearing a charming or exciting story, and given local hospitality, you'll probably be sitting there far into the night. Too, share your own stories.

The ancestor worship of the Chinese is based upon the assumption that a person has two souls. One of them is created at the time of conception, and when the person has died, the soul stays in the grave with the corpse and lives on the sacrificial offerings. As the corpse decomposes, the strength of the soul dwindles, until it eventually leads a shadow existence by the Yellow Springs in the underworld. However, it will return to earth as an ill-willed spirit and create damage if no more sacrifices are offered. The second soul only emerges at birth. During its heavenly voyage, it is threatened by evil forces, and is also dependent upon the sacrifices and prayers of the living descendants. If the sacrifices cease, then this soul, too, turns into an evil spirit. But if the descendants continue to make sacrificial offerings and look into the maintenance of graves, the soul of the deceased ancestor may offer them help and protection.

Inscriptions on oracle bones from the Shang dynasty (1600–1100 BC) and inscriptions on bronze, dating from the Zhou period (1100–476 BC), reveal that an ancestor worship of high nobility, a cult of a high god called *Di*, and an animistic belief in numerous gods of nature had existed early in Chinese history. Originally, ancestor worship had been exclusive to the king. Only a few centuries BC did peasants too begin to honour their ancestors. At first, people believed that the soul of the ancestor would search for a human substitute and create an abode for the soul during the sacrificial ritual. It was usually the grandson of the honoured ancestor who took on the role of substitute. About 2,000 years ago, genealogical tables were introduced as homes for the soul during sacrificial acts. Up until that time, the king and noblemen had used human sacrifices for ancestral worship. Even today, the Chinese worship their ancestors and offer the deities sacrifices of food. This is widely practised, for example, during the Qingming Festival.

The original religion of the people actually focused on the worship of natural forces. Later, the people began to worship the Jade

Preceding pages: Jade Emperor. **Left**, portrait of Confucius. **Right**, demonic tutelary god.

Emperor, a figure from Daoism who became the highest god in the popular religion after the 14th century. Guanyin, the goddess of mercy, originated in Mahayana (Great Wheel) Buddhism. Among the many gods in popular Chinese religion, there were also earth deities. Every town worshipped its own unique god. Demons of illness, spirits of the house, and even the god of latrines had to be remembered. The deities of streams and rivers were considered to be particularly dangerous and unpredictable. Apart from

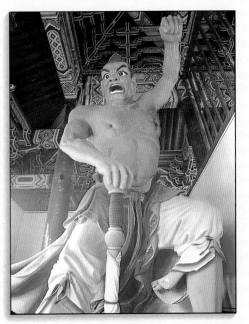

Confucianism, Daoism (or Taoism) and Buddhism, there was also a popular religion known as Daoist Buddhism.

China had been divided into numerous small states. Only after the Qin Empire had won over its rivals in 221 BC did the first emperor over a united China come to power. At the time, there were a number of schools of philosophical thought. Only Confucianism and Daoism gained wide acceptance.

Daoism: Central concepts of Daoism are the *dao*, which basically means way or path, but it also has a second meaning of method and principle; the other concept is *wuwei*, which is sometimes simply defined as passivity, or "swimming with the stream". The concept of *de* (virtue) is closely linked to this, not in the sense of moral honesty, but as a virtue that manifests itself in daily life when dao is put into practice.

The course of events in the world is determined by the forces *yang* and *yin*. The masculine, brightness, activity and heaven are considered to be *yang* forces; the feminine, weak, dark and passive elements of life are seen as *yin* forces. Laozi was the founder of Daoism. He lived at a time of crises and upheavals. The Daoists were opposed to feudal society, yet they did not fight actively for a new social structure, preferring instead to live in a pre-feudalistic tribal society.

years and then gave birth to him through her left armpit. His hair was white when he was born; he prolonged his life with magic.

The classic work of Daoism is the *Daodejing*. It now seems certain that this work was not written by a single author. The earliest, and also most significant, followers of Laozi were Liezi and Zhuangzi. Liezi (5th century BC) was particularly concerned with the relativity of experiences, and he strived to comprehend the dao with the help of meditation. Zhuangzi (4th century BC) is especially famous for his poetic allegories. The ordinary people were not particularly attracted by the abstract concepts and metaphysical reflections of Daoism. Even at the beginning

Laozi, it is said, was born in a village in the province of Henan in 604 BC, the son of a distinguished family. For a time, he held the office of archivist in Luoyang, which was then the capital. But he later retreated into solitude and died in his village in 517. According to a famous legend, he wanted to leave China on a black ox when he foresaw the decline of the empire. Experts today are still arguing about Laozi's historical existence. Since the second century AD, many legends have been told about the figure of Laozi. One of them, for instance, says that he was conceived by a beam of light, and that his mother was pregnant with him for 72

of the Han period (206 BC – AD 220), there were signs of a popular and religious Daoism. As Buddhism also became more and more popular, it borrowed ideas from Daoism, and vice versa, to the point where one might speak of a fusion between the two.

The Daoists and Buddhists both believed that the great paradise was in the far west of China, hence the name, Western Paradise. It was believed to be governed by the queen mother of the West (Xiwangmu) and her husband, the royal count of the East (Dongwanggong). Without making any changes to it, the Daoists also took over the idea of hell from Buddhism.

Religious Daoism developed in various directions and schools. The ascetics retreated to the mountains and devoted all their time to meditation, or else they lived in monasteries. In the Daoist world, priests had important functions as medicine men and interpreters of oracles. They carried out exorcism and funeral rites, and read mass for the dead or for sacrificial offerings. Historical and legendary figures were added to the Daoist pantheon. At the head were the Three Commendables. The highest of the three deities, the heavenly god, is identical to the Jade Emperor, worshipped by the common people. There is hardly a temple without Shouxinggong (the god of longevity), a

friendly-looking old man with a long white beard and an extremely elongated, bald head. There are also the god of wealth (Caishen), the god of fire (Huoshen), the kitchen god (Zaoshen), the god of literature (Wendi), the god of medicine (Huatou) and others. Only the Eight Immortals are truly popular and well-known. Some of them are derived from historical personalities, some are fanciful figures. They are believed to have the ability to make themselves invisible, bring the dead back to life, and do other miraculous deeds.

Left, ancestor worship. **Above**, statue of Laozi, who spread Daoism.

Confucious: While Laozi was active in the south of China, Confucius lived in the north of the country. For him, too, dao and de are central concepts. For more than 2,000 years, the ideas of Confucius (551–479 BC) have influenced Chinese culture, which in turn sculpted the worldview of neighboring lands such as Korea, Japan and Southeast Asia. It is debatable whether Confucianism is a religion in the strictest sense. But Confucius was worshipped as a deity, although he was only officially made equal to the heavenly god by an imperial edict in 1906. (Up until 1927, many Chinese offered him sacrifices.)

Mencius, a Confucian scholar, describes the poverty at the time Confucius was born as follows: "There are no wise rulers, the lords of the states are driven by their desires. In their farms are fat animals, in their royal stables fat horses, but the people look hungry and on their fields there are people who are dying of starvation."

Confucius himself came from an impoverished family of the nobility who lived in the state of Lu (near the village of Qufu, in the west of Shandong Province). For years, Confucius – or Kong Fuzi (Master Kong) – tried to gain office with one of the feudal lords, but he was dismissed again and again. So he travelled around with his disciples and instructed them in his ideas. All in all, he is said to have had 3,000 disciples, 72 of them highly-gifted ones who are still worshipped today. Confucius taught mainly traditional literature, rites and music, and is thus regarded as the founder of scholarly life in China. The Chinese word *ru*, which as a rule is translated as Confucian, actually means "someone of a gentle nature" – a trait that was attributed to a cultured person. Confucius did not publish his philosophical thoughts in a book. They have, therefore, to be reconstructed from fragments of the comments he made on various occasions. The thoughts of Confucius were collected in the *Lunyu* (Conversations) by his loyal disciples. Some of the classic works on Confucianism are: *Shijing*, the book of songs; *Shujing*, the book of charters; *Liji*, the book of rites; *Chunqiu*, the spring and autumn annals; and *Yijing*, the book of changes.

Confucianism is, in a sense, a religion of law and order. Just as the universe is dictated by the world order, and the sun, moon and stars move according to the laws of nature, so a person, too, should live within the framework of world order. This idea, in turn, is based upon the assumption that man can be educated. Ethical principles were turned into central issues. Confucius was a very conservative reformer, yet he significantly reinterpreted the idea of the *junzi*, a nobleman, to that of a noble man, whose life is morally sound and who is, therefore, legitimately entitled to reign.

Confucius believed that he would create an ideal social order if he reinstated the culture and rites of the early Zhou period (1100–700 BC). Humanity (*ren*) was a central concept at the time, its basis being the love of children and brotherly love. Accord-

subordinate (identical to the father/son relationship).

In the 12th century, Zhu Xi (1130–1200 BC) succeeded in combining the metaphysical tendencies of Buddhism and Daoism with the pragmatism of Confucianism.

His systematic work includes teachings about the creation of the microcosm and macrocosm, as well as the metaphysical basis of Chinese ethics. This system, known as Neo-Confucianism, reached canonical status in China; it was the basis of all state examinations, a determining factor for Chinese officialdom until this century.

Buddhism: The Chinese initially encountered Buddhism at the beginning of the first

ingly, the rulers would only be successful in their efforts if they can govern the whole of society according to these principles. Confucius defined the social positions and hierarchies very clearly and precisely. Only if and when every member of society takes full responsibility for his or her position will society as a whole function smoothly.

Family and social ties – and hierarchy – were considered to be of fundamental importance: between father and son (the son has to obey the father without reservations); man and woman (the woman does not have any individual rights); older brother and younger brother; friend and friend; and ruler and

century, when merchants and monks came to China over the Silk Road. The type of Buddhism that is prevalent in China today is the *Mahayana* (Great Wheel), which – as opposed to *Hinayana* (Small Wheel) – promises all creatures redemption through the so-called Bodhisattva (redemption deities). There were two aspects that were particularly attractive to the Chinese: the teachings of *karma* provided a better explanation for individual misfortune, and there was a hopeful promise for existence after death. Nevertheless, there was considerable opposition to Buddhism, which contrasted sharply with Confucian ethics and ancestor worship.

At the time of the Three Kingdoms (AD 220–280), the religion spread in each of the three states. The trading towns along the Silk Road as far as Luoyang became centres of the new religion. After tribes of foreign origin had founded states in the north, and the gentry from the north had sought refuge in the eastern Jin dynasty (317–420), Buddhism developed along very different lines in the north and south of China for about two centuries. During the rule of Emperor Wudi (502–549), rejection and hostility towards Buddhism spread among Confucians. And during the relatively short-lived northern Zhou dynasty (557–581), Buddhism was officially banned (from 574 to 577).

Buddhism was most influential in Chinese history during the Tang dynasty (618–907). Several emperors officially supported the religion; the Tang Empress Wu Zetian, in particular, surrounded herself with Buddhist advisors. During the years 842 to 845, however, Chinese Buddhists also experienced the most severe persecutions in their entire history: a total of 40,000 temples and monasteries were destroyed, and Buddhism was blamed for the economic decline and moral decay of the dynasty.

In the course of time, 10 Chinese schools of Buddhism emerged, eight of which were essentially philosophical ones that did not influence popular religion. Only two schools have remained influential through today: Chan (school of meditation or Zen Buddhism) and Pure Land (Amitabha-Buddhism). The masters of Chan considered meditation to be the only path to knowledge. In Mahayana Buddhism, worship focused on the Bodhisattva Avalokiteshvara. Since the 7th century, the ascetic Bodhisattva has been a popular female figure in China. She is called Guanyin, a motherly goddess of mercy who represents a central deity for the ordinary people. Guanyin means "the one who listens to complaints".

In Chinese Buddhism, the centre of religious attention is the Sakyamuni Buddha, the founder of Buddhism who was forced into the background in the 6th century by the Maitreya Buddha (who was called Milefo in China, or redeemer of the world). In Chinese monasteries, Sakyamuni greets the faithful

Left, worshippers lighting incense at Buddhist temple. Right, Buddha Sakyamuni.

as a laughing Buddha in the entrance hall. Since the 14th century, the Amitabha school had dominated the life and culture of the Chinese people.

The most influential Buddhist school was the so-called School of Meditation (Chan in China, Zen in Japan), which developed under the Tang dynasty. It preached redemption through buddhahood, which anyone is able to reach. It despised knowledge gained from books or dogmas, as well as rites. Liberating shocks or guided meditation are used in order to lead disciples towards the experience of enlightenment. Other techniques used to achieve final insights were long hikes and physical work. The most

important method was a dialogue with the master, who asked subtle and paradoxical questions, to which he expected equally paradoxical answers.

In 1949, the year the People's Republic of China was founded, there were approximately 500,000 Buddhist monks and nuns, and 50,000 temples and monasteries. A number of well-known Buddhist temples were classified as historical monuments.

At the beginning of the Cultural Revolution in 1966, it seemed as if the Red Guards were intent on completely eradicating Buddhism. The autonomous Tibet was hard-hit by these excesses. Only a few important monasteries and cultural objects could be protected, and completely or only partly preserved. Today, there are Buddhists among the Han Chinese, the Mongols, Tibetans, Manchus, Tu, Qiang and Dai (Hinayana Buddhists) peoples.

In the 7th century AD, another type of Buddhism, called Tantric Buddhism or Lamaism, was introduced into Tibet from India. With the influence of the monk Padmasambhava, it replaced the indigenous Bon religion, while at the same time taking over some of the elements of this naturalist religion. The monasteries in Tibet developed into centres of intellectual and worldly power, yet there were recurring arguments. Only the reformer Tsongkhapa (1357–1419) succeeded in rectifying conditions that had become chaotic.

He founded the sect of virtue (Gelugpa), which declared absolute celibacy to be a condition and re-introduced strict rules of order. Because the followers of this sect wear yellow caps, this order came to be known as Yellow Hat Buddhism.

Tsongkhapa had predicted to two of his disciples that they would be reborn as heads of the church. He had therewith anticipated the continuous transfer of powerful positions within the church – for instance, the position of the Dalai Lama and the Panchen Lama. The Dalai Lama represents the incarnation of the Bodhisattva of mercy (Avalokiteshvara), who is also worshipped as the patron god of Tibet. The Panchen Lama is higher in the hierarchy of the gods and is the embodiment of Buddha Amitabha. The present 14th Dalai Lama, who was enthroned in 1940, fled to India after an uprising in 1959 and has been living in exile since then. The Panchen Lama died in Beijing in January 1989, at the age of 50, after he came to an understanding with the Chinese authorities following the uprising.

In Lamaism, a complex pantheon exists; apart from the Buddhist deities, there are figures from the Brahman and Hindu world of gods and the old Bon religion. Magic, repetitive prayers, movements, formulae, symbols and sacrificial rituals are all means for achieving redemption.

Islam: Islam probably became established in China in the 7th century, and its influence has been very long-lasting. Ten of the 56 recognised nationalities in China profess themselves to Islam. They are the Hui, Uzbek, Uighur, Karach, Kirgiz, Tatar, Shi'ite Tadshik, Donxiang, Sala and Bao'an – a total of 14 million people. The Hui are, as a rule, Han Chinese. They are the only group who enjoy the special status of a recognised minority solely on the basis of their religion.

Mohammed was born in Mecca around the year 570 (the exact date is unknown). From the age of 40 onwards, he preached the Koran. Islam soon came to China on two different routes: one was the famous Silk Road, the other from across the sea to the southeastern coast of China. During the Yuan dynasty (1271–1368), Islam finally became permanently established in China. The im-

perial observatory was built in Beijing and the Arab astronomer Jamal-al-Din was in charge of it.

The policies of the Qing dynasty were – though it may be oversimplified to say so – hostile to Moslems. In the 18th century, slaughtering according to Islamic rites was forbidden, and the building of new mosques and pilgrimages to Mecca were not allowed. Marriages between Chinese and Moslems were illegal, and relations between the two groups were made difficult.

Some of the Moslem sects were declared illegal during the Qing dynasty. Later, the Cultural Revolution led to many restrictions for religious people. Over the last few years, the People's Republic of China has been attempting to bring socialism and religion closer together and achieve a harmony between them. Believers (irrespective of their religion) are expected to be patriotic and law-abiding, but not to give up their faith. Today, there are around 21,000 mosques in China. The Moslems celebrate their festivals, and Chinese-Moslem societies organise pilgrimages to Mecca.

Christianity: Christianity was first brought to China by the Nestorians, in 635. The followers of Nestorian Christianity disseminated their teachings with the help of a Persian called Alopen, who was their first

church in China was probably built when John of Montecorvino, a Franciscan monk from Italy, arrived in Beijing in 1295.

During the Ming period, Catholic missionaries began to be very active in China. A leading figure among the Jesuit missionaries who played an important role was an Italian, Matteo Ricci. When he died, there were about 2,000 to 3,000 Christians in China.

The Jesuits had used their excellent knowledge of Western sciences in order to forge links with Chinese scholars. Other Catholic orders were more dogmatic and introduced tensions. The Chinese emperors, fed up with the squabbling, persecuted them all.

At the onset of the 19th century, the Prot-

missionary. The symbol of Nestorianism was a cross with two spheres at the end of all four beams. A stele dating from the Tang dynasty is decorated with such a cross and is on display in the museum of Shaanxi Province.

For a period, in spite of religious persecutions, this religion had spread to all the regions of the empire, and in some parts of the country was practised until the end of the Mongol dynasty. At the same time, initial contacts were made between China and the Roman Catholic Church. The first Catholic

Left, mosques are common in northwestern China.
Right, Virgin Mary shrine, and South Church.

estants began their missionary activities. The methods used to convert people were not always scrupulous. Nevertheless, the number of people converted remained an almost negligible minority. In 1948, the year before the founding of the P.R.C., there were 3 million Catholics and 1 million Protestants.

The Vatican had taken an extremely anticommunist stance after World War II, and as a result, the Chinese government ordered that the Catholic church in China should no longer be accountable to the Vatican. Moreover, the Vatican to this day recognises only the Taiwan government. However, relations are slowing improving.

Beijing cuisine, in contrast to that in other parts of China, tends to be rustic – a sort of good home cooking that uses onions and garlic, but not the great variety of vegetables used in the rest of China. There are geographical reasons for this, since in the winter, Beijing does suffer shortages of vegetables. In the past, it was not unusual to see nothing but lines of cabbage filling the markets. Today, however, much improved transportation means residents can get pretty much anything they need, if not perhaps at a slightly higher price.

On the other hand, during the years when it was the imperial capital city, Beijing attracted people from ethnic groups all over China. The emperor called the best cooks to his court, and the first among them could count on being given the rank of minister. It was in these palace kitchens that dishes were created that belong to the pinnacles of the world's culinary successes, and which were soon being imitated in kitchens all over the country. They were altered and refined, but the basic recipes remained true to their original forms. This is where dishes that belong to every sophisticated Chinese kitchen originated: Peking Duck, Phoenix In The Nest, Mandarin Fish, Lotus Prawns, rice soup, *Mu Shu* Pork, Thousand Layer Cake – all delicious dishes. Additionally, the palace kitchens produced dishes made from rare ingredients, the preparation of which needed the skill of great culinary artists, both of which only the emperor could afford.

Even today, the ordinary citizen can get to know the dishes of so-called palace cuisine only in special restaurants. Beijing cuisine, therefore, is a mixture of the everyday food of northern China, the refined palace cuisine, and culinary skills from across the country.

"Food first, then morals": This quotation from Bertolt Brecht is particularly appropriate in a developing country such as China. During its long history, it has suffered famine again and again. Even today, the problem

Preceding pages: the kitchen team after their work has been completed. Left, *jiaozi*, the filled dumplings. Right, pride at having mastered the use of the chopsticks.

of an adequate supply of foodstuffs to satisfy demand is by no means solved, although one can't help but notice the generous supply of goods on the free markets, permitted once more since 1979.

The great importance of eating in China is even expressed in their everyday speech. A common greeting is "*Chiguolema?*" ("Have you eaten?"). Only about 10 percent of China's surface is arable land. This is not much, compared to the population figures, and explains why in densely-settled areas every

square metre is used for growing something edible, even if there's only space for a single head of cabbage. Pasture or fallow land is hardly ever seen.

This is one of the reasons that China's dairy industry has not taken off. On the one hand, milk cows are far too expensive for an average Chinese farmer to buy, and on the other, there is no pasture. The few existing cows, mostly kept in cowsheds, live off scraps and the meagre grass cuttings from railway embankments and road verges.

Despite the small dairy industry, in Beijing nowadays one can buy milk, cheese, and yoghurt. Beijingers have adapted to the requirements of the foreigners living here, and many Chinese have acquired the taste for yoghurt. However, in general, soya products are still favoured, replacing milk, meat and other animal proteins.

Scarcity of land and of fuel have dictated the way the Chinese handle food and prepare meals. Usually the ingredients are cut small, so that they do not take long to cook. Ovens, which need a lot of fuel, hardly exist in private households. This also explains why there is no bread, in the common sense of the word. Very few utensils are used in cooking. Often the stoves are small, portable affairs, fuelled by bricks of compressed coal dust, which can be set up anywhere outside the

with pickled ginger as an hors d'oeuvre. The taste is, to many Westerners, an acquired one, but demands to be sampled at least once.

Most foreigners have no difficulty adjusting to and enjoying Chinese cooking. The cuisine is varied and, for the most part, tasty and pleasing to Western palates. However, with so many foreigners living here, it was inevitable that Western-style restaurants and bars would arrive.

Today, you cannot walk a block in either the Sanlitun or Jianguomenwai embassy districts without passing at least one Western establishment. And it is obvious by their numbers that many native Beijingers, especially the young, seem to find it fun eating

house, especially if there is no kitchen in it.

According to widespread prejudice, many Chinese do eat fairly obscure things such as snakes, rats, dogs, and cats. All of these may be seen at some time in some markets, but they are by no means the norm. They also eat something called thousand-year-old eggs. These are duck eggs that have been packed raw into a mass of mud, chalk and ammonia and thus kept for two weeks or so – not a thousand years. When fully preserved, the egg white is a transparent, dark greenish black and the yolk is a milky yellow-green. They are then cut into wedges, sprinkled with soya sauce and sesame oil and served

out Western-style. Hence, it is not surprising that the leading fast-food outlets such as MacDonalds, Pizza Hut and Kentucky Fried Chicken are here in full force, each with several branches in Beijing.

Guest of a Chinese family: How does one behave when invited to either a private party or an official function? First of all, it is usual to bring a gift for the hosts. This could be in the form of alcohol or cigarettes, but little things typical of one's own home country are also acceptable. Flowers are less usual. Shake hands when greeting people, a custom adopted from the West. It is no longer usual for the sexes to be separated; however, in rural areas, the women of the house might eat only after the men and the guests have finished. In such cases, the women have to make do with the leftovers.

There will be bowls and chopsticks on the table, sometimes with smaller plates to be used either for sauces, or for leftover food. Cold hors d'oeuvres, consisting of pickled vegetables, meat and small delicacies, are arranged – often very skilfully – on serving dishes, but they don't really count as part of the meal and are only intended to put you in the mood for what is to come. These cold snacks also provide the accompaniment to the alcoholic drinks, which on special occasions, and on not so special occasions, are

person. You can expect such a large quantity of food to be served that you will be quite unable to eat even a third of it. If the guests at a banquet should succeed in clearing every dish, the host would lose face.

When the menu is put together, care is taken that various meat dishes with vegetables, one dish of vegetables only, and often also a fish dish, provide contrasting flavours and colours. In this way, a hot dish can be followed by a less spicy one, and a sour one by a sweet one. Fish is often served, because the word for fish, *yu*, sounds the same as the auspicious word for abundance.

Hot dishes are served freshly prepared, one after the other (which means that when

freely indulged in according to the capacity of each guest.

As soon as the host has noticed that foods appeal most to his guest, he will keep on placing more of them on to the guest's plate. *Manman chi* – eat slowly – is the local equivalent of *bon appetit*.

After the hors d'oeuvres, the hot dishes are served. You will never be served just one main course. Several dishes are served at every meal, but there is at least one per

Left, old and young enjoying a snack at a street restaurant. **Above**, even the most simple meal is a social occasion.

invited to a private house, whoever is cooking will spend most of the time in the kitchen). Eat slowly and steadily, tasting a bit of everything. At the same time, people drink, chat and smoke between courses – which strikes most Westerners as unusual if not unpleasant. It is mostly men who smoke since, except in northeastern China and among certain minority groups, it is still considered improper for a woman to smoke. (Foreigners, however; are excused.)

Mifan, or rice, is one of the last dishes to be served, but not until all glasses of alcohol have been drained. This can sometimes be difficult, as during the meal, you'll probably find your beer glass is never allowed to be less than three-quarters full. If you simply can't manage any more, don't be embarrassed to ask the person next to you to help finish your drink.

In Beijing, light soup ends the meal. There is no dessert in the Western sense of the word, since sweet dishes are served as part of the main meal.

Good head for drink: Alcohol is often an integral part of the meal. A warning to "take care" is not unwarranted here, as most of the drinks are of very strong grain spirits. *Maotai*, named after its place of origin, is famous, as is *wuliangye* from Sichuan, with some 60 percent alcohol per volume. Both spirits are

eat a few of the snacks, but if you don't want to seem greedy, put your chopsticks down now and again.

Refusing to drink can be a tricky manoeuvre in itself. One way to manage is to turn your glass upside down on the table or hold your hand over it. But if your host insists on feeding you more, as he almost undoubtedly will, citing health reasons should get you off the hook. Sometimes their insistence to drink is genuine politeness; sometimes they just want to see how the *lao wai*, or foreigner, will behave.

Mealtime customs: Westerners may, at first, be a little put off by the fact that everyone eats with fairly audible enjoyment, but in

usually found in every restaurant and home, and are in special abundance at any type of official gathering. Sweet liqueurs are also drunk, as is beer, which is a staple mealtime drink. There are also several Sino-Franco joint ventures producing passable wines, the best of which are Dragon Seal and Dynasty. Both are fairly inexpensive and are of a decent standard.

At the meal, the host will encourage guests to help themselves to food and will drink toasts to them. *Ganbei!* means that you should empty your glass in one shot, and turning your glass upside down shows that you have followed this instruction. From time to time,

time one gets used to it. You may even come to appreciate the lack of restraint and practise the same yourself. However, remember that eating is a communal act here. Demonstrate proper social etiquette while eating by taking care of your neighbours at the table, and serving them some of the food, especially from dishes that they cannot reach easily. Remember also not to pick out the best pieces on each dish, but to take food from the side of the dish closest to you.

Apart from such customs, almost everything that furthers your enjoyment is allowed, and if at a loss as to where to discard the bones, simply place them on the table beside your bowl. Many a Chinese table looks like a battlefield after a meal, and the success of three-day wedding celebrations have often been measured by the height of the piles of discards – sweet wrappers, fruit peel, cigarette butts, pumpkin and sunflower seed husks – left on the floor. (Nowadays, though, you should take care not to throw away any litter or to spit in the street and other public places.)

Tea may be served after the meal, mostly green tea scented with fragrant jasmine blossom. Boiling water is poured onto the tea leaves, which are not strained. With green tea, water can be poured on several times, and it is said that the second brew is, in fact, better than the first. However, if water has been poured more than three times onto the same tea leaves, you may take this as a delicate hint that the meal is over and it is time to leave.

Peking Duck: One of the most famous dishes of northern Chinese cuisine is unquestionably Peking Duck. Its preparation requires considerable skill in order to produce the perfectly-flavoured duck with the melt-in-the-mouth crispness that is now known worldwide. There are several duck restaurants in Beijing that have specialised in this dish, but which, unfortunately, have all too often become pure mass production centres.

A prerequisite for true Peking Duck is a special kind of duck bred in and around Beijing. These animals are force-fed before slaughter for about six months. After slaughter, plucking and cleaning, air is carefully blown through a hole in the neck, so that the skin is loosened from the flesh. This process serves to make the skin as crisp as possible after roasting. The duck is then painted with a mixture of honey, water and vinegar and hung up in an airy place for three days to dry. Afterwards, still hanging, it is grilled slowly in a specially-built stove.

Just as important as the preparation of the duck itself are the side dishes served with it: very thin pancakes, little sesame seed rolls, spring onions and *haixian* sauce (also known as *hoisin* sauce, a sweetish bean sauce flavoured with garlic and spices).

An authentic meal of Peking Duck begins

with many hors d'oeuvres, which should ideally all derive from various parts of the duck – fried liver, boiled tongues, variously prepared eggs, and the webbed skin of the feet cut very finely, proving that in Chinese cooking, very little is wasted. After these, the cook brings the finished, grilled duck to the table and arranges bite-sized pieces of skin and meat on a platter. Take a pancake, use the chopped spring onion to spread haixian sauce on it, put a piece of duck over the spring onion, roll the whole thing up, and eat it using your fingers.

This is the combination that provides the highest gastronomic pleasure and makes the often rather fatty meat digestible. For the

final course of such a meal, a soup made of the remains of the duck is a must.

Of course, such opulent, expensive duck banquets are not indulged in very often by most Chinese families, and are usually eaten on very special occasions.

The main meal of a family of four usually consists of rice, noodles or steamed dumplings, soup, and three or four freshly-prepared hot dishes. Cold meals and sandwiches are unknown in China. People eat three cooked meals a day, which makes for a lot of domestic work. For this reason, most working people, especially in the lower economic levels, eat in canteens or cookshops.

Left, ducks being fattened on a farm near Beijing for use in Beijing's restaurants. **Above**, pancakes are being made in this open-air kitchen.

Beijing opera has really only existed for about 200 years, although the origins of theatre in China go back much further. Descriptions of dances dating from the Tang dynasty (618–907) show striking similarities to present-day Beijing opera. During the Ming era (1368–1644), Kunqu opera, a form of musical drama, developed, to which many elements of the song, dance and music of the Beijing opera can be traced.

A living tradition: In the old days, as permanent theatres were a rarity, even in Beijing and the major ports, Beijing opera was performed on the streets and in the market places – a sign of its popularity with ordinary people. The Beijing opera was the only way for them to learn anything about life outside the narrow circle of their own day-to-day existence, and was probably their main source of Chinese history. There was hardly a single temple festival during which a theatre performance was not given, although the opera performances themselves generally had nothing to do with the religious occasion.

The four main branches of Beijing opera are song, dialogue, mime and acrobatics, united categories that are separated in European theatre. There are various forms of Beijing opera. Sometimes music and song are predominant, sometimes mime. In other pieces, fight scenes dominate and the acrobatics are in the foreground, while in others still, the spoken word gets centre stage.

The main division is between *wenxi* (civilian plays), and *wuxi* (military dramas), but there are also comedies and skits. Wenxi pieces are more like our conception of drama. They describe domestic, civilian life. The wuxi, on the other hand, consist mainly of fights, and tell of historical wars and battles by making great use of acrobatics.

Many Beijing operas go back to popular legends, folk or fairy tales, or to classical literature such as *The Three Kingdoms, The Dream of the Red Chamber*, or *Journey to the West*. These works are much better known

in China than one might find most literary classics are in the West.

There are four different types of role in Beijing opera: *sheng*, male lead roles; *dan*, female roles; *jing*, painted-face roles; and finally *chou*, male or female clowns. Each major group is divided into sub-groups and then there are also extras, such as guards, soldiers, ladies-in-waiting, et cetera. Foreigners often have difficulty with the individual roles. For instance, the *xiao sheng*, or young male lead role of the Beijing opera

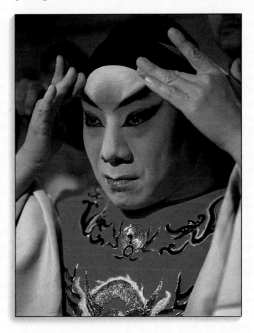

The White Snake, had to be turned into a *lao sheng* (old man) role for tours abroad. There was often inappropriate laughter during the performances, as the speaking part of the xiao sheng role – a very high, artificial voice – with the falsetto singing, the pink-rouged cheeks and the soft movements seemed effeminate to most non-Chinese.

The dan or female role is the most important part. There are two historical reasons for this. On the one hand, in most of the dramas, stories and novels that form the bases for the operas, a woman is the focus of interest. On the other, the central figure in Chinese dramas has been a woman since the days of the

Preceding pages: the fascination lies in brilliant masks and magnificent costumes. **Left**, Sun Wukong, King of the Apes. **Right**, mask colours provide information about the character.

Yuan dynasty (1271–1368). In general, the dan, who were traditionally played by men, have their faces made up with a white base and various shades of carmine, and a little pale pink around the eyes. They move gracefully with soft, flowing steps. Other characteristics are their half-sung, half-spoken dialogue and a kind of mewing singing.

However, for nearly forty years now, the training of men to sing female roles has been prohibited. The reason given is that this practice has led to "sexual perversion".

Jing, or painted-face roles, portray warriors, heroes, statesmen, adventurers and supernatural beings. Their stage make-up is like a skilfully-made, conspicuous mask.

Masks and costumes: The costumes are based on court costumes of the Han, Tang, Song, and especially the Ming dynasties (1368–1644), as well as from the era of the Manchu emperors (1644–1911). Old wall paintings and drawings of the period in question were studied when the costumes were designed. The costumes of the Beijing opera, however, are by no means realistic. Their symbolic characteristics are particularly obvious in the beggar costumes: they wear silk with colourful patches. While the symbolic colours and patterns of their stage make-up reveal details of character, colour may also be used purely for aesthetic reasons, creating harmony between costume, face and head-

Finally, the chou, or the clowns, are easily recognised by their white-painted eye and nose areas. The eyes are also sometimes enclosed in a black square frame. Only real comedies have chou in leading roles, and in other pieces they take secondary parts. They often appear as peasants, servants or other menials, and the coarse colloquial speech used in their dialogues makes the audience laugh. What the other roles achieve through expressive, elevated speech, the chou gains by making use of everyday slang. The jokes of the chou are easy even for a Beijing opera novice to understand, as they are similar to comic characters in theatres worldwide.

dress. The make-up artists can create more than 300 different types of faces.

The history of the mask-like make-up, according to the story, is as follows: Zhuge Liang, a hero from the time of the Three Kingdoms (220–280 AD), had particularly fine, feminine features. For this reason, the great strategist had the idea of painting his face with terrifying colours to frighten his enemies, thus inventing the mask. Red shows a loyal, brave character; black represents a good, strong, slightly rough-diamond and coarse nature; blue symbolises wildness and courage, but also arrogance; yellow indicates a weakened version of the same failing;

green is the sign of an unstable character; orange and grey are signs of age, and a golden mask is worn by gods and goddesses.

Good characters are made up with relatively simple colours, but enemy generals and hostile characters use complicated patterns in their masks. Mysterious characters in the jing roles wear all kinds of colour and pattern combinations. Make-up with the colours green, red and black shows that a character has a limited quantity of the qualities listed above. The addition of green and blue may be a sign that this character rebels before submitting to higher authority.

Cao Cao, one of the main figures from the time of *The Three Kingdoms* and who often

ever said he was going to *see* a Beijing opera, he would have simply sounded ridiculous, for connoisseurs went to listen to an opera. During a lengthy sung portion, they would not watch the stage, but sit with their eyes closed and listening, clapping to the rhythm and thinking about every word in the song."

Beijing opera is a complete work of art, rather than a realistic drama, although in recent years the use of scenery, lighting effects, and more props has led to some change. The form and performance of Beijing opera make it unique. Today, one question in particular is asked: How is this art form to develop, allowing the new to arise without destroying the old?

appears on the Chinese stage, is made up in white, with thin eyebrows and sometimes with many zigzagging lines. This shows not only his great age but also his disgraceful character, as white symbolises treachery, poor self-discipline, cunning and guile.

The art of seeing: In China, you never say you're going to see a Beijing opera; rather, you say that you are going to listen to one. Music and song, after all, are the main elements of opera. A famous performer wrote in his memoirs: "If, in earlier years, anyone had

Left, female general in splendid costume. **Above**, a traitor is accused.

In Beijing opera, the unnecessary is left out and the emphasis is on the essential.

Props are used sparingly. An oar in the hand of a boatman is enough to make it clear that the scene takes place in a boat. A chair can be just a chair, but it can also be high ground in a landscape. An unlit candle can be the sign that evening is coming on. Every soldier carrying a banner represents a whole regiment. Riders almost always play two parts, for they also have to portray the movement of the horse – rearing, galloping, and trotting – through mime and gesture, thus turning themselves into centaurs.

But there is also an art to understanding

and enjoying this kind of theatre. There is great use of convention, so if you want to enjoy Beijing opera, knowing some of the rules is an advantage.

The style of acting is typical of the "non-reality" of Beijing opera. The aim of the actor is not, as in Western drama, to become the character portrayed. The actor distances him or herself from the role and tries to quote it, to portray events that are connected to the role. No Beijing opera performers ever end up "beside themselves." The closest parallels in the West to the ritual style of operatic performance with its fixed gestures are to be found in classic mime, in ballet and among circus clowns.

You will enjoy seeing Beijing opera when the technique of the performers is perfect and when you can follow the stylised methods of expression. Not that this is easy, since there are more than twenty different ways of laughing and smiling alone. The smallest movement of the eyes, the mouth, a single finger, is full of significance. All has been carefully and painstakingly rehearsed: every movement of hand, foot and body are precisely laid down. And they vary from role to role. When a sheng walks, he lifts his feet up and places them slightly to one side. A dan, on the other hand, walks in a slow glide, with little steps, one foot hardly separated from the other. The painted faces take big steps and adopt an upright, proud posture.

In contrast to the other three roles, which demand an upright position, the chou uses his whole body in an expressive, lively fashion. Given the symbolic nature of Beijing opera, this theatrical skill demands excellent coordination from the actors. Just as in a good piece of calligraphy, movement must be both stylish and correct, so every symbol must have its exact counterpoint in real life. The actor has to follow the rules and conventions. How far he or she is able to deviate from them, with delicacy and certainty, without in any way breaking them, is a measure of talent. Using the medium of Beijing opera, actors can swim on the stage, or a battle can be portrayed taking place in water or in darkness. On stage, embroideries can be created or tea prepared using the art of mime. Everyday things can be translated into the language of the stage. Enacting them, the performer of the Beijing opera shows three things: how the process is being enacted according to the rules, what the character portrayed feels about it, and finally, his or her own interpretation of the action.

Modern competition: Under the influence of foreign culture, modern forms of theatre have only begun to develop in China over the last few decades.

Among the influential dramatists are Cao Yu, Tianhan, Guo Moruo and Lao She. The latter wrote *The Teahouse*, performed in Western Europe and Japan.

In the meantime, Western dramatists have also found a sizeable audience in China. Successful performances include – to name but a few examples – Brecht's *Galileo Galilei* and *The Caucasian Chalk Circle*, Arthur Miller's *All My Sons*, as well as various Shakespearean plays. Young dramatists and directors have recently been trying to break with old conventions. London University's Su Liqun's *Zhuang Zi Tests his Wife* was the first play to be staged in English by local actors in over eighty years, while the truly innovative Experimental Theatre of Modern Drama's *Lay Down Your Whip – Woyzeck* combined Chinese street theatre with a German anti-fairy tale to deal with, among other things, violence against women.

Left, elegance and grace on roller skates. **Right**, a novel and acrobatic use of chairs.

Painting, like most other cultural pursuits in China, has a long history; cult murals in tombs, temples and palaces, as well as scroll paintings are known to have existed in the 3rd to 1st centuries BC. Interest in painting is explained by the extraordinary value the Chinese place – and have always placed – on the art of brush painting.

Brush painting: This importance given to brush painting is due to the intimate association between writing and painting, resulting from the original pictographic character of the Chinese script. As Chinese writing is not phonetic, anybody who is literate in whatever region and independent of a local dialect will be able to understand a written text. This nationwide unifying and historically continuous script was therefore always more important than the spoken language; the art of rhetoric – as practised, for instance, in ancient Greece – never developed in China.

The close connection between writing and Chinese painting is evident from the customary incorporation of written words in most Chinese pictures, such as a poem, the name of the painting, the painter's name and date of completion, as well as the painter's and collector's name stamp. There are also examples of calligraphy where the ideograms stray so far from the characters as to virtually become paintings themselves.

In China, painting comprises monochromatic and coloured work in ink on fabric or paper, mural reproductions such as woodblock prints, calligraphy as well as some related techniques such as embroideries, woven pictures, and decorative paintings.

Writing and painting utensils are referred to in China as the Four Treasures of the Study. They consist of the brush, ink, rubbing stone and paper – tools held in high esteem by poets, scholars and painters. There are reliable records of brush and ink already being used in the 1st century BC. Today, a paintbrush consists of a bundle of rabbit fur set in a slim bamboo tube; finer brushes are made of pine marten fur. These brushes differ from the European watercolour brushes by their softness and, above all, by coming to a very fine point at the end, which allows a brushstroke to be gradually broadened by a movement of the wrist – from a hairline to the full breadth of the brush.

As its French name *encre de Chine* suggests, Chinese ink was only taken up in Europe as a distinct kind of paint in the 17th century. There is no doubt, however, that this ink was already widely used in China during the Han period. It is made from the soot of coniferous resin with the addition of glue; ink of good quality even has perfume added – musk in former days, but cloves are now commonly used. The substance is pressed into various wooden moulds, giving it the shape of slabs, bars or prisms. Solid ink gained cult significance early on because it was esteemed as the most important calligraphic material.

Ink in solid form is used both for writing and painting, although liquid ink is now also available. However, this deprives the painting process and calligraphy of some of their contemplative attraction, because the rubbing of ink is not just a practical procedure but also attunes one to the artistic activity and aids concentration. The process involves dripping water onto a stone pestle, rubbing solid ink on it and then diluting the solution with water if necessary.

Paper is the usual medium on which to paint. In former days, silk and fine linen were often used, but are now rarely used because they do not allow as much technical refinement as paper does. Paper – itself another ancient Chinese invention, developed by Cai Lun and used from AD 106 onwards – is now produced in different qualities, each offering the painter alternative possibilities depending on absorption and texture.

In China, painting is learned in much the same way as writing: through copying old masters or textbooks, of which *Flowers from a Mustard Seed Garden* is one of the most famous. A painter is considered a master of his art only when the necessary brushstrokes for a bird, a chrysanthemum or a waterfall flow effortlessly from his hand. The strong emphasis placed on perfection quickly leads to specialization by painters on specific subjects. In this way, for instance, Xu Beihong (1895–1953) became known as the painter of horses, just as Qi Bai-Shi (1862–1957) was famous for his shrimps.

One of the most favoured painting forms in China was landscape painting. Notable characteristics of this form of painting are perspectives that draw the viewer into the picture, plain surfaces (unpainted empty spaces) that give the picture a feeling of depth, and the harmonious relationship between man and nature, with man depicted as a small, almost disappearing, figure in nature.

A peculiar feature is the presentation of the picture as a hanging scroll. It is first painted on silk or on extremely thin paper, backed with stronger paper and mounted in a complicated way on a long roll of silk or brocade. Then a wooden stick is attached at the lower end (or left end, if the scroll is to be displayed horizontally). Typically, the picture was stored away rolled up and brought out only on special occasions to be slowly unfurled, revealing only parts of a scene that was pieced together in the mind of the observer, subtly drawing him into the picture, making him a participant and not just a mere observer. After it had been displayed, the scroll was carefully put away again.

Thus, the picture was handled in order to be looked at – touched by hand while being scrutinized. With horizontal scrolls, always unrolled little by little, the hands were in constant movement. A similarity applies to the other two forms of presenting classical painting – the fan that needed unfolding and the album leaf that needed pages turned. The underlying thought was to create a bond between picture and observer – an intimate merger – whereas Western painting on panel or canvas impose a rational distance. In keeping with this, a landscape painting often has a path or bridge in the foreground to bring the viewer into the picture.

Silk and the less-noble arts: Calligraphy, painting, poetry and music are regarded in China as the noble arts, whereas the applied arts are considered merely as an honourable craft. All the same, in the West, these skilled crafts have always held a special fascination. When thinking of China, one thinks of silk, jade and porcelain.

The cultivation of the silkworm is said to go back to the 3rd century BC. Legend has it that planting of mulberry trees and keeping

silkworms was started by the wife of the mythical Yellow Emperor Huangdi. For centuries, silk held the place of currency: civil servants and officers as well as foreign envoys were frequently paid or presented with bales of silk. The precious material was transported to the Middle East and the Roman empire via the Silk Road. The Chinese maintained a monopoly on silk until about 200 BC, when the secret of its manufacture became known in Korea and Japan. In the West – in this case the Byzantine empire – such knowledge was acquired only in the 6th century AD. The Chinese had prohibited the export of silkworm eggs and the dissemination of knowledge of their cultivation, but a

monk is said to have succeeded in smuggling some silkworm eggs to the West. Today's centres of silk production are areas in the south of China around Hangzhou, Suzhou and Wuxi; in this region, silk can be bought at a lower price. Hangzhou has the largest silk industry in the People's Republic, while in Suzhou, silk embroidery has been brought to the highest artistic level.

Porcelain: The Chinese invented porcelain sometime in the 7th century – a thousand years before the Europeans did. The history of Chinese ceramic artifacts, however, goes back to neolithic times. Along the Huanghe (Yellow River) and the Yangzi (Changjiang),

7,000- to 8,000-year-old ceramic vessels, red and even black clayware with comb and rope patterns, have been found. The Yangshao and Longshan cultures of the 5th to 2nd millennium BC developed new types of vessels and a diversity of patterns in red, black or brown. Quasi-human masks, stylised fish, and hard, thin-walled stoneware, with kaolin and lime feldspar glazes, were created. Later, light-grey stoneware with green glazes, known as *yue* ware – named after the kilns of the town of Yuezhou – were typical designs of the Han period. Even during the Tang dynasty, China was known in Europe and the Middle East as the home of porcelain.

The most widespread form of ancient Chinese porcelain was celadon – a product of a blending of iron oxide with the glaze that resulted, during firing, in the characteristic green tone of the porcelain. *Sancai* ceramics – ceramics with three-colour glazes from the Tang dynasty – became world-famous. The colours were mostly strong green, yellow and brown. Sancai ceramics were also found among the tomb figurines of the Tang period in the shape of horses, camels, guardians in animal or human form, ladies of the court, and officials. The Song period celadons – ranging in colour from pale or moss green, pale blue or pale grey to brown tones – were also technically excellent. As early as the Yuan period, a technique from Persia was used for underglaze painting in cobalt blue (commonly known as Ming porcelain). Some common themes seen throughout the subsequent Ming period were figures, landscapes and theatrical scenes. At the beginning of the Qing dynasty, blue-and-white porcelain attained its highest level of quality. Since the 14th century, Jingdezhen has been the centre of porcelain manufacture, although today, relatively inexpensive porcelain can be bought throughout China. However, antique

pieces are still hard to come by because the sale of articles predating the Opium Wars is prohibited by the Chinese government.

Jade: With its soft sheen and rich nuances of colour, jade is China's most precious stone. Jade is not a precise mineralogical entity but rather comprises two minerals: jadeite and nephrite. The former is more valuable because of its translucence and hardness, as well as its rarity. The Chinese have known jade since antiquity, but it became widely popular only in the 18th century. Colours vary from white to green, but there are also red, yellow and lavender jades. In China, a clear emerald-green stone is valued

Left, painting of the famous contemporary painter Li Keran with calligraphy. **Above**, hand painting on porcelain in a factory.

most highly. According to ancient legend, Yu, as the jewel is known, came from the holy mountains and was thought to be crystallized moonlight. In fact, jade came from Khotan, along the southern Silk Road.

Nephrite is quite similar to jadeite, but not quite as hard and is more common. During the 18th century, nephrite was quarried in enormous quantities in the Kunlun mountains. It comes in various shades of green (not the luminous green of jadeite), white, yellow and black. The oldest jades so far discovered come from the neolithic Hemadu culture (about 5000 BC). The finds were presumably ritual objects. Circular disks called *bi*, given to the dead to take with them, were frequently found. Centuries later, the corpses of high-ranking officials were clothed in suits made of more than 2,000 thin slivers of jade sewn together with gold wire. Since the 11th century, the Jade Emperor has been revered as the superior godhead in Daoist popular religion. Today, the ring disk – a symbol of heaven – is still worn as a talisman; jade bracelets are believed to protect against rheumatism.

In the jade carving workshops in present-day China, there are thought to be as many as 30 kinds of jade in use. Famous among the jade workshops are those in Qingtian (Zhejiang province), Shoushan (Fujian province), and Luoyang (Hunan province). Masters of jade work include Zhou Shouhai, from the jade carving establishment in Shanghai, and Wang Shusen in Beijing, the latter specializing in Buddhist figurines. In government shops, jade can be trusted to be genuine. On the open market and in private shops, however, caution is advised. Genuine jade always feels cool and cannot be scratched with a knife. Quality depends on the feel of the stone, its colour, transparency, pattern and other factors. If in doubt, a reputable expert should be consulted.

Lacquerware: The glossy sheen of lacquerware is not only attractive to the eye but is also appealing to the touch. The bark of the lacquer tree (*rhus verniciflua*), which grows in central and southern China, exudes a milky sap when cut, which solidifies in moist air, dries and turns brown. This dry layer of lacquer is impervious to moisture, acid, and scratches, and is therefore ideal protection for materials such as wood or bamboo.

The oldest finds of lacquered objects date back to the 5th millennium BC. Bowls, tins, boxes, vases, and furniture made of various materials (wood, bamboo, wicker, leather, metal, clay, textiles, paper) are coated with a skin of lacquer. A base coat is applied to the core material, followed by extremely thin layers of the finest lacquer that, after drying in dust-free moist air, are smoothened and polished. In the dry lacquer method, the lacquer itself dictates the form: fabric or paper is saturated with lacquer and pressed into a wood or clay mould. After drying, the mould is removed and the piece coated with further layers of lacquer. Vessels, boxes and plates were already being made in this way in the Han period.

During the Tang dynasty, large Buddhist sculptures were produced by the lacquerware process. If soot or vinegar-soaked iron filings are added to the lacquer, it will dry into a black colour; cinnabar turns it red. The colour combination of red and black, first thought to have been applied in the 2nd century BC, is still considered a classic. In the Song and Yuan periods, simply-shaped monochromatic lacquerware was most highly valued.

During the Ming period, the manufacture of lacquered objects was further refined. The cities of Beijing, Fuzhou, Guangzhou, Chengdu, Yangzhou and Suzhou were renowned for exquisite lacquerware, which was enriched and decorated with carving, fillings, gold paint and inlay.

The carved lacquer technique, which began at the time of the Tang dynasty, reached its highest peak during the Ming and Qing periods. The core, often of wood or tin, is coated with mostly red layers of lacquer. When the outermost coat has dried, decorative carving is applied, with the knife penetrating generally to the lowest layer so that the design stands out from the background in relief. Today, lacquerware is mainly produced in Beijing, Fuzhou and Yangzhou. The most well-known lacquerware is the Beijing work, which goes back to the impe-

ornamentation. The spaces between the rods are filled with enamel paste and fired in the kiln. Finally, metal surfaces not covered with enamel are gilded. During the Yuan dynasty, Yunnan was the centre of cloisonné production. However, the golden age of this technique was the Ming period, when the techniques of melting enamel on porcelain was developed.

Ivory: As a craft material, ivory is as old as jade, and early pieces can be traced to as far back as 5000 BC. During the Bronze Age, wild elephants were not a rarity in northern China, some of them were tamed during the Shang dynasty. The old artist carvers regarded elephant tusks as a most desirable materi-

rial courts of the Ming and Qing dynasties. Emperor Qianlong (1734–1795) had a special liking for carved lacquerware; he was even buried in a coffin magnificently carved using this technique.

Cloisonné: The cloisonné technique – used to create metal objects with enamel decor – reached China from Persia in the 8th century AD, was lost and then rediscovered in the 13th century. In the cloisonné technique, metal rods are soldered to the body of the metal object. These form the outlines of the

al from which to make jewellery, implements and containers. The once-large herds of elephants in the south of China thus shrank to a small remnant, and eventually ivory had to be imported. Ming dynasty carvings exemplified the excellent craft skills and superior taste; then during Qing times, ivory carving was even further refined.

Today's centres for ivory carving are the cities of Beijing, Guangzhou and Shanghai. All the ivory is imported from Thailand and several African countries. When buying ivory in the People's Republic of China, keep in mind that the import of ivory is prohibited in many countries.

<u>Left</u>, the art of carving in ivory. <u>Above</u>, precious ivory carving.

"Seeing is worth a thousand words." Tour guides in China occasionally quote this old Chinese proverb when greeting foreign visitors. In such an exquisite and ancient culture as that of China, words indeed quite often fail. Seeing does, in fact, surpass words.

Most travellers to Beijing make their way to Tiananmen Square, the Square of Heavenly Peace. This square may rightly be seen as the centre of both the old and new China. Here, the eye looks upon open space that is one of the largest public squares in the world. Nearly 50 years of socialism, made manifest in the monumental government buildings and in Mao's mausoleum, as well as centuries of the feudal history of the Middle Kingdom, have come together to surround Tiananmen, which is almost – but not quite – in the centre of Beijing.

What is the centre of Beijing is the Imperial Palace, where generations of emperors have ruled over the world's most complex society. From here, travellers can set out on a journey into the history of the Chinese empire, experiencing it not only through the Palace and surrounding historical sites, but also through the Temple of Heaven, and outside of Beijing, at the Summer Palace and the Great Wall. Unfortunately, like historical structures elsewhere in the world, the decades and the violence have taken their toll on ancient China's monuments – European troops in the 19th century, Japanese soldiers in search of booty during World War II, fanatical Red Guards during the Cultural Revolution. Fortunately, the Chinese government saw the value in returning to these monuments much of their former glory, and the restoration of ancient relics has been an ongoing affair in Beijing. Unfortunately, urban development often eclipses such efforts, overcoming them with progress.

Historical it may be, but Beijing is very much a living and growing city. Nearly 13 million people live here. The changes of the city symbolic of the prosperity and problems that China increasingly shares – have left both people and skyline very much different than a decade ago, or from the preconceptions with which travellers often arrive. While walking along the expansive boulevards or through the *hutong* alleys, remember an old Chinese proverb. "None are as blind as those who don't want to see."

Preceding pages: monumental poster painting; well-organized bicycle park; Tiananmen Square; the Great Wall (but only a short part of it). **Left**, bronze lion in the Imperial Palace.

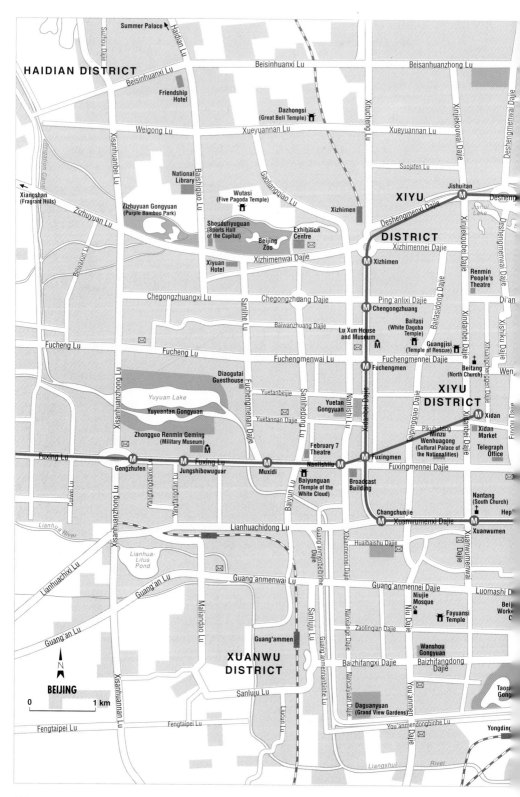

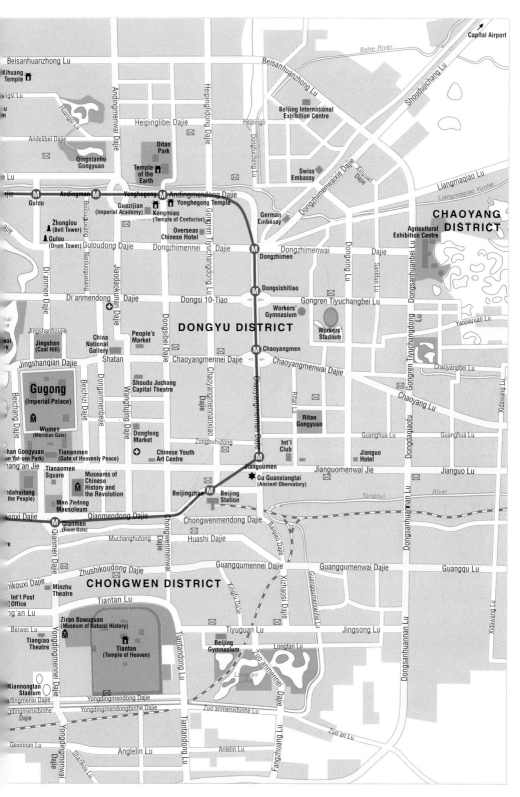

BEIJING

In traditional Chinese thought, the world was not imagined as the flat, round disk of the Ptolomaean vision in the West, but was conceived as a square. A city, too – and especially a capital city – was supposed to be square, a reflection of the cosmic order and following its geometrical norms. In no other city in China was this basic idea realised as completely as in ancient Beijing.

The city did not receive its typical form, which still survives today, until the rule of the Ming dynasty. The Emperor Yongle is considered its actual planner and architect. In 1421, he moved the seat of government from Nanjing to the city of Beiping (Northern Peace), renaming it Beijing (Northern Capital), which, in a rather unfortunate attempt at romanisation, became known as Peking in the West.

The city layout plans of Emperor Yongle followed the principles of geomancy, the traditional doctrine of winds and water that strives to attain a harmonious relationship between human life and nature.

Screened from the north by a semicircle of hills, Beijing lies on a plain opening south. In an analogue to this position, all important buildings in the city are built to face the south, protected from harmful *yin* influences of the north, such as the Siberian winter winds or the enemies from the steppes. It was in the south that the generosity and warmth of the *yang* sphere was thought to reside. As a result, it was not by chance that **Qianmen**, the Outer or Southern Gate to the city, was the largest, most beautiful, and most sacred of its kind. **Jingshan (Coal Hill)**, to the north of the Imperial Palace, which when the air is clear has a beautiful view of the rooftops of Beijing, was probably created according to geomantic considerations.

A line from north to south divides the city into eastern and western halves, with a series of buildings and city features laid out as mirror images to their equivalents on the opposite side of the city. For instance, the Ritan (Altar of the Sun) has its equivalent in the Yuetan (Altar of the Moon). Planned in an equally complementary way were Xidan and Dongdan, the eastern and western business quarters, which today still serve as shopping streets.

Some of the most notable buildings of old and new Beijing are to be found on the gigantic symmetrical axis itself. Going from the north, the **Zhonglou**, **Gulou** (Bell and Drum Towers, the two huge clocks of the city), and Jingshan; from the south, the Qianmen (Outer Gate), and more recently, the **Mao Mausoleum** together with **Tiananmen** (Square of Heavenly Peace) and the "Monument to the Heroes of the Nation" are lined up one after the other.

In the middle of this chain of historically significant buildings lies the heart of ancient Beijing, the **Dragon Throne**. From it, the Son of Heaven held the reins of political power and served as ritual mediator between Heaven and Earth. With his face turned to the south, he attempted to steer the fate of his

enormous empire. The throne of the emperor was considered the centre of the physical world. The Earth was imagined as a gigantic chessboard, its square and mostly walled elements clearly given a defined place in a hierarchy depending on how far they are removed from the centre. The imperial throne is embedded in a majestic palace, which is also square and surrounded by high walls on all sides – the **Forbidden City**. Around it lies the **Imperial City**, which in earlier times also formed a square that was surrounded by walls.

Part of the Imperial City was a huge chain of lakes, its northern part today forming the centre of **Beihai Park**; on the shores of the central and southern waters lies, since 1949, the **Zhongnan-hai (Government Quarter)**, the Party's holy of holies, which foreign observers like to call the new Forbidden City. Only highly-placed officials and important state guests are allowed in.

Crowded around the Imperial City was a sea of mainly single-storeyed houses: the **Inner City**. Its roofs, curved like the crests of waves, were not allowed to rise above the height of the Imperial Palace. Here, the tasteful homes of wealthy and influential officials, important Manchus, and the elegant private residences of princes were to be found. Even nowadays, this part of Beijing is still considered to be the actual Inner City or old city. However, only a few monumental gates of the mighty defensive walls that once surrounded it have survived – gates such as the Qianmen or, in the north, the Deshengmen. They tower up into the sky like impregnable fortresses, remains of a fortification system that had to make way for a fast-lane highway.

Adjoining the Inner City to the south was the **Outer City**. In Qing times, these two residential areas were known as the Tatar City and the Chinese City. In the Chinese City, the doors of the houses were lower, the *hutong* (as the alleys of Beijing were known) were narrower, and the rice bowls were less well filled. Hot water was drunk instead of tea; people wore straw sandals on **Street scene in old Beijing.**

106

their feet instead of satin boots. However, bored officials and wealthy merchants liked to flee their respectable surroundings and come here. There were tea and opera houses, bathing houses and brothels, speciality restaurants and bazaars – all competing for the favours and money of tipsy literati, mahjong-playing monks, lusting mandarins, and the occasional prince in disguise.

Even today, things are livelier to the south of Qianmen (Outer Gate) than they are in other parts of the city. However, the little theatres are no longer reserved for the brilliantly-painted and costumed performers of Beijing opera, nor for supple acrobats. Kung fu films and trite romances bring in more money. The famous gourmet restaurants are usually hopelessly crowded. Dazhalan, a small street running at right angles to Qianmen Dajie, has old established shops and businesses of excellent reputation, and is still an attraction for the people from the Beijing suburbs as well as the provinces. Not far away is **Liuli-chang**, a shopping street restored to its original style for tourists, which offers almost everything that China can offer by way of art and kitsch. The number-one shopping district today is still **Wanfujing**, a street that runs in a northerly direction from the Beijing Hotel.

Outside these historic city districts, huge faceless concrete tower blocks have sprouted. In the northwest lies the scientific and intellectual quarter with the most famous universities – Beijing and Qinghua. The Chaoyang District to the east is the largest industrial area of the city. Traffic on the city streets is still dominated by the never-ending flow of bicycles. The local public transport system is insufficiently developed and hopelessly overcrowded. Up till now, the metro has not been of much help.

The rhythm of the seasons is similar to that in central Europe. The summers are hot and long, winters are cold and dry. When sandstorms whirl through the city in spring, Beijing hardly dares to breathe. The fine dust forces its way through all cracks and crevices in homes, which are badly insulated.

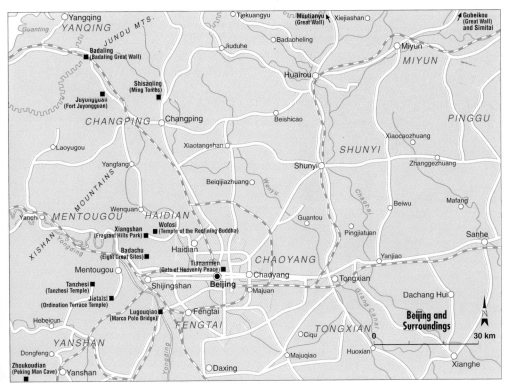

A morning walk through the park offers undreamed-of impressions and acoustic delights: the sound of a moon fiddle accompanied by an aria from a Beijing opera; the chirping of birds, their cages hung in the trees; the sight of graceful sword dancers and noiseless *taiji* practitioners; and more recently, disco gymnastics for the elderly.

Modern Beijing, although transformed, does retain some of the spirit of the Beijing of Ming and Qing times. The ancient city was not just a favoured place for magnificent palaces and broad parks; here also, the great religions of China, this country of many peoples, had their most impressive sacred buildings. Many of the Buddhist, Daoist, and Tibetan shrines, many mosques and churches, and the majority of the small temples, mostly dedicated to local gods, have been destroyed since 1949 or have been turned into factories, barracks or schools. Since the socialist revolution, the religious element of everyday life in Beijing has been pushed into the background. However, the most historically important religious sites have been restored and reopened to the public.

Beyond Beijing: Escape beyond Beijing's physical boundaries to explore its spill-over charm in Tianjin, Chengde and Beidaihe. These towns attract many Beijingers out on a day trip by train.

Tianjin, which used to be romanised as Tientsin, has a population of 7 million and is one of China's major cities. Situated some 140 kilometres (90 mi) to the southeast of Beijing, it is famous for its port and its carpets, and, because of its architecture, it has more of a city atmosphere than the old cityscape of Beijing with its hutong.

Chengde, formerly Jehol, was the summer residence of the Qing emperors, and a politically important meeting place for the leaders of ethnic minorities. The **Eight Outer Temples** were built in the style of the minority peoples (for instance, those of Tibet). The "palace for escaping from the heat" – the Chinese name of Chengde – is surrounded by a magnificent park.

Beidaihe, some five hours away from Beijing on the Bohai Bay of the Yellow Sea, is the most favoured seaside resort for people from Beijing because of its wonderful sandy beaches. In the hot summer months, it is visited by thousands upon thousands of Chinese workers, all in need of a well-earned rest. Seafront hotels overlook beaches reserved for their guests. In out-of-the-way villas, the old guard of party bosses meet for their traditional annual summer conference. At nearby Shanhaiguan, sections of the Great Wall have been restored and are open to visitors.

The quantity and variety of cultural and artistic places of interest in Beijing are enough to warrant a stay of at least a week, without any risk of boredom. But unfortunately, the organisers of group tours generally plan stays of between two and four days maximum for Beijing, as the city is usually one of many stops on a tour of China or Asia that lasts for only a few weeks. Over the last few years, however, the number of business and individual travellers has increased immensely, and they are spending more time exploring this great city.

Left, tired feet. **Right**, military dignitary at the Ming Tombs.

GUGONG:
THE IMPERIAL PALACE

For a long time, the Middle Kingdom was ruled by an emperor residing in **Gugong (Imperial Palace)**, in Beijing, which was considered the centre of the world by the Chinese. The Inner Palace was called the Purple City after the constellation of purplish stars that has the pole star in the centre, thus putting the rulers' residence on an equal footing with the centre of the entire universe.

The life of the emperors, given their position as Sons of Heaven dealing with earthly matters, was strictly regulated. The emperor was the measure of all things in the cosmic trinity of heaven, human beings and earth. He was supposed to be the intermediary between heaven (*yang*) and earth (*yin*), and thus incorporate the Mandate of Heaven on earth. He was responsible for peace, prosperity and orderly life on earth.

The very architecture of the Imperial Palace raised the court above all earthly things. Huge red walls enclosed the inner sanctum, an area forbidden to ordinary mortals. No building in the city was permitted to be taller than the walls of the Palace nor to outshine them in colourful splendour.

The exact geometric pattern of the city that surrounded the Palace reflected the strongly hierarchical structure of Chinese society – a fixed and ordered harmony. The Chinese considered this grid-like ground plan an expression of cosmic order.

According to legend, the Ming emperor Yongle, who began the building of the Imperial Palace in 1409, received the plans from the hands of a Taoist priest who had descended from heaven especially for that purpose.

The buildings were aligned according to north-south lines. The most important buildings face south, towards the sun, and have names mainly based on Confucian philosophy, since those are considered fortunate. Thus there are endless combinations of "harmony", "peace" and "quiet" in building names.

Tiananmen Square (Square of Heavenly Peace) formed the complete complex of the Forbidden City, together with the Imperial Palace. The imperial corridor, following an imaginary north-south line, ran from the square's southern gate (today, Qianmen) via Tiananmen (Gate of Heavenly Peace), to the Imperial Palace and northwards as far as the Bell and Drum Towers.

Palace life: Every time the emperor moved from one part of the palace to another, it was a major expedition. Puyi, the last Emperor of China, whose life Bertolucci depicted in his film, *The Last Emperor*, described a walk in the garden in his autobiography: "At the head marched a eunuch, a herald whose function was like that of a car horn. He walked twenty or thirty yards in front of the others, constantly hissing 'chi, chi' to shoo away any other people in the vicinity. He was followed by two of the higher eunuchs walking like crabs on both sides of the path. Behind them came the main group of the procession, the Dowager Empress and me.

"If I was carried in my palanquin, two of the younger eunuchs walked at my side, ready to attend to my wishes at any time. If I was walking, they held me under the arms to support me. Behind me followed a eunuch with a great silken canopy. He was accompanied by a great crowd of eunuchs, some of whom carried nothing, others with their hands full of all kinds of paraphernalia – a chair to rest on, a change of clothes, umbrellas and parasols; after the eunuchs who personally served the emperor came the eunuchs from the Imperial Tea Office with boxes of cakes and delicacies, with jugs of hot water and the tea sets; they were followed by the eunuchs from the Imperial Pharmacy. The following always had to be included among the medicines taken: the tinctures of lampwick grass, chrysanthemums, red roots, bamboo leaves and bamboo bark; in summer, betony pills for regulating the emotions, six-harmonies pills for the stability of the central organs, gilded cinnabar pills for cooling, pills made of sticky scented rice, an ointment for universal use, medicines against cramps and powders to combat infectious disease; also, all year round the tincture of the three immoralities was available to aid digestion.

"At the end of the procession came the eunuchs carrying chamber pots and pulling commodes. If I went on foot, an open or closed palanquin followed, according to the season. This brightly coloured circus parade of several dozen people progressed in complete order and silence."

History of the Palace: As early as the Yuan dynasty (1279–1368), the palace of the Mongol emperors was situated just to the west of today's Imperial Palace. In 1403, the third Ming emperor, Yongle, decided to move the capital to Beijing. The palace was completely built anew, from the foundations upwards, and this basic structure has remained to the present day. From 1406 to 1420, about 200,000 people were occupied with building the palace. The stones had to be brought in on wagons from the countryside around Beijing. In winter,

Camel train in front of the Imperial Palace.

they were drawn on ropes from the quarries over the icy ground. Wood came from the Yunnan and Sichuan provinces in the southwest of China.

The buildings of the palace – mostly wooden – were constantly being altered. The main enemy was fire, and often entire great halls burned down. For this reason, there were a number of large water containers in the palace, many made of gilded copper. Most of the present buildings date from the 18th century. (Even as late as 1987, one of the smaller buildings in the Imperial Palace fell victim to fire.)

Until the overthrow of the last emperor, the general public had no access to the Imperial Palace. Although the older parts were made into a museum in 1914, the last emperor and his court lived in the back parts of the palace until 1924. The first tourists visited the Imperial Palace sometime in the 1920s, but in 1949, the Guomindang took many of the palace treasures with them to Taiwan. After the founding of the People's Republic, extensive restoration work was undertaken. Today, the Imperial Palace is officially designated a palace museum, and is protected by law.

The Imperial Palace covers an area of 101 hectares (250 acres), is surrounded by a broad moat, and is protected by a wall 10 metres (35 ft) high with mighty watchtowers standing at the corners. The palace is divided into two main areas – the front part, comprising three large halls, in which the Ming and Qing emperors held state ceremonies, and a rear section consisting of three large palaces, a few smaller palaces to the east and west, and the Imperial Gardens. In the central hall of the front section, the Hall of Supreme Harmony, or Taihedian, is the Dragon Throne, the former centre of imperial power. Grouped around the Dragon Throne is a labyrinth of linked palace halls and squares of the Forbidden City, surrounded by walls and moats, and encircled by the government buildings and temples of the Imperial City. Many of the grand houses of the former princely families now house institutions, schools and official departments; the

Water container, originally gilded and intended for extinguishing palace fires.

Central Hospital was once the seat of the princely Yu family.

Tiananmen Square: The best place to start a visit to the Imperial Palace is Tiananmen Square. This centre of Beijing is a square that, with its area of 50 hectares (123 acres), is one of the largest and most imposing urban squares in the world. Its name comes from the Tiananmen (Gate of Heavenly Peace), on its northern boundary.

Tiananmen Square has been the heart of the nation since 1949, when Mao Zedong proclaimed China as the People's Republic in front of a crowd of 3 million. It is in this square – bounded by the Great Hall of the People (capacity 10,000) to the west, the Museum of Chinese History to the east, the Imperial Palace to the north and the "ordinary" city to the south of Qianmen – that classical heritage and revolutionary symbolism meet. A number of demonstrations have taken place here – mass parades organised by the government, the immense gatherings of the Cultural Revolution, demonstrations in April 1976, and especially the democracy rallies for which it became famous in the summer of 1989.

In the middle of the square is the **Monument to the Heroes of the People**, dedicated in 1958. The obelisk commemorates the fallen soldiers of the revolution. At its height of 37 metres (123 ft), it is 4 metres (14 ft) taller than the Tiananmen and it stands on a double pedestal. The lower part of the base is ornamented with bas-reliefs portraying the stages of Chinese revolutionary history, from the first Opium War (1840) to the founding of the People's Republic of China. The stone-paved slabs in the square are numbered in series, so that soldiers taking part in parades can quickly find their places.

To the south of the memorial, in front of Qianmen, is **Mao's mausoleum**. Nowadays, many Chinese regard it as a feudal remnant of the personality cult of Mao. Built in only nine months in 1978 for the deceased party Chairman and founder of the state, Mao Zedong, it now also contains rooms commemorat-

Dragon heads and legendary creatures keep away evil spirits.

ing other state and party leaders. The **Renmindahuitang (Great Hall of the People)**, on the west side of the square, dates from the 1950s. The National People's Assembly, the Chinese parliament, meets in the 50,000-square-metre (19,300-sq-ft) building. Various official departments are housed here, and political delegations from abroad are received in the hall.

On the eastern edge of Tiananmen Square, opposite the Great Hall of the People, are the **Museum of Chinese History and the Museum of the Revolution**, built in 1959 and opened in 1961. They give an overall impression of the development of China from the Old Stone Age, through the primitive societies, the slave-owning society, and feudalism, to more recent history since the Opium Wars and up to present times.

In the southeastern corner of Tiananmen Square is the former **Diplomatic Quarter**. To the north and south it borders on Chang'an Boulevard and Dongjiaomen Street, and to the east on Dongsi Street. In earlier years, it was surrounded by a wall and guarded by cannon. During the Boxer Rebellion, the embassies were under fire from Chongwenmen. Once the rebellion had been crushed, this area was made an extraterritorial concession and was administered by the foreigners. The Chinese could not buy land here, and the rickshaw coolies of the quarter had to have special plates on their carts – QD, for *Quartier Diplomatique*.

Qianmen (Qian Gate), or **Zhengyangmen** as it is sometimes known, borders the square to the south. This gate was built in the 15th century, and was then destroyed and rebuilt in 1905 after the Boxer Rebellion. It is one of the few surviving gates of the old Inner City. Outside Qianmen, the former Outer, or Chinese, City began, which even today is one of the busiest parts of the city. In earlier years, there were brothels and opium dens among the shops and restaurants along what is now Qianmen Street. This is where the "old China hands" continued to meet in the 1920s and 1930s. A stroll from Qianmen into

Filigree woodwork on palace roofs.

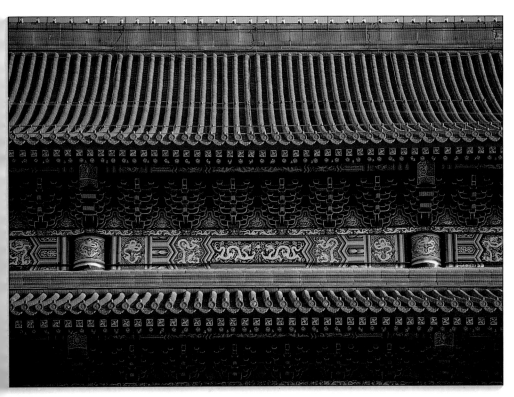

this district is worthwhile. Here you will find interesting shops and restaurants, and you can still get a feel of the old city of Peking.

In earlier times, officials came from the south and had to leave their horses outside Qianmen, or when they reached the side gates of Tiananmen (these were demolished in 1912 in order to open up the square). They then passed through the gates into the Forbidden City.

The gate called **Tiananmen** was itself reserved for the emperors. Today, the Chang'an Boulevard runs past the gate, and traffic roars along the boulevard's 40-kilometre (25-mi) stretch through the central city area. To the west is **Sun Yat-sen Park**. In this part of the city, which used to belong to the Forbidden City, the Altar of the Earth once stood. Opposite the park, on the eastern side of the gate, is the **Laodong Renmin Wenhuagong (Workers' Palace of Culture)**.

Tiananmen was built in 1417, and in 1465 the wooden structure, damaged by fire, was replaced with stone. In 1651, it

was rebuilt after destruction by the Manchu troops. The building, known as Guomen (Gate of the Empire), was then renamed Tiananmen. This was the meeting place of the divided city, where the levels of the traditional pyramid of authority – the city to the south of Qianmen, the Imperial City, and the Imperial Palace (or Purple City, the actual Forbidden City) – touched.

When the emperors left the Forbidden City to celebrate the New Year rites at the Temple of Heaven, they made their first offerings at Tiananmen. On important occasions, imperial decrees were lowered from the gate in a gilded box. The civil servants, kneeling, were to receive them, copy them, and then distribute them all over the country. Thus it was in a decidedly imperial manner that Mao Zedong proclaimed the People's Republic of China from this spot on 1 October 1949, and in the same way received the adulation of millions of Red Guards during the Cultural Revolution (1966–76).

The gate has become the symbol of Beijing, and, indeed, for the whole of the People's Republic of China. It is the only public building still to display the portrait of the founder of the state, Mao Zedong, on the outside.

Five marble bridges lead to the five passages through the gate. The central one follows the imperial route and was once reserved for the emperor. In earlier years, subjects are said to have put up petitions to the emperor, along with suggestions for improvements, on the marble pillars, the *huabiao*. To the left of the portrait of Mao Zedong, which is above the gate in the centre, is a sign in Chinese characters: "Long live the People's Republic of China." The sign on the right says, "Long live the great unity of all the peoples of the world."

Follow Chang'an Boulevard in a westerly direction for a few hundred yards. On the right-hand side and framed by red walls, **Xinhuamen** is the gate leading into **Zhongnanhai**, or, literally, Central and Southern Lake. Zhongnanhai is the seat of the Communist Party of China, and despite offering limited access to visitors, it is a sort of new Forbid-

Lions guard the palace gates.

den City. It was here that Mao Zedong used to reside as the Great Leader.

Imperial Palace: To the north of Tiananmen is **Wumen (Meridian Gate)**. The entrance to the actual Forbidden City, its 38 metres (125 ft) make it the highest gate at the palace. Because of the five pavilions on its U-shaped base, this gate was also known as the Gate of the Five Phoenixes. As everywhere in the palace, the number five is of great symbolic importance as it represents the five Confucian cardinal virtues. The emperor could only represent the *dao* of Heaven, the order that pervades the world, and bring harmony on Earth if he walked the path of these virtues. From Wumen's vantage, the emperor reviewed military parades, announced new calendars, and had rebellious officials punished.

Back then, the only people apart from the emperor allowed to use this gate were the empress on her wedding day, and the best scholars who had passed the palace examinations. Now, each day, hundreds of foreign and Chinese visitors pass through the huge gates with its large lion-head door knockers. Beyond the gate lies the first of the innumerable inner courtyards into which the Imperial Palace is divided. The **Jinshahe (Golden Water River)** runs along the palace's west wall and across the south.

The first courtyard ends to the north at the **Taihemen (Gate of Supreme Harmony)**, which was rebuilt in 1890. In this gate is a large map of the Imperial Palace. Beyond this gate is the largest **Court of the Imperial Palace**. In earlier times, the imperial shops selling silk and porcelain were situated here.

There are three large audience and throne halls at the end of this courtyard. They stand on a marble platform more than 8 metres (26 ft) high, with three levels. The balustrades on each level are decorated with dragon heads that spout water when it rains. The three halls are the Taihedian (Hall of Supreme Harmony), the Zhonghedian (Hall of Middle Harmony), and the Baohedian (Hall of Preserving Harmony).

In the **Taihedian (Hall of Supreme Harmony)**, the largest of the three halls,

Wumen, or Meridian Gate.

stood the **Dragon Throne**. From here, the emperor ruled, and only he could walk up the ramp adorned with dragon motifs into the hall. On the platform in front of the hall are two symbols – a grain measure on the left and a sundial to the right – representing imperial justice and agriculture. Also present are bronze figures of cranes and tortoises – symbols of good luck and longevity.

On state occasions, such as a coronation, the first day of the new year, or the empress' birthday, a formal court ceremony was conducted in the hall. During the Ming and Qing dynasties, its 35 metres (115 ft) made it the tallest building in Beijing. Outside the hall, the officials and the more important dignitaries lined up according to their rank. Incense and bells strengthened the impression of the other-worldly nature of the emperor.

The roof of the hall is supported by 72 pillars, with the inner six adorned by dragons, and the most attractive. Chinese feudal society even had a hierarchy based on roofs. Roofs served to indicate the social position of the householder, and the roofs of the Imperial Palace symbolized the highest degree of power through their colour, construction and material. Their breathtaking beauty makes it worth taking the time to see them again and again from different perspectives. The U-shaped corbels typical of Chinese wooden buildings – all built without the use of nails – were reserved for great palaces and temples.

The Hall of Supreme Harmony has the most imposing roof, with a horizontal ridge, four rooftrees and double eaves. The varnished ornaments are also a sign of the building's status. Its dragons, for instance, at a weight of 4.5 tonnes and a height of three metres (11 ft), are the largest in the palace. These dragons are supposed to attract clouds and water and so protect the building from fire. On the roof are the figures of 10 animals and an immortal, serving as protection against evil spirits.

In the smallest of the three front halls, the **Zhonghedian (Hall of Middle Harmony**, behind the Hall of Supreme Har-

Marble steps to Hall of Supreme Harmony.

mony), the emperor prepared for ceremonies before entering the main hall. Now, visitors can see an imperial palanquin here. The last of the three great halls, the **Baohedian** (**Hall of Preserving Harmony**), was used for the New Year's banquet and examinations.

Once beyond the Hall of Preserving Harmony, stairs lead down from the platform. In the middle of the stairs, along the former Imperial Way, lies a ramp hewn from a single block of marble weighing 250 tonnes and decorated with dragon motifs.

The centre of the rear palace is formed by the **Qianqinggong** (**Palace of Heavenly Purity**). Enter it through the **Qiangingmen** (**Gate of Heavenly Purity**). These palaces were the living and working quarters of the Ming and Qing emperors. In the rear hall of **Kuninggong** (**Palace of Earthly Tranquility**), the Manchu emperors, following their religious traditions, carried out ritual sacrifices that entailed slaughtering pigs and cooking votive offerings. At present, all that can be seen are *kang* (heated beds).

In the eastern wing of the Palace of Earthly Tranquility is the bridal chamber of Qing emperors who married after their accession, namely Kangxi, Tongzhi and Guangxu. The last time the room was used for this purpose was in the winter of 1922, by the deposed emperor Puyi. The emperor wrote:

"After we had drunk the marriage cup at our wedding and eaten cakes to ensure children and children's children, we entered this dark, red chamber. I felt very uncomfortable. The bride sat on the kang, her head lowered. Sitting beside her, I looked about for a while and saw nothing but red: red bed curtains, red bedclothes, a red jacket, a red skirt, red flowers in her hair, a red face… everything seemed to be made of red wax. I felt most dissatisfied. I did not want to sit, but to stand was even less desirable. Yangxindiang (Hall of Mental Cultivation) was, after all, more comfortable. I opened the door and went back to my accustomed apartments."

To the sides of the Palace of Heavenly Purity lie the **East and West Palaces**,

Imperial throne, Temple of Heavenly Purity.

grouped like the constellations around the Pole Star. Here, the emperor was the only adult male, surrounded by concubines, eunuchs, the empress, serving women and slaves. As late as 1900, there were still 10,000 people living in the palace. The servants, without exception, were eunuchs. For many Chinese, especially for the poor, it was lucrative to enter the imperial service as a eunuch. Surgeons stationed themselves at the gates to the Imperial City. They would perform the castration at reasonable rates, but then sell the sexual organs back to the victims at a high price, for the organs had to be presented in a bottle for inspection at the Imperial Palace. The operations were not without complications. Many a young man lost his life during the process. The eunuchs were the only people allowed to enter the city during the day. Thus, they were not only well-informed, but also skilled at intrigues. Some of them were very powerful people indeed.

One of the most important halls is the **Yangxindiang (Hall of Mental Cultivation)**, in the western part of the rear palaces. This is where Emperor Qianlong and the Empress Dowager Cixi lived. The last emperor, Puyi, also had his private apartments here. The working, living and sleeping rooms can be seen, as can the room in which Cixi prompted and controlled the child emperor Guangxu from behind a curtain.

Continue on with a look at the **Jiulongbi (Nine Dragon Screen)**, built out of 1773 glazed bricks. The dragon is a symbol of heaven and, therefore, of the emperor, as is the number nine, the highest unit. It is no surprise that the dragon had, according to Chinese mythology, nine sons. Each of these nine dragons had different skills. We have already met Chao Feng, for instance, who loves danger and is set on the roof to protect against fire.

Opposite the Dragon Screen is the **Gate of Peace and Longevity**, through which you enter **Ningshougong (Palace of Peace and Longevity)**. The Emperor Qianlong (1736–1796) had this complex built for his old age. The **Imperial Treasury**, which gives some idea

of the wealth and magnificence of the Qing emperors, can be found today in the adjoining halls to the north. One can see golden cutlery and table silver, jewellery, robes, porcelain, cloisonné, hunting equipment, and golden religious objects (many of the Qing emperors were followers of Tibetan Buddhism), as well as pictures made of precious and semi-precious stones, usually depicting animals and landscapes – symbols of longevity, health and good fortune.

On the way to the northeastern exit is a small well, the **Zhenfeijing (Well of the Concubine Zhen)**. Zhen Fei was the favourite concubine of the Emperor Guangxu. She supported him in his efforts to push through reforms in the Imperial Palace and in the empire as a whole. For this reason, Zhen Fei was hated by the "Old Buddha," as the vain Cixi called herself, and Cixi gave her eunuchs instructions to have Zhen Fei executed by drowning.

Now follow the mighty red walls in a westerly direction to the northern exit, Shenwumen. Before passing through the gate, however, take a quick look at the **Yuhuayuan (Imperial Flower Gardens)**. Laid out during the Ming period, it is a typical example of the traditional Chinese skill at landscape gardening. The artificial rocks, pavilions, pines, cypresses, flowers and bamboo work together to produce a harmonious whole. This garden was the only chance for many of the people who lived in the Palace to catch a glimpse of nature.

Leave the Imperial Palace by way of **Shenwumen (Gate of Spiritual Valour)**, built in 1420 and erected during the Kangxi era. Today, there is a car park outside of this gate, and on either side along the moat there are free markets. There is a great panoramic view of the Imperial Palace from Jingshan, or Coal Hill, as it is sometimes called, across the street. Although skyscrapers and modern buildings can be seen on the periphery, and although the yellow-gold curved roofs of the Imperial Palace are no longer the highest in Beijing, the palace complex, together with Tiananmen Square, makes an impressive picture of past glory.

Right, taiji practitioner with sword.

BEIJING IN THE MORNING

As soon as the day dawns and Beijing awakens, the first of the old men shuffle out of their homes to escape the morning chaos in the tiny apartments. In their hands are bird cages, which they swing back and forth as they make their way to the nearest park.

In the parks, the shapes formed by the shadow boxers can only be guessed at. Silent – with slow, flowing movements – they act out their dance with an invisible opponent. They seem to float above the ground as they practice the "monkey's retreat" or "send the tiger over the mountain", as the exercises are picturesquely, but aptly, named. Arms arch upward gracefully in a giant circle that symbolically splits the primordial unity of the cosmos into *yin* and *yang*. *Taijiquan*, or shadow boxing, is especially popular with older Chinese, although being only 300 years old itself, taijiquan is something of a newcomer.

Nearby, with drawn swords in hand, women and men wearing track suits leap gracefully with strong, deliberate movements. These are the sword fighters. They, too, are "fighting" unseen opponents, using only their powers of concentration and the suppleness of their limbs.

Some old folks may jog by in a soft shoe shuffle that barely beats a walking pace. Still other early risers, in a trance-like state, are practicing *qigong*. Using precise breathing that trains their bodies to focus all strength in one place, they are thus able to make great demands of it. The most fundamental element of this art form, and a trait it shares with Chinese medical theories, is *qi* (pronounced "chee"), which translates as vital energy or life-force. But it also means air and breath. Qi is an intangible element contained in air, food, water and every living thing on earth. Empiricists – people who deny the existence of anything that cannot be seen and measured – have trouble accepting the concept of qi, but it is the force that fuels Chinese life and martial art exercises like taijiquan and qigong.

After the qigong practitioners have dissipated, elderly ballroom dancers – male and female – take over the open space. With a leader in their midst issuing instructions, couples whirl to Western symphony music spewing forth from distorting loudspeakers. Ballroom dancing, relatively new to China, has become a favourite form of morning exercise for the elderly. It's popularity is obvious when the entire scene is seen once again at dusk.

The bird lovers, meanwhile, have hung their cages on the trees and are having a chat. They have their own philosophy, deeply-rooted in tradition. These *lao* (old) Beijingers go walking with their *huamei* (Chinese thrushes), swinging the blue-covered cages backwards and forwards in a counter-rhythm. "The birds need exercise too!" they say, and mean it quite seriously. In fact, the Chinese thrushes do sing a lot once their cages are hanging in the trees.

Meanwhile, two old men spread out an improvised chess board and begin a game of ancient Chinese chess. Others incessantly roll gleaming steel balls around in the palm of their hands – a method of preventing rheumatism and loss of memory. A moon fiddle player accompanies a singer, whose piercing falsetto voice is rendering songs from well-known Beijing operas. A grateful audience has collected.

In the school compounds, children exercise together before lessons begin, massaging their eyes in a routine to counteract eyestrain from too much studying.

By now, morning streets are crowded with commuters on buses and bicycles. Beijing has fully awakened. ■

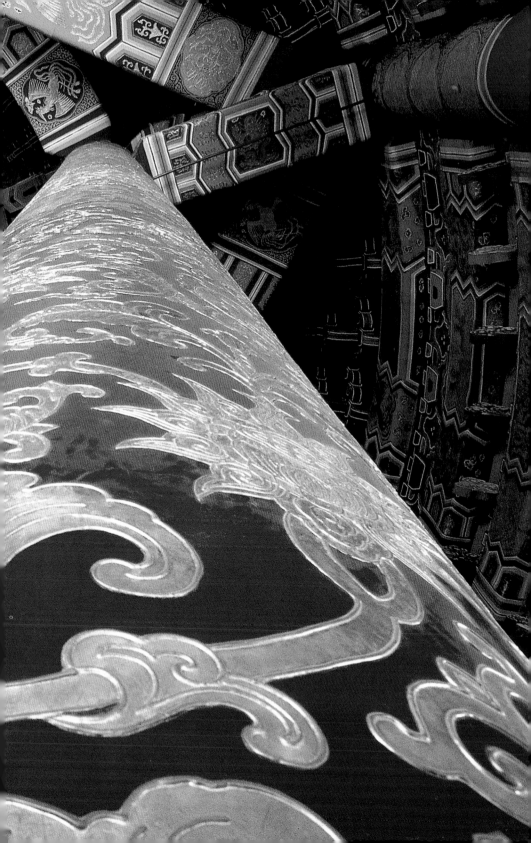

TIANTAN: TEMPLE OF HEAVEN

The Tiantan (Temple of Heaven) lies almost due south of the Imperial Palace, in the Chongwen district. The temple complex – **Tiantan Park** – with its total area of 273 hectares (675 acres), is one of the city's most visited parks, both by the people of Beijing and by tourists. Visitors can easily get to the complex from the Inner City by bus or by taxi. Here is one of the most impressive buildings in China, the Qiniandian (Hall of Prayer for Good Harvests), with its magnificent blue roof. In the centre is the Hall of Heaven, and to the south, the round Altar of Heaven.

Built in 1420, **Tiantan (Temple of Heaven)** served as a place of ceremony and ritual for the Ming and Qing emperors. Every year at the time of the winter solstice, the emperor came here in a magnificent procession lasting several days, in order to honour the imperial ancestors and to pray to heaven for a good harvest. The emperor was the "Son of Heaven" and administered heavenly authority. The sacred nature of his rule had been established in the 3rd century and, as high priest, the emperor alone was responsible to heaven. Originally, honouring the ancestors was reserved for the emperor, but due to the influence of Confucianism, ancestor worship became important to the general population in the late first century BC.

Ancestor tablets were introduced some 2,000 years ago. They were based on the idea that during the religious ceremony, the spirit of the dead person would be present in the tablet, which was engraved with the name, birthday and date of death of the deceased. (The imperial ancestor tablets were kept in the Huangqiangyu, or Hall of Heaven.) According to the Chinese, natural catastrophes, bad farming practices and harvests, or increasing corruption were all signs that the emperor had lost the favour of heaven and of his ancestors. Therefore, it was legitimate to overthrow him and then invest another emperor with the Mandate of Heaven. Exact attention to the practice of the sacrificial rites in the Temple of Heaven was given the appropriate importance.

The procession began at the Palace's southern gate, Qianmen. Once the emperor had arrived at the Temple of Heaven and changed his robes in the Hall of Heaven, he meditated. Then he fasted in the **Zhaigong (Palace of Abstinence)**, in the southwestern part of the complex, until the solstice. With the first rays of the sun, he offered the actual sacrifices and prayers at the Altar of Heaven. In the middle of the first lunar calendar month, the emperor prayed once more to heaven in the Hall of Prayer for Good Harvests. This ceremony was last carried out in 1914 by the self-proclaimed emperor Yuan Shikai.

Lay of the land and temple: The Temple of Heaven can be divided into northern and southern parts. The northern part, with its semi-circular layout, represents Heaven, whereas the southern part, which has a square layout, symbolises Earth. The park can be entered through

Preceding pages: Hall of Prayer for Good Harvests. **Left**, Temple of Heaven. **Right**, temple gate.

several gates. Start the tour in the north with the **Qiniandian (Hall of Prayer for Good Harvests)**, which is built on a three-level marble terrace. Each level is surrounded by a balustrade. First constructed in 1420, the hall was struck by lightning in 1889 and burned to the ground. It was rebuilt according to the original plans.

The pointed roof with its three levels and its 50,000 blue glazed tiles – blue symbolises heaven – and its golden point were constructed without using a single nail and has no spars or beams. It is supported by 28 wooden pillars; the central four, the Dragon Fountain Pillars, are almost 20 metres (66 ft) tall and represent the four seasons. The first ring of pillars surrounding them represents the 12 months; the outer ring, also of 12 pillars, the 12 divisions of the day. The wood for the pillars came from the southern Chinese province of Yunnan. In the centre of the floor is a marble plaque with veining showing a dragon and a phoenix (symbolizing the emperor and the empress).

Echo stones and altars: Proceed south and follow a raised path to the **Huangqiongyu (Hall of Heaven)**. Built in 1530 and restored in 1730, the hall also has a round, pointed roof with a golden spire. The ancestor tablets of the emperors were kept in this hall.

A brick wall surrounding the courtyard has become famous as the **Echo Wall**. If you stand facing the wall and speak to a partner who is also standing by the wall, your partner can understand every word at every point anywhere along the wall. Of course, it is necessary to wait until only a few people are present, which, unfortunately, is very rarely the case. The three stone slabs in front of the stairs to the main temple are the **Sanyinshi (Echo Stones)**, which produce another peculiar effect. If you stand on the first slab and clap your hands, you will hear a single echo, on the second, a double, and on the third, a triple. The secret of this ingenious phenomenon has to do with the different distances at which each stone slab is placed from the wall.

View from the Hall of Heaven, and the Echo Wall.

Further south, pass through an arch of honour to Hanqiutan, the **Altar of Heaven**, a stone terrace of three levels surrounded by two walls – an inner round one and an outer square one.

The lowest level symbolises the Earth, the second, the world of human beings, and the last, Heaven. The altar is built around the number nine, for in earlier times, odd numbers were the attribute of Heaven or *yang*. The number nine, as the highest odd unit, was the most important, and therefore became the imperial number. Accordingly, the altar was built from stone slabs, based on nine or multiples of nine.

The innermost circle on the top level consists of nine slabs, the second of 18, the third of 27 and so on until the final ring on the lowest level, which, as the 27th circle, contains 243 slabs.

If you stand in the middle of the upper level on the round stone slab and speak in a normal voice, your voice is heard more loudly than those of any other people around you. This effect is caused by the echo retained by the balustrades, and by a hollow space within the stone slab that functions much as a resonating cavity. This stone in the centre was considered by the Chinese to be the most holy place in the Chinese empire, indeed the centre of the Earth.

Leave the Temple of Heaven via the west gate, and then follow Tianqiao Street to a sports park, which only dates back to the post-1949 years. Previously, the former **Xiannongtan (Temple of Agriculture)** stood here, symmetrically opposite the Temple of Heaven.

Tianqiao means Heavenly Bridge. However, the bridge has not been in existence for a long time. Before 1949, this was a meeting place of acrobats, fortune tellers, sellers of miraculous elixirs, and other shady characters. Even today, the free markets around the Temple of Heaven still bustle with life, and the residents of this district are considered a separate breed.

Apart from the Temple of Heaven, there were eight altars that played a great role in the ritual life of the Ming and Qing emperors.

The Temple of Agriculture, mentioned above, was dedicated to the legendary Emperor Shennong, the "first farmer" in China. The names of these altars indicate their former roles: the Tianshentan (Altar of the Gods of Heaven), in the grounds of the Xiannongtan altar; the Diqitan (Altar of the Gods of Earth), in the western part of Tianshentan; Shejitan, the Altar of the Land and the Grain, in what is now Sun Yat-sen Park next to the Imperial Palace; the Ditan (Altar of Earth), in the north and to the west of the Andingmen Gate near the Lama Temple; Yonghegong; Ritan (Altar of the Sun), in the Jianguomen diplomatic quarter not far from the Friendship Store, is also a public park now (with a restaurant).

Situated symmetrically opposite it to the west is the Yuetan (Altar of the Moon), also a public park in which the telecommunications tower was built in 1969; and finally, to the north of Zhongnanhai Lake, the Xiancantan (Altar of the Goddess of the Silk Moth), dedicated to Leizu, consort of the legendary Yellow Emperor Huangdi.

The Hall of Prayer for Good Harvests in the Temple of Heaven.

YIHEYUAN:
THE SUMMER PALACE

Yuanmingyuan, the Old Summer Palace, is an historic idyll found only a few hundred yards to the east of the existing Summer Palace, Yiheyuan. Northwest of central Beijing, past the zoo and not far from the elite Beijing and Qinghua universities, its northern entrance is guarded by two stone lions, and unassuming little paths make their way through an overgrown park. Past a wide depression in the landscape is a broad field of ruins, where the remains of ornate pillars and frescos could more easily be associated with European baroque buildings, rather than with imperial China.

The place is mostly deserted, except for student joggers from the nearby sports college, shy lovers, little groups of cyclists on excursions, or foreigners who live in Beijing, although it has recently become a favourite weekend picnic spot for all Beijingers.

The great aesthete and architect, the Qing emperor Qianlong, who ruled from 1736 to 1795, had a huge masterpiece of landscaping and architecture created in the northwest of Beijing. Built as a place of retirement for his beloved mother, this was the paramount "Garden of Gardens". Named Yuanmingyuan (Garden of Perfect Purity), it was a huge and astonishingly magnificent park of three independent but harmonious examples of classic Chinese landscape gardening.

For over 150 years, the Qing emperors, when they were not spending the summer months in Chengde, came here to escape from the heat of the Forbidden City. Dozens of palaces, pavilions and temples stood in idyllic spots amidst artificial hills, lakes and canals. The few European visitors, almost without exception Jesuits, enthused over this park in paeans of overwhelming praise.

In the first phase of the Yuanmingyuan's construction, the southern and western parts were refined and extended in accordance with Qianlong's aesthetic ideas. Once the work was finished, the court artists had to capture 40 spots of scenic beauty and grace in Yuanmingyuan on their rice paper, while Qianlong composed a poem for every one of these landscapes. The island of Penglai (Home of the Immortals), in Fu Hai (Lake of Fortunate Life), which can still be seen today, was compared by Qianlong to a "jade palace in an elfin kingdom." On the eastern shore of the lake stood the Hut of the Beautiful View, long since destroyed. From here, Qianlong could see the Western Hills and enjoy the quiet peace, surrounded by pines and bamboo – the "old friends" mentioned in one of his poems.

Qianlong was an enthusiastic admirer of southern Chinese landscape gardening. Six times he set out on the long and difficult journey to the south of the Yangzi river in order to delight in its fascinating landscape, the quiet beauty of the West Lake in Hangzhou, or the bizarre gardens and canals of Suzhou.

The court artists who accompanied him made innumerable sketches that were then used to transform the northwest surroundings of Beijing, including the area of the present Summer Palace, into a gigantic masterpiece of landscape gardening. Here, natural landscape and the work of human hands merge into a perfect whole.

But that wasn't enough. Inspired by pictures of princely French and Italian palaces, Qianlong gave orders for buildings in the European style to be constructed in the northeastern part of the park. The architect was a Jesuit missionary and artist, Guiseppe Castiglione, from Genoa, Italy, later to be the confidant and teacher of Qianlong.

In an area comprising only two percent of the Garden of Perfect Purity, a complex of buildings unique in China was created between 1747 and 1759. There were little rococo palaces with horseshoe-shaped staircases, marble halls, fountains and even a maze – a bit of Versailles in the Middle Kingdom, the counterpoint to the Chinoiserie of European princes.

The rooms in these unique buildings were equipped with European furniture, and there were even European toys.

Qianlong and his court listened to Western music and ate Western food, making him feel like the "Emperor in Rome". During the Mid-Autumn Festival, he sat in a raised pavilion in the centre of his maze. His court ladies, with torches in their hands, had to find their way to the emperor. The first to reach him was rewarded with a present.

Qianlong was particularly fond of European fountains, simple or elaborate. The fountains – the remains of which can still be seen just south of the present palace museum – were composed of several levels of water-spouting figures. The water sprayed out from stone lion heads and stag antlers, as well as from dogs' mouths.

An interesting symbiosis of Chinese thought and European architecture was the water clock, designed by the French Jesuit, Benoit. Close to the Palace of the Quiet Sea, the ruins can be seen between the museum and the restored maze. Traditionally, the Chinese divided the 24-hour day into 12 segments, with every segment attributed to an animal. Benoit designed a construction with 12 stone animals, each of them spouting water for two hours.

Qianlong had brought Princess Xiangfei, an Uighur beauty and Moslem from the extreme west of China, into this earthly paradise. As the new concubine was wasting away with homesickness, a mosque was built especially for her. Castiglione and other artists were commissioned to paint scenery representing the landscape of east Turkestan. However, all this care could not prevent the "fragrant concubine" – the literal translation of her name – from committing suicide after only one year's stay at the Manchu court.

In Qianlong's time, the French court contributed to the decoration of the buildings "in the Western style" and sent rare gifts. Ironically, roughly a hundred years later, it would be French troops, together with the British, who destroyed these very palaces in Yuanmingyuan.

During the Second Opium War (1858–1860), when China vastly overestimated its strength and tried to throw the

Palace hall in the Old Summer Palace.

unscrupulous foreign merchants out, the Europeans took brutal revenge. The imperial house was considered personally responsible for the xenophobic policies, and Lord Elgin, the commander-in-chief of the British forces, ordered the destruction of Yuanmingyuan. It was said that he wanted to spare the common people and only punish the imperial court, and indeed, the Garden of Perfect Purity was exclusive to the emperor and his court. Before the troops stormed the Old Summer Palace in October, 1860, the emperor Xianfeng, together with his womenfolk (among them was the concubine Cixi), just managed to escape to Chengde in safety.

The allied soldiers plundered, taking away anything they could carry. Then they set fire to the palaces. For three days and three nights, the Summer Palace blazed in fierce flames. Black clouds of smoke rose, terrifying the inhabitants of Beijing. The "Chinese" part of the Summer Palace, completely built of wood and which formed the major part of the palace complex, was almost com-

Ruins of the Old Summer Palace.

pletely destroyed. As for the Western-style buildings, only a few survived.

Later attempts to restore Yuanmingyuan failed because of the chronic lack of finance suffered by the dynasty. These feeble attempts at restoration were then destroyed for the second time – this time completely – after the Boxer Rebellion. In the period that followed, peasants from the surrounding countryside took away valuable ceramic tiles and marble to build houses and chimneys. Today, historians are trying to reconstruct the original appearance of the park in model form. The results can be seen in the small exhibition hall in the area, together with a short, historical summary.

Today, the centre for excursions and activities is the great lake of **Fu Hai**. In the summer, hundreds of paddle and rowing boats bob in the water, and in the winter, skaters glide over the ice. The spaciousness of Yuanmingyuan, however, is inviting for all. Given the crowded nature of Beijing, it is surprising that it is not more crowded than it usually is. Renovations are ongoing, but at a slow

pace, and it has not yet been decided how far they will proceed. At any rate, one will find peace and quiet, especially during the week, and plenty of time to meditate on the greatness of, and the fall of, a unique palace and park.

Today's Summer Palace: Although the old summer palace was never again seen in its original splendour, it was replaced by a new summer residence, known as the **Yiheyuan (Garden of Cultivated Harmony)**, built on the same imperial grounds laid out by Qianlong for his mother a century earlier.

This new summer palace was made possible by the corrupt schemes of the famous (or infamous) Empress Dowager Cixi, in 1888. Originally a concubine of the third rank, she rose to power after the death of the emperor Xianfeng in 1861. The emperor's only heir, Cixi's son Tongzhi, was six years old and too young to rule, thus enabling Cixi to organise a coup and place herself on the Dragon throne. The Empress thus ruled in an unscrupulous and self-centred way in the name of her child.

In 1874, the Emperor Tongzhi died before his twentieth birthday. His mother moved quickly once again. Cixi had a new child placed on the Dragon Throne, for whom she was to take over the regency as long as he lived. The Emperor Guangxu, four years old at the time, was not only a blood relative, being the son of her sister, but his father, Prince Chun, was also extremely loyal to the Cixi. Shortly afterwards, he was appointed Chief of the Navy.

The ruthless Empress Dowager used Chun's parental loyalty, and in 1888 she blackmailed him for money that was intended to build a Chinese naval fleet. (This was to be the cause of China's defeat in the Chinese-Japanese war of 1895.) The fleet money was used instead to build the new imperial summer residence, far from the heavy and dwarfing proportions of the Forbidden City.

With masterful skill, Cixi's builders and architects followed Qianlong's beautiful landscaped gardens when building the new palace. The flower beds typical of Europe were rare in

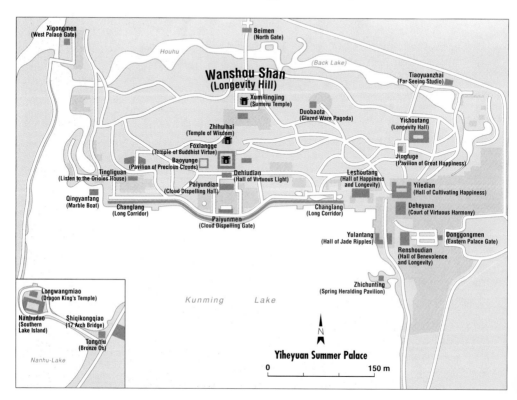

Chinese gardens, and in the Summer Palace, too, blossoming shrubs and a colourful, though skillful, arrangement of flowering plants in tubs were preferred. As in every Chinese garden, it is water and mountains, or rocks, actually, that determine the design of Yiheyuan.

Kunming Lake covers about two-thirds of the area of the summer residence (30 square kilometres or 12 sq mi). The water is not intended to express movement, as with fountains or waterfalls. In China, the emphasis is on its peace and quiet. In summer, Kunming Lake is covered with a carpet of huge, round green lotus leaves, while pale pink lotus flowers rise between them and turn the surface of the water into a breathtaking flower bed.

A Daoist myth, more than 2,000 years old, tells of the three islands in the eastern sea that are supposedly inhabited by immortals. The dearest wish of the Chinese emperors seemed to be to live forever, so they equipped their gardens with reminders of the legend. Hence, the three islands in Kunming Lake, divided by dams. An artificial hill about 60 metres (200 ft) in height was named by Qianlong, **Wanshoushan (Longevity Hill)**, in honour of his mother on her 60th birthday.

Today, it still divides the park of the Summer Palace like a giant screen into two completely different landscapes. The southern part, with the broad lake in the foreground, is reminiscent of the idyll of the West Lake in Hangzhou; the northern part with its romantic groves and canals creates an atmosphere like that of Suzhou.

Visitors cannot see all the splendours and the sheer variety of landscaping in the palace gardens at just one glance. This is because there has been a conscious use of walls and parts of buildings to screen sections of the complete masterpiece from view. Small pieces of the landscape appear like framed pictures through windows in chequered, rhomboid, fan, vase and peach shapes. Sometimes a sudden and dramatic change of scene is possible within only a few yards. A walk through the Sum-

A bridge on the western part of Lake Kunming.

mer Palace can be likened to the slow unrolling of a Chinese scroll painting.

The main path leads through a mighty wooden *pailou*, a kind of Chinese triumphal arch, past the ghost wall that is supposed to ward off all evil influences, directly to the main gate in the east of the palace. Visible beyond it is the **Renshoudian (Hall of Benevolence and Longevity)**, with its opulent furnishings and decorative *objets d'art*. This is where young Emperor Guangxu dealt with state business when the imperial court resided in Yiheyuan during the summer months; here, grand audiences were held for imperial ministers, advisers, mandarins, and later for foreign diplomats as well.

At first, Cixi sat behind a screen in order to listen and to prompt the emperor. Later, she flouted imperial customs, sat on the Nine Dragon Throne herself, and ordered her powerless nephew and adopted son to sit at her side. After the failure of attempts at reform in 1898, she did without his presence altogether. Guangxu then joined a reform-minded group of intellectuals who were proposing a politically, socially and culturally renewed China, and planning a coup against Cixi. Kept extremely well informed of the plans of her opponents by her exemplary network of spies, the "Old Lady" and her counter-coup preempted the emperor's move. The Son of Heaven, deathly ill according to official sources, was kept under palace arrest and imprisoned for no less than 10 years in the luxurious **Yulantang (Hall of Jade Ripples)**, near the audience hall. His apartments were surrounded with a high wall, and he was not even allowed to see his wife or his concubines. The latter were accommodated in the Yiyunguan (House of Fragrant Herbs), not far from the Xijialou (Pavilion of Beautiful Sunsets), at the point where the shore of the lake curves westwards.

Not far from here, on the southeastern slopes of Longevity Hill, were Cixi's private living and sleeping apartments, the **Leshoutang (Hall of Happiness and Longevity)**. Given the age of its inhabitant, the name was truly pregnant

An arch of honour (pailou) on Lake Kunming.

with symbolism. However, it is doubtful whether life was very joyful here. Cixi led an extravagant life of wasteful consumption, and her hard-hearted, ruthless regime made life a misery for the hundreds of eunuchs, serving maids, lady's maids and ladies-in-waiting in her service.

Sometimes her more cunning servants took advantage of her wastefulness. For instance, Cixi expected exactly 128 dishes for the midday and evening meals. She was particularly fond of shark's fin soup, sea cucumbers, duck's feet, and steamed butterfly-shaped buns, and so she only ate from some of the dishes ordered and always the same ones. As time passed and this continued, her cooks used the food not favoured by Cixi on the table day after day, until the maggots crawling in them became too obvious – an interesting way of reducing their workload and increasing their pocket money.

The Lady Ruler of the Western Palace – the translation of the name Cixi – was also addicted to the theatre, namely, to Beijing opera. There was an excellent ensemble at court, composed of 384 eunuchs. Cixi herself was supposed to have appeared in some operas as Guanyin, the goddess of mercy. She had an impressive open-air stage built in the **Deheyuan (Garden of Virtue and Harmony)**. Its three stages, one above the other, were connected by trap doors, so that supernatural beings, saints and immortals could swoop down into the operatic scene and evil spirits could rise from the depths of the underworld. There was even an underground water reservoir for "wet" scenes. Cixi followed the fascinating theatrical performances from the **Yiledian (Hall of Cultivating Happiness)**, which was located opposite the theatre. She sat on a gold-coloured throne, a precious piece of lacquered furniture that portrayed a hundred birds doing homage to the phoenix – the symbol of the empress.

Today, the Deheyuan has been turned into a **theatre museum**. Costumes can be seen in glass cases, and the female museum attendants wear the clothes and

One of the Summer Palace's many temples.

hairstyles of the Qing dynasty. Under their Manchu shoes are high platforms, which gave women a swaying walk. In contrast to women among the Han Chinese, the Manchu women – the palace elite of the Qing dynasty – did not have their feet bound. Apart from the theatre collection, there are also some of Cixi's private possessions on display. Some of her jewellery and cosmetic implements can be seen, as can the first automobile imported into China.

Here, one can also see the famous portrait in oils painted by the American artist Catherine Carl when the Empress Dowager was seventy. The picture shows the Old Buddha, as Cixi was respectfully known, in a Manchu silk robe of imperial yellow, covered with the ideogram *shou*, for longevity. In one hand she is holding a precious fan painted with peonies, and golden sheaths protect her outsize fingernails. Her face seems idealised, flatteringly bathed in a youthful glow.

It was unheard of for the vain Cixi to model for a portrait during her lifetime.

Emperors were only allowed to be portrayed after their deaths. Artists never saw their model, either dead or alive, and had to ask the help of the mourners to point out the appropriate eyes, nose, mouth etc. from samples laid before them – much like building up an identity photo of a suspected criminal.

A jewel in the further eastern part of the palace gardens is the **Xiequyuan (Garden of Harmonious Interest)**, a complete, perfect and beautiful replica of a lotus pool of the Wuxi area. When Cixi came here to fish, devoted eunuchs would dive under the water to hang a catch onto the old lady's hook, for she was impatient and given to outbreaks of temper. They not only attached fish, but sometimes put a precious piece of jewellery on the hook in order to keep her in a good mood. Here, by the way, is where Bertolucci filmed the only Summer Palace scene in *The Last Emperor*.

Covered walkways and galleries are established features of Chinese landscape gardening. These light, elegant, wooden structures link scattered indi-

Spring at the Summer Palace.

vidual buildings to make a composite whole. The **Changlang (Long Corridor)** in the Summer Palace is more than 700 metres long and runs along the foot of the hill parallel to the shore of Kunming Lake. The original walkway dated from the time of emperor Qianlong, but as with many other parts of the park, it was destroyed during the Second Opium War (1860-1862) and then rebuilt under Cixi.

The ceilings and rafters of the walkway are decorated with countless bird and flower motifs. If humans or human-like creatures appear in the pictures, they are either in scenes from famous legends, episodes of Chinese history, or scenes from classical novels such as *The Dream of the Red Chamber*, *The Bandits of Liangshan Moor* or *The Journey to the West*, with its hero, admired by old and young alike – the Monkey King, Sun Wukong.

To prevent the ceiling paintings from fading until they are unrecognisable, the colours have to be renewed every 12 years. Here, as in some other parts of the palace, it is unfortunate that the work of restoration has not been done very well. The glaring colours are somewhat irritating, and much of the complexity and wealth of detail in the original paintings has been lost.

In the middle of the walkway, where the east-west axis of the palace park meets the north-south axis, **Paiyunmen (Cloud-Dispelling Gate)** – a great triumphal arch, or pailou – marks the start of the climb up Longevity Hill. Next to 12 massive, bizarre-shaped stones symbolising the signs of the Chinese zodiac is an elegant pair of lions cast in bronze – perhaps the most beautiful in all of Beijing – guarding an imposing Buddhist temple complex, which is surrounded by a red wall. Go through two gates and over a bridge to reach **Paiyundian (Hall of Dispelling Clouds)**.

A temple once stood on this site during the Ming dynasty. The Emperor Qianlong had it rebuilt and, on his mother's 60th birthday, renamed it the **Temple of Gratitude for a Long Life**. It was destroyed in 1860, and the present

Pagoda of the Incense of Buddha, Longevity Hill.

form of the complex dates from Cixi's time in 1892. This was where she celebrated her birthdays with rejoicing, luxury, extravagance and elaborate court ceremonies. Many of the presents given to her on these occasions are on exhibition in the rooms of the Paiyundian, often with the yellow paper labels attached, marked with words of adulation such as "Given in honour and respect by your true and loyal subject ..."

Go past the Paiyundian, through the **Dehiudian (Hall of Virtuous Light)**, and up a steep stone staircase to reach the massive, 38-metre (125-ft) tall, octagonal **Pagoda of the Incense of Buddha**. This is the highest point of the entire palace and park. From here is a lovely panoramic view of the Summer Palace: the blue of Kunming Lake, the green of the trees, the red of the pillars and the grey-blue of the tiled roofs. Only the most important buildings have yellow roofs. There are hardly any stern, hard colours or symbols; a clear, elegant atmosphere predominates.

To the east is a group of buildings, the **Zhuanlunzang (Repository of Sutras)**, once used as the archives for copies of Confucian classics and Buddhist scrolls. To the west is a rare and quite extraordinary masterpiece of Chinese architecture – the **Baoyunge (Pavilion of Precious Clouds)**, framed on all four sides by smaller pavilions and walkways. In Cixi's day, Lamaist monks gathered here to pray on the 1st and 15th day of every lunar month. Its stepped roof, and its beams, columns and struts, make it look like a wooden building, yet they were all cast from bronze in 1750 with the help of wax moulds. This is why it is usually called the Tongting (Bronze Pavilion). It is one of the few buildings of the Summer Palace to have survived the wanton destruction of 1860 and 1900 reasonably undamaged.

Behind the pagoda on Longevity Hill, a narrow path leads to the **Zhihuihai (Temple of Wisdom)**. There are countless little statues of Buddha in the niches of its greenish-yellow ceramic facade.

The emphasis on Buddhism in Yiheyuan may seem surprising – especially in

Wooden ceiling, Summer Palace hall.

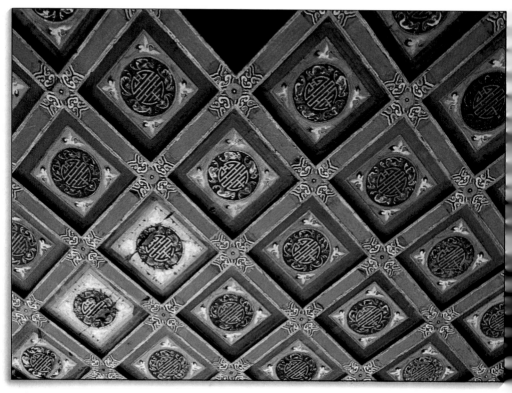

view of the fact that temples and shrines of the ancestor cult are missing. But Cixi had no point of contact with the veneration of ancestors who prescribed a male succession and excluded women from ritual and political life. She felt attracted to Buddhism, and in particular to the goddess Guanyin, who played, and still plays, a role in the spiritual life of Chinese women, similar to that of the Virgin Mary among Catholics.

It was part of the Buddhist rites at court that Cixi had to release 10,000 birds every year on her birthday. This pious gesture would, she hoped, improve her chances when she was reborn into another life. She was inexpressibly happy when some of the freed birds refused to leave her and returned again and again to rest on her shoulders. Little did she suspect that this loyalty was not due to her charisma, but instead was due to the training skills of some of her eunuchs. Nor did she guess that these very eunuchs, once Cixi had returned to her apartments, climbed into the trees to recapture the recently freed birds, then shut them into cages and sold them for a good price in the markets. These days, it is fairly quiet in the northern part of the Summer Palace along the smaller, adjacent lakes.

On a fine summer Sunday, thousands, indeed tens of thousands, of people will walk along the shores of Kunming Lake or crowd around the buildings near the main eastern gate. Relatively few, however, will venture to the other side of Longevity Hill, where the northern gate now sits, and where, near the end of the 19th century, there was a market street. Held especially for the Imperial family, it was intended to recreate, in harsh Beijing, the lively southern Chinese atmosphere of Suzhou. Book and antique shops and tea houses were intended to give the inhabitants of the palace, forbidden to take part in life outside the walls, the illusion of participation in everyday trade and exchange. When the imperial dignitaries approached, the eunuchs, dressed as traders, became very busy and spread out their wares, praising them with theatrical gestures. Like

Cixi's marble boat.

many other buildings in the further part of the Summer Palace, this market street fell victim to the destruction that followed the Boxer Rebellion in 1900. However, it has since been rebuilt.

The Boxer groups and societies were part of a militant movement, at first based mainly in rural areas of China. They wanted to preserve Chinese traditions at all costs and to expel all things foreign, and the foreigners themselves, from China. Missionaries were murdered and the Diplomatic Quarter in Beijing was besieged. The European powers sent an army that took Beijing, at the same time plundering and partially destroying the Summer Palace. Cixi, fleeing to Xi'an, became ill with rage along the way when she heard that her throne had been flung into Kunming Lake, her robes stolen, and the walls of her bedchamber scrawled with obscene words and drawings. Once she had returned to Beijing, she set about restoring the Palace to its former glory with her typical energy. Some things, however, were not restored. The Lama Temple, on the far side of Longevity Hill, has only been partially rebuilt in the last few years.

At the foot of Longevity Hill, almost at the end of the long walkway, a restaurant extends an invitation to eat an exquisite meal, in the style of the Imperial cuisine, and in traditional surroundings. This is the **Tingliguan (Listen to the Orioles House)**. Visitors can put on old Chinese silken robes and have their photographs taken in an imperial pose. In the picturesque buildings behind the restaurant, the Emperor Qianlong used to invite his friends to a cup of rice wine and demonstrate his poetic talents by reciting his verses.

As in many other attractively landscaped areas, pavilions invite the thoughtful visitor to stay. This pretty spot is called "as if walking through a picture", **Huazhongyou**, and the view into the distance does indeed create such an illusion.

"Borrowing a landscape from outside" is part of traditional Chinese landscape gardening, and means that attractive elements of the natural scenery outside the walls of the gardens are carefully incorporated into the view. From Huazhongyou, for example, the walls of the Summer Palace are invisible, and the distant Jade Spring Hill seems to have been delicately painted with watercolour and brush.

A little further to the west, in the waters of Kunming Lake, lies the famous **Qingyanfang (Marble Boat)** with its two stone wheels on either side. It's a reminder of the patriotic generals who collected money to finance a Chinese fleet. Cixi used the donations instead to restore the Summer Palace, yet still had the cynicism to have a ship of marble built. From here, one can cross the lake by ferry, landing either on the **Nanhudao (Southern Lake Island)**, or on the neighbouring mainland. Nanhudao is where the famous **Tongniu (Bronze Ox)**, with its sad eyes, crouches. Its task, as the characters engraved on its back make clear, is to pacify the water spirit and to protect the surrounding land from floods.

Shiqikongqiao (Seventeen Arches Bridge) crosses the water in a graceful curve and links the island with the mainland. Some 500 stone lions keep watch on the balustrades. On the little island itself lies the **Longwangmiao (Dragon King's Temple)**.

The old Manchu dowager of Kunming Lake would surely turn in her grave if she could see the globe-trotters, male and female, with hairy legs or plunging necklines, or the Japanese constantly snapping with their cameras as they follow their tour guide who waves a little flag. Add to these the Chinese children up from the country with their parents, trotting day after day across the palace paving, and finally the fashionably dressed honeymooners and the noisy participants on company outings, sticking their noses into every corner of what was once the private domain of the imperial family.

But perhaps what might bother her most, and you, for that matter, are the seemingly endless number of conspicuous vendors selling the tackiest of souvenirs, both outside and inside the palace grounds.

Portrait photograph of the Empress Dowager Cixi.

IMPERIAL GARDENS AND PARKS

In the 15th century, the large lake in the middle of Beijing was divided in two. Today, the park around the Beihai (Northern Lake) is one of the most beautiful and popular places for excursions in the Inner City of Beijing. In summer, the lake is used for boating, and in winter, for skating. The very youngest enjoy themselves on ice sledges – daring constructions consisting of a wooden chair, or sometimes just a large plank, fastened onto two runners. For imperial ice celebrations, by the way, the ice was smoothed with glowing irons.

Even more than the northern lake, the southern part of the lake – or **Zhongnanhai (Central and Southern Lake)** as it is named – and its surroundings were a pleasure garden for the court. Right next to the Imperial Palace, this is where horse races and hunts, birthday receptions, and celebrations of the Lantern Festival took place. After 1949, Mao, Zhou Enlai, Liu Shaoqi and other prominent comrades lived here. Mao's private library can still be seen today. Surrounded by a thick wall, Zhongnanhai has been, since 1949, the seat of the Politbureau and the State Council, the communications centre of the political leadership of the state with its population of billions. Foreign visitors are not admitted to the seat of government unless they are invited to an audience. It is not infrequently whispered that Zhongnanhai is the new "Forbidden City."

In the centre of Beijing sprawls **Beihai Gongyuan** (Northern Sea Park), just west of Jingshan and northwest of the Imperial Palace. Its location marks the ancient centre of Khanbaliq, the Western name of the Mongol capital. The Khan had the island and the surrounding area landscaped and, according to Marco Polo, ruled from this spot in inimitable splendour.

Even now, the **Qionghuadao (Jade Island)** is the most impressive part of the park as far as scenery and history are concerned. Going from the main south gate leads to a bridge more than 600 years old, across which is the **Yong'ansi (Temple of Eternal Peace)**, and beyond it, the **Falundian (Hall of the Wheel of Law)**. From there, a twisting path leads up uneven steps to the 35-metre (115-ft) high **White Dagoba**, an onion-shaped shrine in the Tibetan style, built in honour of the fifth Dalai Lama on the occasion of his visit to Beijing in 1651. In 1679, and again in 1731, the dagoba was destroyed by earthquakes, but was rebuilt on both occasions. The view from here of the Imperial Palace, Beihai and Zhongnanhai lakes, and the *hutong* of the Inner City of Beijing, is only surpassed by the view from the peak of Jingshan (Coal Hill).

On the northern side of the dagoba, the path leads through a labyrinth of stairs, corridors, pavilions, and bizarre rock formations with grottos intended to resemble the houses of Daoist saints, and goes steeply down to the shore, which is bordered by a long, semi-circular covered walkway. Halfway up the northwestern slope is a statue, nearly 4

metres (13 ft) high, rising above the tangle of landscape and buildings, and representing one of the Eight Immortals. It is a reminder of a legend from the life of the Emperor Wudi, who ruled early in the first century. He is supposed to have heard that drinking dewdrops would make him immortal. He commanded a slave to sit out outdoors overnight with a bowl and catch the dewdrops falling from heaven, so that His Majesty, the Son of Heaven, could refresh himself with them and partake of immortality.

Right below this statue is the **Yuegolou (Building for Reading Old Inscriptions)**. A collection of 495 stone tablets, engraved with the work of famous Chinese calligraphers, dating mostly from the 18th century, is kept here. Some of the inscriptions, however, are 1,500 years old.

Just next door is the Fangshan Restaurant with its stylish interior and its menus based on the imperial cuisine. It is one of the best, and most popular, restaurants for banquets and celebrations, as well as being one of the most expensive in Beijing. It is advisable to reserve seats well in advance.

From here, a ferry will take visitors to the **Wulongting (Five Dragon Pavilion)**, on the northwest lakeshore. These buildings from the Ming era are built in a zigzagging line over the water and are connected by walkways. The foremost and largest pavilion, with its double-stepped, curved roof, forms the head of a curving dragon when seen from above. The emperors used to fish from this point. Beside the point where the boats tie up is the **Tieyingbi (Iron Wall)**, 700 years old and some 4 metres (13 ft) broad, with impressive reliefs of mythological figures. Like the other gardens and parks around the Forbidden City, Beihai Park was reserved for the imperial household's private pleasures.

The path leads on in a westerly direction to the **Wanfolou (Tower of 10,000 Buddhas)**, built by the Emperor Qianlong in the 18th century on the occasion of his mother's 80th birthday. The statuettes of Buddha, made of pure gold,

Entrance to the Communist Party and government compound of Zhongnanhai.

that filled the niches inside the tower were stolen, like so many other treasures in 1900, by European troops.

To the south stands what is probably the biggest pavilion in China, the **Xiaoxitian (Miniature Western Heaven)**. In the Mahayana Buddhist tradition that established itself in China, the idea of the "Western Heaven" is similar to Christian concepts of Paradise. Inside, Buddhist paintings are exhibited, and the pavilion still has a semi-religious air. The **Jiulongbi (Nine Dragon Screen)**, which once protected a temple entrance from evil spirits, now only serves to screen the football goal posts in the playing fields outside the park walls. A few steps to the east of the Dragon Screen, in the **Tianwangdian (Hall of the Celestial Kings)**, is an exhibition of gifts brought here by foreigners during state visits over the centuries to the Middle Kingdom.

The **Jingxinzhai (Place of the Quiet Heart)**, just beyond, invites walkers to rest and pause in contemplation. It is a delightful garden, complete in itself, with lotus pools, halls to walk in, pavilions and living quarters. Indeed, it is a stylish and well-preserved example of the popular garden within a garden.

Right in the south of Beihai Park, separated from the rest of the park and with its own entrance, is the **Tuancheng (Round Town)**. Once it was one of three islands in the Beihai (northern lake); later it became the centre of the Mongol capital of Dadu. However, only the trees remain from that time, all the architecture of the Yuan dynasty having been destroyed. Only the exquisite 1.5-metre (5-ft) wide nephrite container, in which the Kublai Khan kept his wine, survives from that period.

Later, a poem by Qianlong praising the beauty of this work of art was engraved on the inside of the vessel, which stands next to the entrance in a pavilion of white marble pillars and a blue roof. A second jewel in this Round Town is a 1.5-metre (5-ft) tall, white jade statue of Buddha with inlaid jewels. It can be seen in the **Chengguandian (Receiving Light Hall)**.

Bird fanciers discussing their pets.

Above the Palace: Jingshan, the so-called **Coal Hill**, came into existence at the beginning of the 15th century, when the Ming emperor Yongle had moats dug all around the Forbidden City. Geomancy probably played a decisive part in the choice of a suitable spot for the spoil. The science of the winds and waters, *feng shui*, as this branch of traditional Chinese philosophy is also known, aims to site buildings in harmony with the natural topography, and by this means, to influence them positively. Jingshan (View Hill) served to protect the Imperial Palace from malignant influences from the north. Pragmatism must also have played a role in the choice, as any approaching enemy could be seen at a distance from such a height.

Its five crests – the middle one is the highest – make a view of Jingshan look like a Chinese scholar's brush holder. There are five pavilions, dating from the 16th century, crowning the chain of hills and emphasizing its zigzagging lines. Each pavilion housed a bronze figure of Buddha, four of which were plundered by European troops in 1900.

The surrounding park was not opened to the public until 1928. Before this, it was a private imperial garden, and eunuchs, palace ladies and the imperial family members spent their leisure hours strolling in its picturesque scenery.

Here – or to be more precise, on the eastern slopes – is where Chongzheng, the last Ming emperor, committed suicide in 1644, after the rebellious peasant armies had stormed Beijing. Bareheaded, with only one shoe and wearing a gown with sleeves smeared with the blood of the empress and two princesses, Chongzheng fled to this place and, abandoned by eunuchs and ministers, hanged himself by tying his silken belt on a tree.

The hill is no longer the highest point in Beijing. Yet the view from the **Pavilion of Everlasting Spring** on the central one of the five peaks is superb. Looking straight along the north-south axis of Beijing, one can see to the south a sea of curved golden roofs: the Forbidden City; to the west, the White Dagoba

View of the city from Jingshan (Coal Hill).

towers over the picturesque lake of Beihai Park; to the north are the massive Drum and Bell towers; and on a clear day you can see, on the horizon to the northwest, the silhouette of the Western Mountains.

Shouhuangdian (Hall of the Emperor's Long Life), in the north of the park, is now a children's cultural centre, where courses in music, dance, theatre and painting are available.

South of the Palace: Just west of Tianamen and separated from the Imperial Palace by a wall and a moat, **Zhongshan Gongyuan (Sun Yat-sen Park)** is a fine example of the fusion of imperial architecture and garden design.

Sun Yat-sen was one of the great personalities of the 1911 Chinese revolution, which brought about the fall of the Manchu dynasty and the end of imperial China. After the successful revolt, he became the country's first president and chairman of the Guomindang, the National People's Party.

Sun Yat-sen's widow, Song Qingling, came from one of the wealthiest and most powerful families in the country. She remained in the People's Republic of China, where her name is still greatly respected today. Sun himself is still known with great respect by all Chinese on both sides of the Straits of Taiwan as the Father of the Country.

Sun Yat-sen Park received its name in 1928. Originally – more than 1,000 years ago – this was the site of the Temple of the Wealth of the Land. None of the building remains, and only the ancient cypresses are reminders of that time.

The park is a popular refuge for Beijingers, who are often plagued by stress and dust. Kindergartners walk through the park in lines, and visitors from across the country rest under its shady trees, exhausted by tours of the Imperial Palace and Mao's mausoleum.

Because the leisure facilities in the southwestern part of the park – fun fairs, flower show, billiard hall and (perhaps less of an attraction) a family planning centre – are very popular with local visitors, this place of quiet and worship has lost something of its original char-

Arch in Sun Yat-sen Park.

acter. From the main entrance to the park in the south, the path first goes through a white marble arch.

This arch has had a varied history. In 1900, the German ambassador Baron von Ketteler was shot dead on his way to the Chinese Foreign Ministry by one of the rebellious Boxers. In reparation, the imperial family had to have a triumphal arch built on the spot, with the inscription "In memory of the virtuous von Ketteler." However, after 1919, Germany no longer existed as an imperialist power, and the arch was moved to its present position and inscribed "Justice will prevail." In 1953, it was reinscribed again. The present calligraphy is the work of the famous poet and translator of Goethe, Guo Moruo, and reads: "Defend peace."

Further north, in the centre of the park, is a great square area, where in 1421 the Ming Emperor Yongle had the Altar of Earth and Harvests built. It sat directly opposite the temple to his ancestors, which is now in the Laodong Renmin Wenhuagong (Workers' Pal-

ace of Culture). Its shape is a reminder of the old Chinese concept of the earth as square. Twice a year, in the grey light of dawn, the Ming and Qing emperors brought their offerings in the hope of obtaining divine support for a good harvest. During the sacrifice, the altar was covered with five different types of coloured earth, and these colours can still be seen today, repeated in the coloured tiles that cover the low surrounding walls. The symbolism of the five colours is not absolutely clear. It may be that they stand for the five points of the compass (north, west, east, south and centre), or the five elements of metal, wood, water, fire and earth, which, according to traditional Chinese thought, form the basis of all beings. To the north of the altar is the **Shejitian (Hall of Prayer)**, built of wood, a typical example of Beijing's classical architecture.

Hiding behind the name the Worker's Palace of Culture is a venerable temple complex dating from the 15th and 16th centuries – the **Taimiao (Temple of the Imperial Ancestors)**. If entering the

Old and young find recreation and enjoyment in the parks.

area from the south, from Tiananmen Square, cross a bridge fitted with marble balustrades, and come to the three mighty halls of the complex.

Five times a year, the wooden ancestor tablets, upon which the names of the dead forefathers of the imperial family were recorded, were taken from the central hall in which they were kept to the southern hall, where the Son of Heaven paid his respects to his forefathers. The rear (northern) hall was reserved for the ancestor tablets of those "posthumously" declared to be "imperial ancestors." In other words, they were members of families who were not the ruling dynasty at the time when they were alive.

The veneration of ancestors is one of the oldest practices in the Chinese spiritual tradition. Central is the concept of a mutual interdependence of the physical and spiritual worlds. The transcendental well-being of those in the spirit kingdom depends upon the offerings and the veneration of their descendants. At the same time, however, they can influence the fates of their children and their children's children, who, for their part, try to gain the loyalty of their ancestors by being as generous as possible with their offerings and with the observance of rituals.

This ancestor worship is part of the daily life of every Chinese household. The imperial ancestors received extraordinary honours and respect, of course, as they were believed to be responsible for the well-being of the whole country. The Taimiao (Temple of the Imperial Ancestors) was thus one of the country's most important ritual sites.

After 1949, the temple complex was restored and equipped for its new life as a workers' college and pleasure garden. Now, the "sacred halls" are used for leisure activities and further education courses. Where the tablets of the imperial ancestors once rested, there are now profane ping-pong tables.

However, an atmosphere of awe, and of the sacred and sublime, still hovers over the Ming rooftops. There is an almost reverential silence here. If you want to grieve over the beauty, the splendour and the quiet dignity that the Forbidden City has lost, or if you want to get away from the crowds of visitors, this is the place to revel, undisturbed, in the imperial atmosphere.

Northwest of the Palace: The northwestern site of the present-day **Beijing Zoological Gardens** is one of the oldest parks in the city. It had, however, become dilapidated and was not restored until the reign of the Empress Dowager Cixi. Around the year 1900, a Manchu high official returned from a long journey abroad and brought a special gift for the Empress Dowager. He gave her a great number of animals, especially birds, which were mainly bought in Germany. The decaying park proved to be the ideal accommodation for them and was thus renamed the Park of 10,000 Creatures.

The wide area covered by the Beijing Zoo is ideal for long walks. The main attractions of the zoo, of course, are the giant pandas, whose quarters are right by the entrance. If venturing into the zoo, be forewarned: standards are not

A giant panda in the Beijing Zoo.

up to those of most Western zoos. Next door, in the panda souvenir shop, you can admire and buy the polyester variety. Among the cuddly pandas, the unavoidable silhouettes, the water colours and the T-shirts with panda designs, one can find silk embroideries framed in brocade and wall hangings – not unlike the Stag At Bay so popular in European living rooms. Panda handbags, panda stickers, panda thermometers and red lacquer sticks with panda motifs complete the wide-ranging, mind-numbing assortment of souvenirs.

About half a kilometre to the west of the zoo, between the Shangri-La and the Xiyuan hotels, is the **Zizhuyuan Gongyuan (Purple Bamboo Park)**. Around its three lakes, 10 different varieties of bamboo, rare in northern China, can be seen growing. A total of 160,000 bamboo plants and trees are supposed to have been planted. This place is mainly frequented by families with children because of the small children's amusement park and playground.

About 100 metres (300 ft) to the west of the southwestern gate is a very special performance every Sunday morning. Hundreds of Chinese men and women, mostly young people and especially students, gather in the "English Corner" to practise their English with one another, since there are not enough genuine native speakers to go around. Unsuspecting foreigners taking a walk will soon be surrounded by a large crowd of talkative and curious Beijing Anglophiles. With the number of Chinese now learning English, this activity has become increasingly popular, and "English Corners" may be found on weeknights in various locations, especially around the universities.

"There was a sound of music in the distance. And now the procession was approaching, two by two: Dragon Banner, Phoenix, pheasant-feather fans and court parasols swayed past. They were followed by bearers of golden incense burners, then a mighty canopy of yellow-gold silk; a crown, a cloak, belt and shoes were borne on a cushion… and finally there came, carried by eight men, **Autumn walk.**

the great yellow-gold silken state palanquin." Yuan Chun, eldest daughter of the wealthy house of Jia, was married to the Son of Heaven as one of his lesser wives. Usually, any contact with their parent's clan was forbidden to those women who entered the imperial harem, but the concubine Yuan Chun received the extraordinary favour of being allowed to visit her family after a lengthy separation. The family was commanded, however, to receive their daughter and his Imperial Highness in appropriate style. So, especially for this occasion, they had the opulent **Daguanyuan (Grand View Garden)**, laid out.

The above story is an episode in the famous Qing era classic, *Hongloumeng* (*The Dream of the Red Chamber*), an extremely popular book in China. The novel describes the gradual downfall of the aristocratic Jia family through their ambition, their opulent and decadent way of life, and their remarkable capacity for family intrigue. The story centres on the tragic love between the highly sensitive and poetically talented Jia

Baoyu, the younger brother of the imperial concubine, and his fragile cousin, Lin Daiyu, whom he worships.

The actual Grand View Garden, between Beihai Park and the zoo, was laid out only a few years ago. It is therefore not an ancient monument, not even a new edition on an existing historic site. The pretext for the creation of this park was that appropriate scenery was needed for filming several episodes of a TV series based on the novel. A work of literature thus became reality: "Right behind the entrance a broken hilly landscape opened out. These hills, which blocked the view at this point, increased expectation," as the novel describes its garden. And indeed, as soon as visitors enter the south gate, they are confronted with a bizarre artificial rock formation, a very common stylistic element in classical Chinese landscape gardening.

"The path went on through dark grottos into bright glades, over meadows scattered with bushes and trees, and sown with flowers, past a lively stream... A white marble balustrade surrounded

The Western Mountains in the mist.

the lake, and across the narrow part the triple arch of a marble bridge curved like the jaws of a water monster."

Following the garden's path, you come to a delightful water pavilion, the entrance of which bears, in the novel as well as in the "reality" of southwestern Beijing, the inscription: "Through fragrances." It was customary in old China to increase the atmosphere of beautiful landscapes and buildings by providing them with a suitable poetic couplet, inscribed next to, or above, the entrance.

Around the lake there are elegant pavilions, colourful walkways, zigzagging bridges and jetties, a temple, and the main scenes of the novel. To the northwest of the entrance is the **Court of Red Fortune**, the residence of the male hero of the novel, Baoyu, and his servants. To the northeast is the **Bamboo Pavilion**, the home of his beloved Daiyu. The bamboo plantation is not only a rarity in Beijing, given the harsh climate, but the plant is also a symbol for loneliness, pride and sadness. As such, bamboo illuminates the character of the heroine,

who is broken by the fact that her beloved does not marry her, but is given by the family to a bride they find more suitable. The Grand View Park thus offers visitors the opportunity to enjoy a bit of literary history while strolling through the grounds.

Fragrant Hill Park: A good hour's drive from downtown Beijing to the northwest, in the range of the Western Mountains, lies one of the most popular places for excursions for the people of the Chinese capital: **Xiangshan (Fragrant Hill)**. Even in earlier times, the nobility and wealthy merchant families fled the summer heat in Beijing to the shady coolness of their country houses on the slopes, or rented guest quarters in the temples. The journey was undertaken on mule at an easy pace, travelling through the woodlands, getting accommodation in Daoist or Buddhist shrines, and enjoying the feeling of communion with nature.

Today, Xiangshan is particularly popular in late autumn because of the blazing red of the sycamore leaves. As early

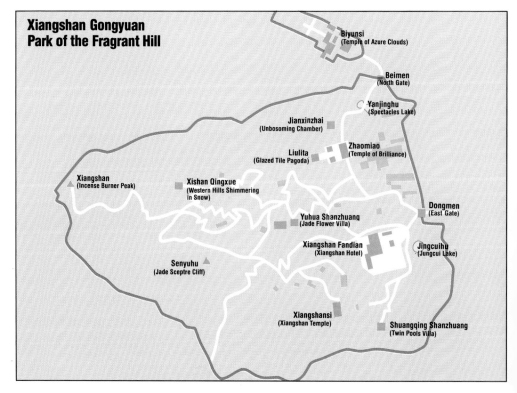

**Xiangshan Gongyuan
Park of the Fragrant Hill**

Biyunsi
(Temple of Azure Clouds)

Beimen
(North Gate)

Yanjinghu
(Spectacles Lake)

Jianxinzhai
(Unbosoming Chamber)

Zhaomiao
(Temple of Brilliance)

Liulita
(Glazed Tile Pagoda)

Xiangshan
(Incense Burner Peak)

Xishan Qingxue
(Western Hills Shimmering in Snow)

Dongmen
(East Gate)

Yuhua Shanzhuang
(Jade Flower Villa)

Xiangshan Fandian
(Xiangshan Hotel)

Jingcuihu
(Jungcui Lake)

Senyuhu
(Jade Sceptre Cliff)

Xiangshansi
(Xiangshan Temple)

Shuangqing Shanzhuang
(Twin Pools Villa)

as the Tang dynasty, poets were singing praises of the frost-sprinkled red of the trees, an unforgettable natural wonder.

The strange-sounding name "Fragrant Hill," as it is commonly translated in European languages, is probably due to an error in translation. The summit of the hill, 550 metres (1,830 ft) high, has two peaks of rock that are often veiled in fog or cloud, and from a distance it resembles a sacred incense burner with smoke rising out of it. As there is no semantic difference in Chinese between "incense" and "fragrance," the "incense burner hill" became the "fragrant hill."

In the past, the area was an imperial game preserve. As recently as 300 years ago, the Qing Emperor Kangxi is supposed to have killed a tiger here. Qianlong turned it into a landscaped park, which was destroyed by foreign troops in 1860 and again in 1900. Few of the buildings have survived.

If entering the park through the main eastern gate and turning right, you come to the **Zhaomiao (Temple of Clarity)**, built in 1780 in the Tibetan style for the Panchen Lama. In its grounds is the octagonal **Liulita (Glazed Tile Pagoda)**. There are little bells hanging from the corners of the eaves, and the lightest breeze makes them tinkle delicately. **Jianxinhai (Chamber of Introspection)**, to the east of the pagoda, has a courtyard in the southern Chinese style with a semi-circular pond, as well as the usual walkways and pavilions. Only a few steps ahead lie the two lakes, separated by a jetty and known because of their shape as the **Spectacles Lake**.

If you have time for an excursion to Xiangshan, don't miss the chance of travelling to the summit on the chair lift. The view goes past steep, thickly wooded slopes and deep ravines to the **Temple of the Azure Clouds** (in a side valley to the northeast), and one can see further to the Jade Spring Hill with its ancient pagoda, the Summer Palace and Kunming Lake, all the way to the skyscrapers of the Haidian district of Beijing. On a clear day, the immensity of Beijing, with its ever growing population and increasing modernization, is

Temple of the Reclining Buddha.

more than evident. If choosing to climb by foot, you will need good shoes.

The steepest part of the hill bears the fitting name of Guijianchou, which means "Even the devil is afraid of it!" Your reward will be a visit to the **Xiang-shan Hotel**, definitely the most beautifully-situated hotel in Beijing. Over a decade ago, the famous Chinese-American architect I.M. Pei attempted to translate the ancient Chinese court style into modern forms of architecture – with much success. The southern part of the park beyond the hotel is excellent for picnics. Only a few visitors ever find their way here, past the remains of the once-massive Xiangshan Temple that rose over six levels, to the remote Shuang Qing Shanzhuang (Twin Peaks Villa), and the Banshanting (Pavilion Halfway Up the Hill). Here, a little tower has been restored, and from it one can find a good view of the park and nearby hotel grounds.

The Western Hills in the vicinity of the Fragrant Hill Park are inviting for walkers. To the north, beyond the **Wo-fosi (Temple of the Reclining Buddha)**, is the **Yingtaogou (Cherry Ravine)**, a romantic spot often sought out by lovers. On the way to the Temple of the Reclining Buddha, one will pass the greenhouses of the Botanical Gardens (on the left, or western, side).

Eight Scenic Sites: About 20 kilometres (12 mi) to the south of the Xiangshan Park lie the **Badachu (Eight Scenic Sites)** – eight former temples and monasteries lying on the slope of a hill. You can climb and visit one right after the other. In the pagoda of the second temple, the **Lingguangsi (Temple of the Sacred Light)**, there is a holy relic reputed to be a tooth of the Buddha. The **Dabeisi (Temple of Great Compassion)** is famous for its 18 Lohan statues. The temple below the peak, the **Cave of Precious Pearls**, in fact is built around a cave, in which a hermit is supposed to have lived for 40 years during the Qing dynasty. Badachu used to be in a restricted military area and thus was only open to visitors with special passes, but are now open to the public.

Occupying 5.7 hectares (14 acres) on the north shore of Shisha Lake in central Beijing, the **Gong Wang Fu**, or **Prince Gong Palace**, is the world's largest courtyard house. While much of the grounds are now home to the China Conservatory of Music, its lush gardens and historic structures, including Beijing's only preserved Qing dynasty theatre, are still open to the public. The theatre, whose walls, ceiling and beams are spectacularly painted, is still used for special performances. Here, guests served by women wearing traditional costumes of the period may be treated to a sample of Beijing opera, much as the city's elite were during the over 250-year span of the Qing dynasty.

The palace itself consists of three lines of buildings, each line containing one main building and smaller side buildings. Aside from the Main Hall and the Rear Hall is a 140-room, 48-metre (160-ft) long building. The garden, which is one of the best in Beijing, is at the rear of the residence and has over 20 separate sections, each with its own unique layout and style.

Left, preparations for a souvenir photo in the Fragrant Hill Park.

TRAFFIC SNARLS

The inexorable stream of hundreds of thousands of bicycles, always gliding by in exactly the same manner. A stranger dives in and is carried away by a pedal-pushing green and blue uniformed throng, above which the continuous shrill sound of a thousand bicycle bells can be heard. An ostentatious older-style limousine, behind whose closed curtains you suspect are the peaked caps of high-ranking cadres, tries to win some respect for its progress by honking loudly.

If one comes to Beijing with this preconception, gleaned from books or anecdotes, disappointment awaits. The above may still be true in provincial Chinese cities, and perhaps even in some of the smaller lanes of inner Beijing. But after a visit to today's Beijing, one will probably want to forget the traffic as quickly as possible.

But if truly adventurous, take heart and rent a bike to join the flood of bicycles! Beijing is as flat as a board, and cycling is easy. Don't try and prove to the Chinese that you have better calf muscles than do they. Indeed, there are two types of cyclists who race along and cause accidents: the young hotheads who get rid of surplus energy by speeding along with their torsos bent over the handlebars, and the foreigners, who vigorously push the pedals as if they were being paid for it, made even more noticeable by their heated red faces and light hair. Beijingers literally glide instead.

Bicycle traffic in Beijing illustrates the Chinese proverb that the soft and gentle will defeat the hard and obstinate, with the latter qualities symbolising the growing amount of motorised traffic. With a few exceptions, traffic regulations are the same as in Europe, though they are interpreted differently. Unfortunately, car drivers pay little attention to these rules, the amount of attention given is in inverse proportion to the size of their car. The stream of cyclists stops when faced with an obstacle approaching from the right or the left, opens up and divides to swallow the foreign element, then spits it out again and carries on as before. In general, move with the masses and expect no courtesy from automobiles.

There are traffic police at every major crossroads, unfriendly fellows who try to master the chaos with arrogant gestures. They manage it, too, as long as they look straight at the traffic. If they turn away even for a moment, cyclists and pedestrians move right out into the flow of traffic, even when there is a red light. This forces traffic from the opposite direction to move slowly or to stop, but it also ensures that their own even, communal progress is not interrupted for too long. Thus, the one true traffic law is illustrated: whoever cuts off the other first has the right of way.

Undoubtedly, this anarchic behaviour on the roads has its price. In fact, approximately 90 percent of the victims in fatal traffic accidents in Beijing are cyclists or pedestrians.

If you don't have a bicycle available and taxi rides prove either too expensive or boring, get a feeling of what it's like to live in Beijing by travelling on a public bus. You will come into close – very close – contact with the people of Beijing. At peak traffic times, 13 people try and squeeze into every square metre of every bus. So don't be foolhardy: avoid the rush hour. Most Western visitors are not up to this situation when they arrive, and for them, bus trips are made longer by the simple fact that they can't push their way on.

Organized chaos, indeed, but a significant part of the true Beijing experience is definitely in its traffic. Do jump in feet first and with eyes closed! ∎

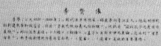

王夫之像

王夫之（公元1619—1692年）明末清初进步思想家，湖南衡阳人。他和顾炎武和黄宗羲等反对道学空谈，提倡"经世致用"之学。他认为世界的根本是物质性的，是自然界固有的，朴素唯物主义的观点战胜了唯心主义，具有朴素辩证法的思想。

顾炎武像

顾炎武（公元1613—1682年）明末大将爱国学者，清代实朝学家以及史籍等，此书学说极广博，深受后世朴学的影响，主张经世致用，当时颇高，学有《日知录》、《天下郡国利病书》等。

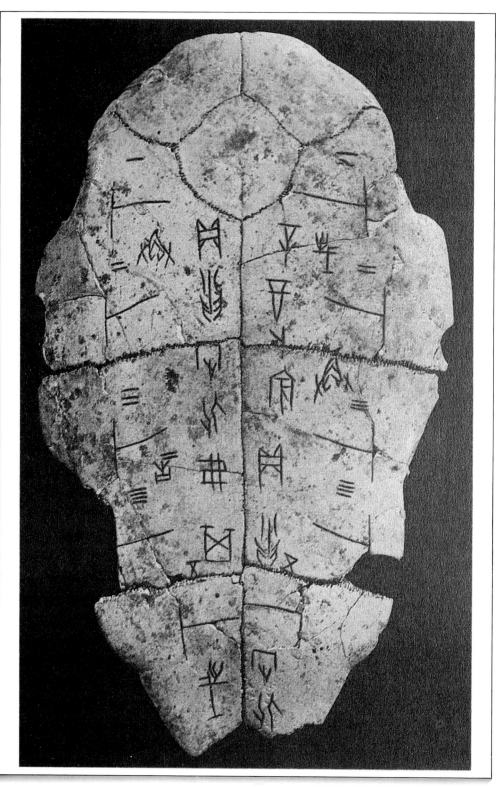

MUSEUMS, GALLERIES AND MEMORIALS

In the eastern district of the city, where Jianguomenwai meets the second ring road, is the **Gu Guanxiangtai**, or **Ancient Observatory**. Originally constructed in 1279 north of its present-day site, the observatory now sits atop a watchtower that was once a part of the city walls. Built in the mid-15th century, the observatory has serviced both the Ming and Qing dynasties in making predictions based on astrology, as well as helping navigators headed to sea.

This was the work place of the famous astronomer, hydraulics engineer and mathematician Guo Shoujing. The name of the observatory has been changed several times. In the Yuan period it was known as the Terrace to Bring Down the Heavens, while in Ming times it was the Terrace for Watching the Stars. It was an astronomer's terrace.

The bronze astronomical instruments that stand atop the observatory and that are exhibited around the grounds and in the exhibition halls, are, scientifically speaking, extremely precise and are examples of the skill of Chinese craftsmen. Seven of the original 15 instruments from the watchtower were taken to Nanjing in 1931, where they are on exhibit in the Zijishan Observatory. The remaining instruments are: three armillary spheres, a quadrant for finding stars, a celestial globe, an equatorial theodolite for determining horizontal angles and angles of elevation, an altazimuth for determining the height of stars in the sky, and a sextant.

Science museum: Beijing's natural history museum, **Ziyan Bowuguan**, is in an unattractive building opposite a department store in the Yongdingmen district, just to the west of the Temple of Heaven in Tianqiao Street.

It has, however, an exhibition of more than 5,000 species in palaeontology, zoology and botany.

In the hall of palaeontology, one can see fossils from the Palaeozoic, Mesozoic and Cenozoic periods, such as the piece of ochre-coloured marble with the cloud pattern formed by fossilised seaweed – a silent record of life in prehistoric times, about 500 to 100 million years ago.

In the centre of the hall is the skeleton of the high-nosed Qingdaosaurus, which had a horn on its nose. The skeleton of Mamenchisaurus, which is twice the size, was dug up in the village of Mamenxi in Sichuan Province. In contrast to these giants, there are the remains of a Lufengsaurus (2 metres high, 6 metres long) from Yunnan Province, and a parrot beaked dinosaur that was no bigger than a cat.

History and revolution: Museums on Chinese history and revolution share a complex of buildings on the eastern edge of Tiananmen Square. The four-storey house with two side wings was built in 1959 as part of a building project involving 10 monumental buildings. Two pillars on either side of the entrance are shaped like torches, symbolising the words of Mao Zedong: "A spark can start a fire in the steppe."

From the entrance hall, walk south into the main hall of the Museum of Chinese History, or north into the Museum of the Chinese Revolution. The central hall is dedicated to the memory of Marx, Engels, Lenin and Stalin, whose portrait busts can be seen here.

The **Zhongguo Lishi Bowuguan (Museum of Chinese History)** was opened in 1926. After 1949, the objects on display were increased to more than 30,000. A few came from state sources such as the Department of the Administration of the Cultural Objects of Northern China, but more than 16,900 pieces came from private collections in China and elsewhere in the world. Among them is the valuable blue-glazed lamp from the Southern Dynasties period (420–589), Tang figures and an embroidered silk portrait of the Celestial Kings.

Among the continuous exhibitions are Peking Man, Lantian Man from Shaanxi, and Yuanmou Man, whose remains were found in Yunnan Province. Ancient bronzes, jade pieces and bones, and ceramics from the Tang and Song dynasties are also on show. Chinese discoveries such as printing, gunpowder, the compass, and paper manufacture are also on display.

The **Zhongguo Geming Bowuguan (Museum of the Chinese Revolution)** provides information about the history of the Communist Party in China, the revolutionary civil wars, as well as the campaign of resistance against the Japanese. During the time of the Cultural Revolution, the exhibition had to be constantly readjusted to fit in with the current campaign (rather like in the Ministry of Truth in George Orwell's novel, *1984*), but today the aim is to provide an objective record.

The **China National Gallery** is another of the 10 monumental buildings of the project realised in Beijing in 1959. It stands where Wusi Dajie Street meets Wangfujing Street, a little to the east of Jingshan, or Coal Hill. The building incorporates the architectural style of a traditional palace and has a roof covered with yellow glazed tiles. The 14 exhibition halls cover an area of 6,000

The Ancient Observatory.

square metres (64,600 sq ft) and exhibitions of Chinese and foreign art are held regularly. One can also see individual artists at work. A shop sells folk art, reproductions, artistic prints and postcards, and art supplies.

West of the Imperial Palace, in Fuxingmen Street, is the **Minzu Wenhuagong (Cultural Palace of the Nationalities)**. The ground plan of this building is based on the Chinese character *shan* (mountain). The pagoda-shaped tower is of exactly the same height as the famous White Dagoba in Beihai Park. Colours predominate: the earth-gold of the granite base, the white of the unglazed tiles and the blue of the roof tiles of the tower. The palace is divided into six sections: museum, library, auditorium, dance hall, restaurant and guest house. Two great bronze doors, adorned with the Chinese ideographs for solidarity and progress, form the entrance.

Beyond them is the central hall, four storeys high, in white and green marble. A bronze chandelier hangs from the octagonal ceiling, and reliefs on the

Long waits for the museums.

walls depict the many minorities of China. The relief on the southwestern wall portrays spring, with Tibetans, Miao and Buyi. The southeastern wall depicts Zhuang, Li and Yao at the rice harvest. On the northwestern wall a herd of sheep can be seen, together with Hui and Uighurs harvesting wheat, cotton and grapes. On the northeastern relief people in colourful clothing are grouped around a range of industrial products.

The museum in the northern part of the building has five exhibition halls and 35 smaller exhibition rooms. The library, with 600,000 volumes, is situated on the ground floor and is the basic source of information for studies of the 55 minorities of China.

The eastern wing of the Cultural Palace contains the auditorium with 1,500 seats, each fitted with headphones for eight channels. There are also facilities for radio and TV programmes, as well as a recording studio. The western wing with the dance hall, restaurant and music rooms is devoted to entertainment. Here you can get very good Russian food, among other dishes.

The **memorial hall for Sun Yat-sen** (1862–1925), founder of the National People's Party, the Guomindang, and charismatic leader of the middle-class democratic movement, lies in **Biyunsi (Temple of the Azure Clouds)**, at the foot of the **Xiangshan (Fragrant Hills)**, located about 10 kilometres (6 mi) west of Beijing.

The Buddhist temple is about 600 years old and comprises four great halls, the innermost being the memorial hall for Sun Yat-sen. Here lies an empty coffin, a gift from the Soviet Union, which could not be used because it did not arrive until two weeks after the funeral of Sun Yat-sen. To the left of the main entrance of the hall, letters and manuscripts left by Sun Yat-sen can be viewed. On the wall is an inscription in marble: a letter from Sun Yat-sen addressed to the Soviet Union.

There are exhibition rooms on both sides of the memorial hall. The first shows photos from Sun Yat-sen's youth; the second contains photos from the period of his active involvement in the democratic revolution. Beyond the memorial hall is the pagoda courtyard. The marble **Jingangbaozuota (Pagoda of the Diamond Throne)** was built in 1748 under the rule of Emperor Qianlong, and is modelled on the Wutasi (Five Pagodas Temple), in the northwest section of Beijing.

In March 1925, Sun Yat-sen's coffin lay in state in the pagoda, before being moved in 1929 to Zhongshanling, the Sun Yat-sen mausoleum in Nanjing. His clothing and personal belongings, however, remained in the pagoda. In front of the building is a stele with an inscription by Hu Hanmin, one of the older leaders of the Guomindang. The pagoda itself is 35-metres (114-ft) high, and its base is adorned with numerous statues of Buddha.

Song Qingling's house: The former home of Song Qingling, honorary president of the People's Republic of China, and wife of Sun Yat-sen, is at No. 46 Beiheyan Street in the Houhai area of Xicheng, Beijing's West City district. The residence was once a garden, part of the palace grounds of a prince of the Qing dynasty.

Song Qingling moved into the house in 1963 and lived there until her death in 1981. The former guest room houses an exhibition of photographs, documents, and objects from Song Qingling's childhood, her years as a student, her marriage to Sun Yat-sen, her political activities, her work for the Society for the Protection of the Rights of the Chinese People, and her support for the resistance to Japanese occupation. An extract from her most famous speech, the essay, "Sun Yat-sen and his cooperation with the Communist Party," is also on exhibition.

Mao's mausoleum: After the death of Mao Zedong in 1976, political circumstances dictated the building of a memorial that would outlast the centuries to honour the great leader of the Chinese revolution. President Zhou Enlai, who died in the same year, had his ashes scattered to the winds. Mao's body, however, was embalmed – by Vietnamese experts, it is said.

Socialist Realism in front of Mao's mausoleum.

The memorial hall, built in a record time of nine months, lies on the south side of Tiananmen Square. The small open space to the south of the hall was famous during the Ming dynasty as Chessboards Street, once a busy market area. There are massive group sculptures by the front and rear entrances, depicting the people's common struggle for socialism – typical examples of the style of Socialist Realism.

Of the building's two floors, only the ground floor is open to the public. Visitors have to queue in lines of four in front of the building, and no bags, cameras or other objects may be taken inside. In the entrance hall is a marble statue of Mao. The wall behind it is covered with a 24-metre (79-ft) long tapestry depicting the rivers and mountains of this huge country.

The body of Mao lies in state in a crystal coffin in the Central Hall of Rest. He is dressed in the typical blue suit and covered with the flag of the Communist Party. In the southern hall beyond, calligraphy by Mao Zedong can be seen, bearing the title "Reply to Comrade Guo Moruo." The mausoleum was visited by countless Chinese in the months after it was opened, with people queuing patiently across Tiananmen Square, but is now much less frequented.

It is only open in the mornings, three days a week. Tourist groups should officially announce their intention to visit prior to arrival.

Lu Xun's house: Lu Xun (1881–1936) was one of the greatest Chinese writers of this century and lived in Beijing from 1923–25. The typical Chinese courtyard house, which he bought with borrowed money, is situated near **Fuchengmen**, an old imperial gate in the western district and due west of Beihai Park. The most eastern room in the northern part of the courtyard belonged to Lu Xun's mother, the western room to his wife. The rooms to the south served as living rooms and a library. The small room added on to the north side was the study and bedroom that Lu Xun called the "tiger's tail." Here he wrote the two stories, *The Tomb* and *Wild Grasses*.

The memorial to Lu Xun.

On the 20th anniversary of Lu Xun's death, the house was opened as a museum. On exhibition are photographs, unpublished manuscripts, letters and a copy of the entry he made in his diary on the day of his death.

Xu Beihong memorial: Xu Beihong (1895–1953), one of the most famous modern Chinese artists and teachers, was well known for his numerous paintings of horses.

The Xu Beihong Memorial Hall was originally housed in his former apartment. Xu Beihong's wife, Liao Jingwen, had left the house and all his works, books and calligraphy to the People's Republic, which built a memorial to Xu Beihong on the grounds. Later, when the house had to be demolished because of the building of the subway, the memorial hall was moved to No. 53 Northern Xinjiekou Street.

In the new hall, Xu's studio was rebuilt exactly as it looked shortly before his death. Hanging on the walls are a copy of Xu Beihong's painting, *Rich Harvest*, and works by Ren Bonian and Qi Baishi, and a photograph of Xu, taken in 1913 by Rabrindranath Tagore, the Indian poet and Nobel Prize winner.

The works of art exhibited in this memorial hall were almost all collected by the artist himself during his lifetime, and among them are more than 1,200 examples from the Tang, Song, Yuan, Ming and Qing dynasties, as well as works from the time of the May Fourth Movement (1919). One of the most valuable works is a cartoon of the Tang painting, *The Scroll of the 87 Immortals*, by Wu Daozi.

The tomb of Xu Beihong is in **Babaoshan (Heroes' Cemetery)** in Shijingshan Street, the western extension of Chang'an Boulevard.

Li Dazhao's tomb: A noted activist of the May Fourth Movement of 1919, and also a co-founder of the Chinese Communist Party, Li Dazhao was condemned and subsequently hanged in 1927. He is buried in the **Warian Gongum (Cemetery of Eternal Peace)**, in the Jade Springs Mountains, 15 kilometres (9 mi) west of Beijing.

Tomb of Xu Beihong.

DISCOVERIES AND INVENTIONS

The concept that the emperor was the Son of Heaven – and that extraordinary celestial and earthly events were the expression of approval or criticism from above – was the cause for the very early development of astronomical observation in China. The imperial court had its own Office of Astronomy, and in the 13th century, there were 17 different astronomical instruments at the astronomer's disposal in the Beijing Observatory. Hence, Halley's Comet was first recorded as early as 467 BC. A calendar of 360 days was in use by the 3rd century BC, which successive dynasties tried to improve. In the 13th century, they fixed the length of the year as 365.2424 days, less than a thousandth off from modern calculations.

The Clock Tower of Su Song, built in 1088, is an early example of the highly-developed art of the clockmaker. Chain-driven and powered by a water wheel, it is fitted with a kind of escapement to regulate the wheels to show astronomical movements very precisely. The oldest *Book of Mathematics* dates from the 3rd century and gives the answers to many astronomical problems. It also deals with the multiplication and division of fractions and the formation of square roots. Imperial geographers were busy with the deviation of magnetic north from true north even before Europeans were aware that the earth had a magnetic field. The Chinese compass originally consisted of a metal plate with a metal spoon on it, the handle of the spoon pointing to the south. Around the year 132, Zhang Heng built a seismograph that could show in which direction an earthquake had taken place.

Around 1100, iron foundries in China were already producing quantities of iron and steel every year that were unmatched in Europe until the 18th century.

The use of block and tackle shows that the Chinese understood the laws of mechanics in the 5th century. The so-called Archimedean Screw was used to pump water in the 1st century, and the water wheel in the 4th and 5th centuries. Irrigation, essential for Chinese agriculture, was important in development of technology.

The written word was always accorded more importance in China than the spoken. This may have been the reason for the early development of paper. Made of mulberry tree bark around AD 200, and of bamboo some 200 years later, paper is still made today all over the world, according to the Chinese method: the fibrous material is soaked, the fibres separated, and a pulp formed; the pulp is thinned, pressed into pages, and then dried and smoothed.

Printing, however, was not developed until some eight centuries later. Stone rubbing and printing with stamps seem to have been the more economic methods of reproduction of the written word, not least because Chinese script consists of thousands of characters.

In the 9th century, Daoist monks, looking for the elixir of eternal life, mixed charcoal, saltpetre and sulphur, thus discovering black powder, or gun powder. This was not used only for fireworks; imperial troops in fact used bombs and grenades filled with black powder.

The invention of silk goes far back; excavations show that silk moth cultivation can be traced back to the 3rd century BC. Up until AD 200, the Chinese had a monopoly on silk manufacture, ensured by the fact that passing on its secrets counted as high treason. It was not until the 6th century that the method of manufacturing silk textiles become known in the West. ∎

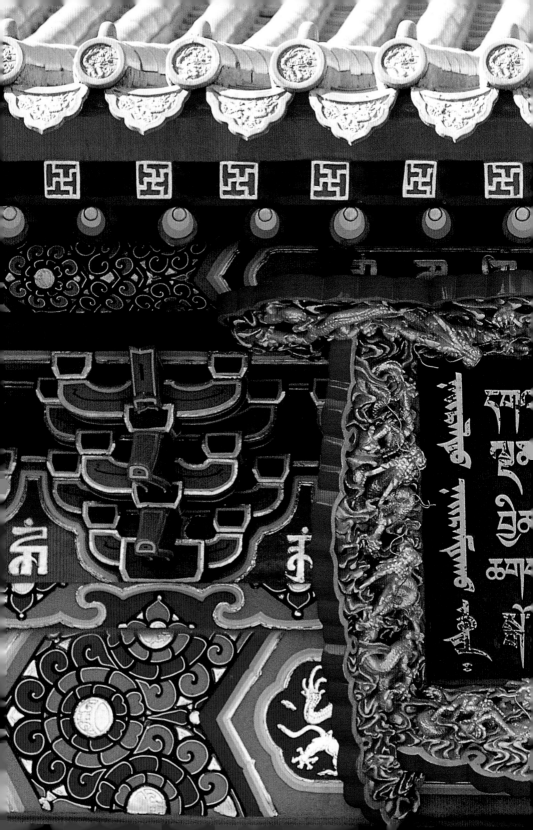

TEMPLES AND MONASTERIES

Although most temples, monasteries and churches were closed during the Cultural Revolution (1966–1976), many of these buildings were reopened to the public in the early 1980s. Even those destroyed by the Red Guards are being rebuilt, and most of them are filled with new life. Today, an increasing number of monks, priests and worshippers can be found in them.

Buddhist temples: While the Temple of Heaven and the many Confucian temples acted as sites for the rituals of the official state religion, the Buddhist temple was the home of popular religion. Buddhism began in India in the 6th century BC and gradually spread. After travelling along the Silk Road to China in the early centuries AD, Buddhism became the most important religion of the Chinese people. However different the various schools of Buddhism may be, their central aim is the attempt to overcome suffering and even pleasures caused by human desires.

The Buddhist goal is to escape from the cycle of death and rebirth and enter nirvana. Particularly influential in China is Mahayana (Great Vehicle) Buddhism. For this reason, the main hall of most Buddhist temples in China contains the historic Buddha Sakyamuni (or Buddha of the present), flanked by Buddhas of the past and future. Despite much destruction, there are still quite a number of Buddhist temples in Beijing.

Bodhisattvas – believers who have achieved great moral and spiritual wisdom and can therefore enter nirvana, but have chosen to remain to help suffering humanity – also play an important part in Buddhism.

Guanyin, goddess of mercy, is especially honoured by Buddhists throughout China. She fulfills a role in Chinese Buddhism similar to that of the Virgin Mary in Christianity. If you want children, or are praying for good health, you turn to this female Bodhisattva believed to be merciful and compassionate.

Probably the oldest temple in the Inner City of Beijing is the **Fayuansi (Temple of the Source of Buddhist Teaching)**, in the Xuanwu district, west of Tiantan (Temple of Heaven) and southwest of the Imperial Palace. A visit to Fayuansi is not on the programme of most group tours, but it is worthwhile for the quiet of the beautiful garden courtyards, and also for its extraordinary sculptures. Fayuansi is in the middle of the old city of Beijing, and if there is enough time, walk from Fayuansi to the **Niujie Mosque** in the Muslim quarter. Here, you are in the genuine old part of Beijing with its *hutong* and courtyard houses, and where the people still speak the authentic dialect.

Fayuansi was built on the orders of the Tang emperor, Li Shimin, in honour of soldiers killed in battle. It took over 40 years to build, was completed in 696 and named Minzhongsi, but since 1734 it has been known as Fayuansi. The temple houses the **Buddhist Academy**, formed in 1956 by the Chinese Buddhist Society. The Academy is devoted

to the teaching and study of Buddhism, and trains young monks for four to five years before they can enter other monasteries in China.

Enter Fayuansi through Shanmen, the Mountain Gate, which is guarded by two stone lions. In the first temple courtyard are two bronze lions in front of the **Tianwangdian (Hall of the Celestial Kings)**. The Celestial Kings rule the four points of the compass and can keep away all evil spirits and the enemies of Buddhism. Enthroned in the middle is a Milefo, a laughing, fat-bellied Buddha, who encourages the faithful: "Come in, follow me on the way to release in nirvana." Such Milefo Buddhas can be seen at the entrance to almost all Chinese Buddhist temples, and are always flanked by the four celestial guardians.

The laughing Buddha figure represents Maitreya, the Buddha of the Coming Age. His depiction as a laughing, fat-bellied figure dates from about 800. In the popular conception of Buddhism, his belly and his laughter seem to promise the Chinese peasants the good life in nirvana. In fact, his belly represents an enlarged centre of life, achieved by deep meditation and an ascetic life.

Behind the Milefo Buddha is the Guardian of Buddhism, with his face turned to the main hall of the temple, the **Daxiongbaodian (Hall of Heroes)**. The four Celestial Kings and the fat Buddha in Fayuansi are Ming dynasty bronzes, a rarity in Chinese Buddhist temples.

In the Daxiongbaodian, which is reached by leaving the first hall and crossing a garden with a bronze cauldron and stone steles, is a Buddha flanked by two Bodhisattvas and surrounded by 18 Lohan, or saints, the lowest rank in the Buddhist divine hierarchy. The Lohan are still alive on earth, but each individual has achieved salvation, which is why they seem marvellous to the observer. The second rank is formed by the Bodhisattvas, who have rejected nirvana to help humanity, while Buddha, the Enlightened One, has already achieved nirvana and is, in his many forms and appearances, the embodiment of Buddhist wisdom itself.

Mythical animals protect against evil spirits.

Leaving the main hall, you will pass a small hall with stone tablets and come to the **Hall of a Thousand Buddhas**. Here, on a stone base, is a 5-metre (15-ft) high sculpture dating back to the Ming dynasty. On the round, spherical Thousand-Buddha base, the Buddhas of the five points of the compass are seated, and towering over all of them is the Dharma Buddha.

In the last hall, with its Reclining Buddha, there is an excellent exhibition of Buddhist sculpture, with some pieces dating back to the Han dynasty (206 BC to AD 220). The most recent examples are bronze figures dating from the Ming and Qing periods (14th to 20th century). A splendid Guanyin Bodhisattva with 1,000 arms is also on display. Finally, it should be noted that the Fayuansi Temple contains a library of more than 100,000 valuable books.

To the northwest of Fayuansi, the **Wutasi (Temple of Five Pagodas)** is not far from the zoo (along the bus route 332 in the direction of the Summer Palace). Basically, it is just north of the **Shoudutiyuguan (Sports Hall of the Capital)**, close to the Purple Bamboo Park. In earlier years, when driving towards the Summer Palace, one used to be able to see the tops of the pagodas on the right-hand side, but now the area has been built up with new apartment blocks. A path behind the sports hall leads to this temple, which, until 1980, was closed and falling into ruin.

The temple, which dates back to the time of the Ming emperor Yongle in the 15th century, was restored during Qianlong's reign but destroyed by European troops in 1860 and again in 1900. The building, with five small pagodas standing on a massive square base, is in a style known in Buddhism as the "Diamond Throne Pagoda" style. Worth seeing above all else are the bas-reliefs on the outside, with Buddha figures, symbolic animals, lotus flowers, heavenly guardians, the wheel of Buddhist teaching, and other Buddhist symbols.

Go up two flights of stairs to the terrace with the pagodas, which are themselves adorned with reliefs around

Buddha's footprints are honoures in the Temple of the Five Pagodas (Wutasi).

the bases. In the cloisters down below, visitors can study the various styles of pagoda architecture in China through an exhibition of photographs. An impressive collection of steles also awaits in the courtyard. The nice thing about this temple is that it does not get as crowded as some of the others in Beijing.

After visiting, relax with a boat trip in the **Zizhuyuan (Purple Bamboo Park)**, and then admire one of the newer monumental Chinese buildings, the **Beijing Library**, next to the park. You can also take a bus ride on route 332 or 302 in a westerly direction to **Renmindaxue (the People's University)**, not far from the Friendship Hotel. Then travel east on the outer third ring road for about two kilometres (just over 1 mi), where you will see on your left, squeezed in among the new buildings and the factories, the **Dazhongsi (Temple of the Great Bell)**.

The temple, built in 743, is famous above all for its huge bell. Made in 1406 on the orders of the Ming emperor Yongle, the bell is 7 metres (23 ft) high, has a diameter of 3 metres (10 ft) and weighs

46.5 tonnes. This bronze bell is in the further part of the grounds, in a 17-metre (56-ft) high tower. Inscribed on the bell – which is among the oldest bells in the world – is the entire text of the Huayan Sutra, consisting of some 200,000 characters.

The Huayan sect (translated as the Garland sect) had great influence in the Far East. It has been responsible for influencing the Asian attitude to nature and for inspiring many artists. It was founded in 630 and endured until about 1000. Its teaching states that all creatures and things are imbued with a cosmic principle, that everything exists in harmony with everything else, and that every grain of dust contains all the wealth of Buddha.

As the secrets of truth can be seen at all times and in all places, this teaching did not feel the need to influence the cosmic powers or to use magic, as is the case with Tantric (Tibetan) Buddhism. It relied, instead, on the contemplation and observation of things and living creatures, and felt that it sufficed to perceive their beauty and their essence.

The temple, much damaged during the Cultural Revolution, has now been restored and is used as a museum. Some 160 ancient bells, weighing from 150 grams (6 oz) to a 46.5-ton giant, can be seen here.

Southeast of Dazhongsi, in the direction of the Imperial Palace and west of Beihai Park, **Baitasi (Temple of the White Pagoda)** was built in 1096 during the rule of the Liao dynasty, and restored in the Tibetan style by Kublai Khan in 1271. Destroyed by fire shortly afterwards, the monastery was rebuilt in 1457 and received its official name of Miaoyingsi (Temple of Divine Justice). This temple is famous for its white dagoba (a Tibetan-style shrine). Its top is adorned by an engraved copper canopy, from which little bells hang, moving in the wind in order to drive away evil spirits. In the fourth hall there are sculptures of the three Buddhas and two Buddha pupils, as well as *thangka*, or Tibetan scroll pictures.

The temple and grounds were restored after 1978. During the renovations, val-

Bell in Dazhongsi.

uable objects were found in the dagoba. Among them were boxes of Buddhist manuscripts and calligraphy by Emperor Qianlong, as well as jewellery and coins from various dynasties.

In the three other halls, there is an exhibition about the city of Dadu, the name Beijing was known by at the time of the Mongol Yuan dynasty. There are models showing the layout of the city and of the canals and other water works that existed at that time, whilst the social, economic and political systems of Mongol rule are described on display boards and posters. Marco Polo is, of course, mentioned.

A 10-minute walk away from Baitasi, at the eastern end of Fuchengmei Street jammed in between apartment blocks and warehouses, lies the **Guangjisi (Temple of Universal Rescue)**. It is currently the headquarters for the Buddhist Association of China, and visits are generally restricted to Buddhist groups or scholars. But it may happen that the doorkeepers at the entrance will be friendly and permit a chance passer-

by to take a quick look inside. Under the Ming emperor Tianshun, an existing Jin dynasty temple on the site was renovated and in 1669, under Emperor Kangxi, it was restored and extended. In 1931, the temple, which in Qing times had acquired a 3-metre (10- ft) high sandalwood statue of Buddha, was destroyed by fire. In 1935, it was rebuilt, and was restored in 1952, although it was kept closed during the Cultural Revolution. The design of the temple follows the classic Buddhist architectural plan. In the third hall, the **Hall of Guanyin**, is a thousand-armed statue of the goddess of mercy, Guanyin, gilded during the Qing period, together with a copper Guanyin figure and a Guanyin on a lotus blossom dating from the Ming period. Stored in the library of the monastery are valuable handwritten sutras from the Tang dynasty, along with more than 30,000 old historical rubbings of stone inscriptions.

Lamaist Buddhism: In the northeastern part of the city is the largest and best-known, and certainly one of the city's

Guangjisi altar.

most beautiful and interesting Tibetan (Lama) temples – **Yonghegong**, the **Palace of Eternal Harmony**.

Located at the second ring road on Yonghegong Street, the Lama temple is about a half hour walk from the Great Wall, Kunlun and Huadu hotels; you can get there by bus on routes 13, 44 and 116, or even more easily by subway, because the Yonghegong station is directly opposite. A visit to Yonghegong can easily be combined with a walk in the northern Earth Altar Park on the other side of the ring road, or a tour of the **Kongmiao (Confucius Temple)**, to the west. In earlier years, the Lama temple used to be part of the city wall.

The name Yonghegong – Palace of Eternal Harmony – points to the courtly and imperial origins of the temple. Built in 1694, it first served as a residence for the fourth son, Yongzheng, of Emperor Kangxi, before the former ascended to the throne in 1722. In the past, the palace of a ruler had to be turned into a temple when the said ruler came to power, and so Yongzheng's successor,

his son Qianlong, sent for 300 Tibetan monks and 200 Chinese pupils and installed them in the palace. The former palace remained a monastery from 1744 to 1960, and was considered one of the most notable centres of Lamaist Buddhism outside Tibet.

It is no coincidence that the Manchu emperors favoured a Tibetan monastery, as many of them were officially followers of Confucius, but privately were attracted to Tibetan Buddhism.

During the Cultural Revolution, the monastery was closed. At first, groups of Red Guards took over the monastery, but were forbidden to destroy or plunder it by orders of the former president Zhou Enlai. However, many monks were ill-treated and sent away to do manual labour in the countryside. In the early 1980s, Yonghegong was reopened and completely restored. Now the monastery houses more than 70 monks.

Study and training in the monastery are thorough. According to an often-told anecdote, one of the young novices, who work by day as supervisors in the

Altar and ancestor tablets in Guangjisi, Temple of Universal Rescue.

temple halls, answered the question, "How long do you have to study?" with, "I don't have to at all. Learning lasts a lifetime." A philosopher, indeed.

The monks, who live in the rear part of the complex bordering the ring road, have the use of washing machines and TV sets and are, in short, a well-equipped collective of Lamaist bachelors. The temple festivals and dances, for which the temple became famous, now belong permanently to the past.

The Yonghegong monastery belongs to the Yellow Hat or Gelugpa sect, predominant in Tibet, whose spiritual head is the Dalai Lama. Whilst the Dalai Lama lives in exile, the second spiritual head of Tibetan Buddhism, the Panchen Lama, resides in Beijing. In contrast to the Dalai Lamas, the Panchen Lamas have recognised Chinese authority since the beginning of this century. The 10th Panchen Lama died in early 1989, and in 1993, the Chinese government invited the Dalai Lama to help in the search for the next Panchen Lama.

Coming from the south, enter the temple grounds through a gate. After crossing the temple gardens, you come to the inner courtyard with its bell and drum towers and two pavilions with steles in them. To the north is the **Tianwangdian (Hall of the Celestial Kings)**, with statues of the Maitreya Buddha and two guardian divinities.

Beyond the pavilion is a stone representation of the World Mountain, Sumeru. In the second of five halls that lead into yet another – **Yonghedian (Hall of Eternal Harmony)** – there are three statues of Buddha surrounded by 18 Lohan. The buildings to the left and right of this inner courtyard house valuable thangka, figures representing the founder of the Yellow Hat sect, Tsongkhapa, and a mandala. Crossing the next courtyard, you come to the **Yongyoudian (Hall of Eternal Protection)**, with statues of the Buddhas of longevity and medicine.

The halls to the left and right of the following courtyard contain, among other items, Yab-Yum figures, a male and a female divinity whose intimate sexual

Chinese palace architecture in the Lama Temple Yonghegong.

connection symbolises the cosmic unity of all opposites. This courtyard is bounded by the **Falundian (Hall of the Wheel of Dharma)**, in the middle of which is a 6-metre (20-ft) high statue of Tsongkhapa. Along the walls, Lamaist manuscripts are stored, and behind the figure of Tsongkhapa is the monastery's valuable treasure – a miniature mountain of sandalwood together with 500 Lohan figures of gold, silver, copper, iron and tin. The fifth inner courtyard ends at the **Wanfuge (Pavilion of Ten Thousand Happinesses)**. This pavilion contains an 25-metre (80-ft) high Maitreya Buddha made from a single piece of sandalwood. The three-storey pavilion is linked by bridges to the two-storey side buildings that flank it.

Also in the Andingmen area is the **Huang Si (Yellow Temple)**, at the terminus of bus route No. 8. This temple – also a Tibetan Buddhist temple – was nothing but ruins a few years ago. It has now been fully restored, and is divided into a western and an eastern temple. The western Yellow Temple was built by the Qing emperor Shunchi, in 1652, for the fifth Dalai Lama on the occasion of the latter's visit to the imperial court. Later, the Yellow Temple became the official residence for high dignitaries of Tibetan Buddhism when they visited Beijing. Apart from the **Hall of the Guardian Divinities**, the most remarkable feature is the **White Pagoda**, which Qianlong had built in honour of the sixth Panchen Lama in 1780. The Huang Si Temple is not open to the public and is now said to be the property of the Panchen Lama.

Not too far to the west and a bit south, nestled in *hutong* surrounding the Drum and Bell towers of Gulou, is the **Guang Hua Buddhist Temple**. Constructed during the Yuan dynasty, this active temple is now home to the Beijing Buddhist Society. While it is only medium sized in relation to some temples, it is well-preserved and well-stocked with the usual colourful array of Buddhist statues and artifacts.

Finally, the following is a list of other temples worthy of note: the **Bailinsi (Cypress Grove Temple)**, to the east of Yonghegong; the **Shengansi (Temple of Imperial Security)**, in Nanheng Street in the Xuanwu district; the **Zhihuaisi (Temple of Perfect Wisdom)**, in the Chaoyang district; and the **Tianningsi Temple** in Guanganmenwai Street, in the southeastern part of Beijing, and where there used to be a flourishing market in the old days. Many of these little temples are no longer open to the public. During the Cultural Revolution, it was not unusual for them to be turned into factories.

Outside of central Beijing: The oldest Buddhist temple of Beijing is not in the city centre, but in the Mentougou district on Tanzheshan Hill. If you have time, you should not shy away from the two-hour drive to the **Tanzhesi Temple**. From the bus station at Zhanlanlu (near the zoo), bus No. 336 will go right to the terminus at Mentougou, where you have to change buses. Or you can drive west along Chang'an Boulevard. It is easy to combine a visit to the Tanzhesi Temple with a side trip to the Jietaisi Temple. Both are delightful because of

Tibetan stupa in the Yellow Temple (Huang Si).

their rural settings and the peaceful isolation, which you can, however, only enjoy on weekdays.

The Tanzhesi Temple is terraced into the quiet, densely wooded scenery of the hills to the west of Beijing. Both Buddhists and Daoists used to withdraw into such beautiful and quiet places in order to meditate. Tanzhesi Temple was built between 265 and 316. Over the centuries, its name has changed several times, until finally Tanzhesi prevailed. *Tan* refers to the Dragon Pool, Longtan, above the temple, and *zhe* to the wild mulberries that grow in the hills. There is an old proverb that says, "First came Tanzhe, then came Youzhou", as the Beijing region was known in the 6th century.

The temple itself is built in three parts along a north-south line on the hill slope. Enter following the central axis from the south, through the **Pailou (Gate of Honour)**, and the adjoining **Shanmen (Mountain Gate)**, also known as the Main Gate. The path is lined by many old pine trees, which are sometimes compared by the Chinese to flying dragons. Beyond the Mountain Gate, one behind the other, lie **Tianwangdian (Hall of the Celestial Kings)**, the **Daxiongbaodian**, the **Zhaitang**, and the **Piluge Pavilion**, which is dedicated to the Buddha Vairocana.

On the roof of the main hall are legendary beasts, sons of the Dragon King, who are supposed to have captured a monk and chained him to the roof. You can get the best view of Tanzhesi and the surrounding country from this highest point in the grounds.

Beyond the main hall of Daxiongbaodian are two **gingko trees**, the Emperor's Tree and the Emperor's Companion's Tree. Both are supposed to date from the Liao dynasty (916–1125). On the western path, go past the **Temple of Guanyin**. Inside, the **Paving Stone of Beizhuan** is kept, on which the nun Miaoyan, a daughter of the Mongol emperor Kublai Khan (1260–1294), is supposed to have prayed to Buddha daily in penance for her father's misdeeds. This leads to the Temple of the

Guanyin, goddess of mercy.

Dragon King and the Temple of the Founding Father of this monastery, all of which belong to the distinct Buddhist sect of Huayan.

In the eastern part of the grounds are a white dagoba dating from 1427, two groups of 12th-century pagodas, a bamboo grove and the **Liubeige (Pavilion of the Moving Cup)**, in which the Emperor Qianlong stayed during his visits to the monastery.

It was somewhat of a tradition for the nobility of the city to meet here on the third day of the Chinese New Year festival. The water of the mountain spring pours out of a lion's mouth into a twisting, dragon-shaped runnel and then flows away. Everyone would place his filled cup in the runnel. If the cup fell over, the person who owned it had to drink a cup of wine and recite a poem.

Today, in the Tanzhesi Temple, there is a reasonably priced restaurant serving good and wholesome food.

Eight kilometres (5 mi) to the south of the Tanzhesi Temple, at the foot of **Ma'anshan (Saddle Hill)**, is the **Jietai-si Temple**. This imposing temple dates from 622 and owes its name to the three-level stone terraces, which were surrounded by statues and upon which the dedication ceremony of monks took place. The terraces can still be seen today. The Main Hall is the Daxiongbaodian, and beyond it is the Thousand Buddhas Pavilion. Steles with Buddhist inscriptions dating from the Liao and Yuan dynasties can be seen in front of the Mingwang Hall. There is no longer much to be seen inside the halls, but it is worthwhile taking a walk to enjoy the temple grounds with their old pine trees.

If you haven't yet had your fill of Buddhist temples, more can be found in the Western Mountains. Apart from the **Wofosi (Temple of the Reclining Buddha)**, which is among Beijing's oldest temples, there are the **Biyunsi (Temple of the Azure Clouds)** – also in the style of the Diamond Throne Pagoda (it has a hall with 500 Lohan figures); the **Zhiaomiao (Luminous Temple)**, built in 1780 as a residence for the Panchen Lama, hence the Tibetan style; and to

Temple of the Azure Clouds (Biyunsi) in the Western Mountains.

the south of the Western Mountains, the **Badachu (Eight Scenic Sites)**, eight temples and monasteries.

In the western suburbs of Beijing are the **Dajuesi (Temple of Enlightenment)**, at the foot of Yangtai Hill, and the **Fahaisi Temple**, famous for its wall paintings, near Cuiweishan Hill.

Daoist temples: A scene in the Baiyunguan (Temple of the White Cloud), the largest Daoist temple in Beijing, during the summer of 1988: An old Daoist priest with the typical hair-knot and beard explains the links between microcosm and macrocosm to a group of young people in front of one of the temple halls. The young Chinese, obviously tourists from another part of the country, are amused at first, and then listen to the words of the priest with increasing fascination.

In earlier times, the Daoist priests were considered in China to be charlatans, magicians and wonder-workers. They were supposed to have attained immortality, and able to flout the laws of time and space. It was therefore believed that they could fly through the air and walk through walls, and Daoist priests were practising exorcism to cure the sick as late as the 1940s. Some of them even had the reputation of gaining their extended lives through eccentric sexual practices. This may be among the reasons for the serious persecution of Daoists after 1949.

During the course of Chinese history, Daoists have appeared again and again in the ranks of rebellious peasants, and they have sometimes organised secret societies. Their teaching may be summed up in the concept of *wuwei* non-active doing that takes a critical view of all temporal authority.

Early Daoism – a philosophy described by Laozi in the book *Daodejing*, and in the book *Master of the Southern Flowering Land* (c. 500–300 BC) – and the later development of the popular religion of Daoism, which dates from the Han dynasty (c. 200 BC), do not have a lot in common.

The early Daoism, which has found increasing numbers of followers in the

A procession in the Daoist temple of Baiyunguan.

West in recent years, had a great influence on Chinese culture, particularly on its medicine and methods of healing.

The central concept of this doctrine is *dao*, the Way, which describes a general cosmic law applying both to the natural world and to human beings. Daoism sees nature as the macrocosm and human beings and other living things as the microcosm. The aim of all human beings, therefore, should be to live in harmony with this all-embracing law, to take the path of introspection and let dao work within themselves. Thus freed from the constraints of their individuality, their own lives will fit spontaneously into the great cosmos.

In addition, a Daoist heaven with countless divinities was created. Daoism is considered a religion of purely Chinese origin and has had great influence on traditional Buddhist and Confucian thought.

Today, there are only a few Daoist temples left in Beijing. The largest and most important is the **Baiyunguan (Temple of the White Cloud)**, in the southwest of Beijing, behind the Radio Beijing building, 15 minutes south of the Yanjing Hotel. A factory site during the Cultural Revolution, the temple was restored to its original use some years ago. By the end of 1988, it housed some 50 Daoist priests, mostly younger men. The temple dates from the Tang dynasty and is the centre of the Daoist Dragon Gate sect. Daoist temples on the grand scale were not built until the Yuan dynasty and the reign of Kublai Khan. The latter appointed a priest named Qiu Chuji, "National Teacher." From that time on, the temple – Qiu Chuji lived here – has been the centre of Daoism in northern China.

The Baiyunguan temple complex contains several courtyards. The overall design is similar to Buddhist temples in that the following elements lie one behind the other along a straight line: the memorial arch, the main gate, the pond, a bridge, the **Hall of the Officials of Celestial Censorship** (which is equivalent to the Hall of Celestial Kings in Buddhist temples), the **Hall of the Jade Emperor** and the **Hall of Religious Law** (equivalent to the rear halls of a Buddhist temple).

In the centre of the furthest courtyard is the **Hall of the Four Celestial Emperors**, and on its upper floor is the **Hall of the Three Purities**. Daoist manuscripts are kept here in a compendium similar to Buddhist ones.

In a hall in the side courtyards of the western section there are old bronze guardian figures, and in a building behind this one there are 60 newly-made figures of Daoist divinities, each one appointed to one year of the 60-year calendar cycle. Here, visitors can find their personal Daoist divinity according to the traditional Chinese calendar. The Daoist priests who reside there will be pleased to help.

Although Daoist temples are similar in design to Buddhist ones, the former use obvious symbolic motifs more frequently in their decoration, such as the Lingzhi mushroom, which is supposed to prolong life, Daoist immortals, cranes and the eight trigrams from the Book of Changes. In this temple, there is also a stele with calligraphy by Emperor Qianlong, telling the history of the temple and its founder.

Another temple in Beijing that belongs to the Daoist faith is the **Dongyuemiao (Temple of the God of Tai Mountain)**. On Shenlu Street in the Chaoyang district, it was built to honour the highest celestial ruler of the Tai mountain, one of the five Daoist holy mountains in China. Founded by Zhang Daoling during the Yuan dynasty, it was the largest Daoist temple in northern China and belonged to the Zhengyi sect of Daoism.

The temple complex consists of three courtyards. In the main courtyard is the **Daizongbaodian (Hall of Tai Mountain)**, and the **Hall of Moral Perfection**. In the centre of the Hall of the Tai Mountain is a statue of the god of Tai Mountain, surrounded by his high-ranking servants.

The temple has more than 100 stone tablets that date from the Yuan, Ming and Qing dynasties. As for the buildings that can be seen today, all of them date from the Qing period.

TEMPLE OF CONFUCIUS & IMPERIAL ACADEMY

Kongmiao (Temple of Confucius), right next to the Imperial Academy in the northeast of the city, is only a few hundred yards away from the Lama Temple Yonghegong. It was built during the Yuan dynasty (1206–1368), and lengthy ceremonies were held here every year in honour of the great scholar.

In front of the main entrance to the temple is a memorial arch of glazed tiles, the **Xianshimen (Gate of the First Teacher)**, which leads to the first of four courtyards. Shaded by pine trees and cypresses, 188 stone tablets are housed in a series of pavilions. They bear the names of the scholars who passed the imperial examinations, held every three years.

At the northern end of this courtyard is the **Dachengmen (Gate of Great Achievements)**, housing copies of stone drums with inscriptions. These are re-

puted to be odes from the decades of Emperor Xuan (828–782 BC), of the Zhou dynasty.

A footpath then leads visitors to the **Dachengdian (Hall of Great Achievements)**. The path is flanked by 11 pavilions of steles, bearing stone tablets with reports of various military expeditions under the command of Qing emperors. The hall was restored in 1906 during a period of Confucian renewal.

The roof is formed with yellow-glazed imperial tiles, and the hall is surrounded by a stone balustrade. Between the two flights of stone stairs leading up to the hall is a marble plaque with a relief showing two dragons playing with a pearl, in the midst of which a twisting dragon spews forth fog and clouds. A memorial tablet to Confucius is found in the plain, unadorned hall. The exhibition rooms next door once displayed stone tablets with all the names of Confucius' pupils and famous followers.

Behind the central hall is the **Chongshengci (Shrine of the Great Wise Man)**, erected to honour the ancestors of Confucius during ceremonies.

The **Guozijian (Imperial Academy)** is directly connected to the temple by a side gate. It was the highest educational institution in imperial China, where, above all, the classical Chinese writings were taught. The academy, built in 1287 during the Yuan dynasty, was extended repeatedly until its impressive present dimensions were reached during the 18th century under Emperor Qianlong (1736–1796), of the Qing dynasty.

After the founding of the People's Republic of China, the academy was completely restored and equipped as a library for the capital. In 1956, the academy was renovated once more. Beyond the main entrance, the visitor comes to the **Taixuemen (Gate of Highest Learning)**. Next to it is a memorial arch of glazed tiles, with a drum and bell tower to either side. Directly opposite the gate is the famous **Biyong (Jade Disk Hall)**. The square pavilion in the centre of a round pool, which may be crossed using marble bridges, is crowned by a golden ball. Here, the emperor occasionally explained the works of the

Entrance courtyard to Kongmiao.

classical writers in front of an audience of civil and military dignitaries and students of the Imperial Academy.

The eastern and western exhibition rooms of the Biyong Hall once held the stone inscriptions of Qianlong, who in the mid 18th century ordered that 13 complete classics be carved in stone. To carry out this command, Jiang Heng, a scholar from Jiangsu, cut 630,000 Chinese characters into 189 stone tablets over a period of 20 years. These tablets can now be seen to the east of the Gate of Highest Learning.

Beyond the Biyong Hall is the former **Pavilion of Exalted Literature**, used during the Yuan dynasty as a library. Later, the name was changed to the **Hall of Moral Teaching**. Before the Biyong Hall was built, the emperor and scholars sometimes gave students instruction here. Today, the pavilion is one of the reading rooms of the Beijing Library.

Imperial Archives: The **Huangshicheng (Imperial Historic Archives)** is situated on the east side of the southern end of Nanchizi Street, to the east of Tiananmen Square. It was built in 1534 under the Ming dynasty, and is said to be the oldest surviving court archives in the world. The structure of the main part is essentially unaltered, although the archive was rebuilt in 1807 under Emperor Jiaqing. In earlier centuries, it contained among its varied collection an edition of Emperor Yongle's encyclopaedia, *Yongle Dadian*.

The complex is neatly laid out along a north–south line, with the entrance in the western side of the front courtyard. At the northern end of the square courtyard lies the actual library, or archives, a long building with an overhanging roof. In order to lessen the danger of fire, only stone was used in the building, and it is now the only beamless hall of its kind in northern China. However, the stone arches with their five arched entrances in the southern facade copy the wood structure.

Inside the building, on a low marble platform, sit 152 golden dragon-carved cases originally constructed to hold the archive's documents.

Bronze statue in courtyard of Kongmiao.

188

CONFUCIUS

Next to Daoism and Buddhism, Confucianism is the great doctrine that has left a lasting impression on life in China for more than 2,000 years. It has determined behaviour for all areas of social life right down to the smallest detail. Even today, certain ways of behaviour and certain views in China can be explained with reference to Confucian tradition.

Confucius is known in Chinese as Kong Qiu. (It was the Jesuits who latinized the Chinese title Kong Fuzi, "Master Kong", to Confucius.) He was born in 551 BC, a member of an impoverished aristocratic clan in the state of Lu, in the southwest of modern Shandong Province. China did not yet exist as a single unified nation, and states within its territory were constantly struggling for supremacy.

In this age of great social upheaval, Confucius appeared, a travelling teacher who tried to influence the fate of the country through his group of pupils and through direct contact – as adviser or minister – with the ruler. His ideal was the virtuous ruler whose example would lead all his subjects to keep moral standards. The kingdom whose ruler did not measure up to this moral standard must inevitably fall. Natural catastrophes and bad harvests were a sign that a ruler's mandate had been withdrawn.

Apart from this belief, the recognition of hierarchy, whether expressed in family relationships or in loyalty to the ruling house, is the cornerstone of Confucian thought. Relationships between human beings, and not speculation about the existence of any God, are the focal point. Confucius tried to restore the *li* customs and rites, which were believed to date back to the wise rule of the Zhou dynasty, but which had fallen into disuse. In these matters he could be considered a traditionalist.

Yet he was ahead of his time in his rationalism and enlightenment, which caused him to dismiss the mysticism connected with rites. A human being should try to be truly good. Nobility is not determined by birth, but by an attitude of mind and the actions resulting from it. Nobility of mind and a hierarchical order of ruler and subject, ancestor and descendant, father and son, man and woman, old and young, teacher and student, form the basis for right action that keeps in mind the well-being of all humanity.

Confucius died in 497 BC and was buried in Qufu, in Shandong Province, where the temple built in his honour can still be visited. Even today, generations of Kongs are able to trace their descent in a direct line from Confucius.

During Confucius's lifetime, his teachings met with little response from the rulers. Under Emperor Qin Shi Huangdi (221–206 BC), followers of Confucius were even buried alive and their writings burned. However, the Han dynasty raised Confucianism to a state doctrine, for it offered them a problem-free system of administration and a strengthening of the power structure. Apart from a short predominance of Buddhism, Confucianism has been inextricably bound up with the imperial system ever since, and has formed the ethical basis of Chinese society.

The Communists, however, saw an ideological opponent in Confucianism. During the Cultural Revolution, their struggle came to a head with an Anti-Confucius Campaign, which was, however, less of a debate about the contents of his teaching than a defamation of his character.

Over the last few years, attempts have been made to hold an examination of, and debate about, Confucianism. ∎

Portrait of Confucius in the robes of court official (presumed to date from the Tang dynasty).

MOSQUES AND CHURCHES

Mosques: There are more than 200,000 Chinese Moslems living in Beijing today. Known as the Hui minority, they have 6 million members throughout China. Many of them are no longer orthodox Moslems, but, whether believers or not, they share one custom important to all Moslems: They don't eat pork. For this reason, there are in Beijing, as in many other Chinese cities, *Huimin Fandian*, or Hui restaurants, in which ritual-clean hands prepare snacks and meals, substituting mutton for pork. If you should be invited home by a Hui family in Beijing and served *jiaozi* (dumplings), these too, will be filled with mutton.

The Hui are known as Chinese Moslems because they use the Chinese language and can hardly be distinguished from Han Chinese. However, if you have the opportunity to visit a mosque in Beijing during prayers, or to take a stroll along Niujie Street, you will see many non-Han faces.

The largest concentration of Hui in Beijing is along Niujie Street and in its many little side streets. Even the name points to the association with the Hui community: Niujie means Ox Street.

One can get to Niujie Street, west of the Caishikou crossroads, on bus route No. 10 from the subway station, Changchunjie. More than 10,000 Hui live here. If you take a stroll up Niujie Street from the south, you will pass Hui butchers, Hui shops and a Hui elementary school before arriving at a mosque on the east side of the street.

The mosque, with curved eaves and colourfully painted support and cross beams, looks more like a Chinese temple than a Moslem place of worship. On the outside, many Chinese mosques are built in the Chinese palace style, with main and side buildings laid out symmetrically. The buildings are wooden with roofs of glazed tiles, and the roof arches and posts are often adorned with

Preceding pages: Beitang, the North Church. **Below,** Chinese Moslems at Niujie Mosque.

texts from the Koran or other Islamic motifs. The **Niujie Qingzhensi (Ox Street Mosque)** was built in 966 in the style of a Buddhist temple, after the Islamic faith had entered China during the rule of the Tang dynasty (618–907). Today, there are many Moslems, particularly among the minorities of northwestern China, such as the Uighur and Kirghiz people. The Hui also have their largest settlements in this area, namely in the Autonomous District of Ningxia.

The Niujie Mosque was renovated under Emperor Kangxi (1662–1722). On a stone tablet is the following inscription: "Tell the provinces of the country that the governor will have anyone who spreads false tales about the Moslems executed and then bring a report to me. All Hui shall follow Islam and may not disobey my commands."

The proclamation was the reaction to a report that the preparations and celebrations leading up to a day of fasting were the beginnings of a rebellion. The emperor did not believe the story, visited Niujie Street and the Mosque in disguise, and discovered that the accusation was quite groundless.

Right behind the entrance to the mosque is a hexagonal building, the **Wangyuelou (Tower for Observing the Moon)**. Every year, at the beginning and at the end of the fasting month of Ramadan, the *imam* climbs the tower to observe the waxing and waning of the moon and to determine the exact length of the period of fasting. Even nowadays, it is the duty of orthodox Moslems in Beijing to fast during Ramadan, although many can no longer keep this up if they work in factories by day. The same applies to the strict observance of praying five times a day, which can usually be followed only by those Hui who spend their days near a mosque.

Beyond the Tower for Observing the Moon is the **Main Hall of Prayer**. This is where the faithful come for their religious ceremonies, after ritual cleansing in the washrooms. Like all rooms in mosques, the hall has no adornment or pictures inside. In the front is the pulpit for the imam. Since Islamic tradition dictates that Moslems have to pray facing Mecca, the front of the hall faces west. Women can only take part in the prayers in a niche screened off with curtains. They also have to cleanse themselves ritually beforehand and put on a white robe and a white head covering.

Beyond the Main Hall are a few smaller religious buildings and steles. In the centre is the minaret. In the little courtyard garden that runs east is the tombstone – with Arabic inscription – of the founder of this mosque. During the Cultural Revolution, the faithful had buried it by the wall.

Also in the Niujie Mosque is a Koran school. As there is no religious instruction in Chinese schools, Hui children, if their parents insist on it, have to come here to receive religious instruction. During the Cultural Revolution, this was strongly forbidden and the mosque was closed to the public. With state support, the mosque has been restored in recent years and today it is once more a meeting place for Moslems. The Hui are not the only ones who come here; so do the staff of the embassies of Islamic

Islamic Hui.

countries and the Uighurs from Xinjiang who are living in Beijing. Some of these Uighurs are studying at the Central Institute for National Minorities, which is not far from the Friendship Hotel in the Western City. This institute trains officials for areas inhabited by minorities and has a Moslem canteen.

Another mosque in Beijing that also has an active religious life is the **Dongsi Mosque**. Not open to the general public, an appointment must be made for a visit. From the street after which the mosque is named, which lies in east Beijing, one would hardly notice that there is a mosque. It was built in 1447, and in 1450, the Ming emperor Jiangtai gave it the title **Qingzhensi (Temple of Purity and Light)**, which is how all mosques are now referred to in Chinese. Although the mosque is in the middle of the noisy city centre of Beijing, perfect peace reigns in its inner courtyard. While the front part of the main hall is built of wood in the Chinese fashion, the rear has a vault-like roof of tiles. In the front is a tablet with an Arabic inscription. The mosque can hold over 500 people and has a women's "corner".

The library of the Dongsi Mosque has many valuable Islamic manuscripts, among them a Koran manuscript that is almost 700 years old. Since 1949, the Dongsi Mosque has been the seat of the Islamic Society, with the qualifying of, and further training courses for, imam held here. Restored in the early 1950s and closed during the Cultural Revolution, the mosque is now self-financing.

The Hui also have their own cemetery in Beijing. However, non-Moslems are not allowed to enter it. Cremation is the general rule for funerals in China, but the Hui have special exemption.

Churches: The Chinese government has no relations with the Vatican, hence Roman Catholics who remain true to the papacy have to practise their religion in secret. Only the Patriotic Catholic church is officially permitted. It does not recognise the pope and insists on autonomy. Catholic churches in Beijing belong to this branch. The Protestant churches are united under the Chinese Christian Council.

The oldest church in Beijing is the **Nantang (South Church)**, at 181 Qianmenxidajie, which runs parallel to Chang'an Boulevard, one block to the south. One can get there by taking a walk from the Xidan crossroads southwards along Xuanwumennei Street, which leads past a row of small shops and restaurants. The church was founded in the period between the end of the Ming dynasty and the beginning of the Qing dynasty, when Christianity began to establish itself with the arrival of Matteo Ricci (1552–1610) and Johann Adam Schall von Bell (1592–1666).

The current structure of the cathedral dates from 1904, as the old building was destroyed in 1900 during the xenophobia of the Boxer Rebellion. The original church on this site was built as a result of the efforts of Schall von Bell, to whom permission to build was granted in 1650.

In 1775, the original burned down, but was afterwards rebuilt with money from the emperor Qianlong. However, the increasingly hostile attitude of the imperial court towards the Jesuits delayed the work. The last bout of destruction took place during the Cultural Revolution. The building has been open to the faithful again since the early 1980s, and is also the seat of the Patriotic Society of Chinese Catholics.

Not far from the Xizhi Gate stands another Catholic church, the **Xitang (West Church)**. Built in the 18th century, it was destroyed during the persecution of Christians in 1811. A second church, built in 1867, was in turn a victim of the Boxer Rebellion. The present building dates from the turn of the century.

Dongtang (East Church), on Wangfujing Street, was also burned to the ground in 1900, and the present church also erected at the beginning of this century. In previous years, the site was part of the house of Schall von Bell, who died here in 1666.

Beitang (North Church) is near the Beijing Library in a side street, Xishiku Dajie, off Xianmen Street. Its history is as troubled as that of the other churches. The Jesuits, with the support of the Western powers, managed to gain permission for the rebuilding of the church in the middle of the last century, but because of pressure from the Empress Dowager Cixi, who permitted no churches to be built near the Imperial Palace, a new site had to be chosen.

In 1889, the present North Church was finally built. In 1900, it was besieged for seven weeks by the rebels before Japanese troops rescued the 3,000 Christians and 50 allied soldiers under the care of Bishop Favier, who had remained in the church.

The two important Protestant churches in Beijing are the **Mishitang (Rice Market Church)**, in Northern Dongdan Street (this street was previously known as Rice Market Street), and the **Ganwashitang (Earthenware and Brick Market Church)**, in the western district of Beijing, in Xisi Street. The grey brick building of the Mishitang, with its Chinese roof and the double wooden eaves, dates from the 1920s. At that time, the church was the seat of the Bible Society and today it is home to the Beijing branch of the Chinese Christian

Council. The Ganwashitang was built at the beginning of this century for the London Bible Society.

The first Christian missionaries appeared in the imperial capital at the time of the Mongol Yuan dynasty, but the spread of Christianity really only began in the 16th and 17th centuries, with the arrival of the Jesuit missionaries, particularly Matteo Ricci, Adam Schall von Bell and Ferdinand Veerbiest.

The old **Jesuit cemetery**, in which they and 61 other Jesuits lie buried, is in the courtyard of the Party School of the Beijing City Committee of the Chinese Communist Party (on Maweigoulu, in the Fuchengmen district).

Another cemetery, the **Babaoshan**, near the subway station, has been reserved for heroes. Most of the tombs date from the 1950s and 1960s and are those of dedicated or long-serving Communists, but there are also some of famous people, such as the tomb of the well-known artist Xu Beihong. A crematorium and several halls for memorial services form part of the complex.

The former Jesuit cemetery at Party School.

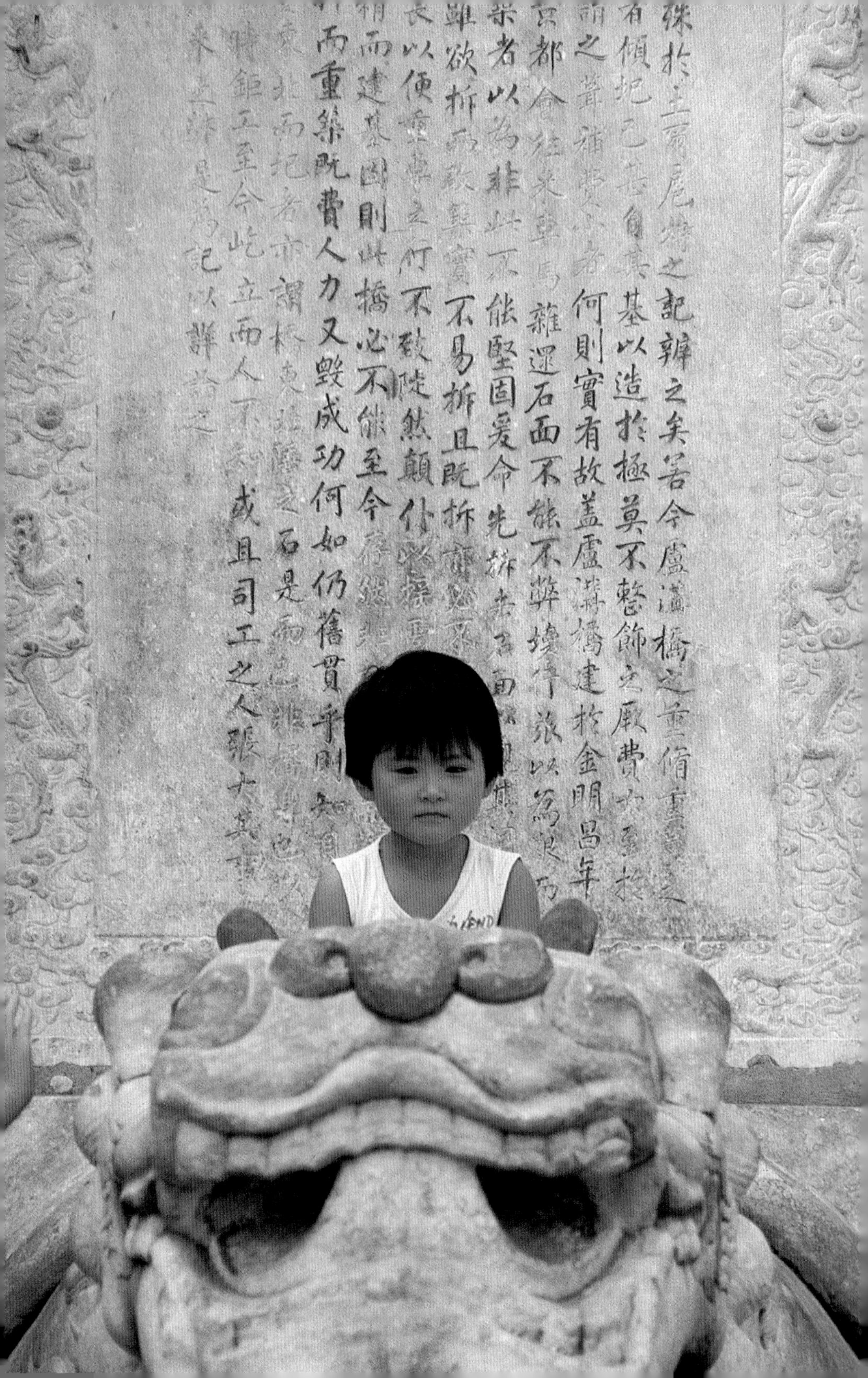

PLACES OF SPECIAL INTEREST

Cave of Peking Man: The site of the discovery of Peking Man, *Sinanthropus pekinensis*, lies close to the small town of Zhoukoudian, about 50 kilometres (30 mi) southwest of Beijing. As early as the Ming dynasty, workers digging for lime found many animal fossils, which were believed to be the bones of dragons. The cave of Peking Man lies on the northern slopes of **Longushan (Dragon Bone Mountain)**. About 450 million years ago, there was an ocean on this site, and as it receded, limestone caves gradually developed. Over 500,000 years ago, for about 300,000 years, hominid lived in this place. Then the caves were completely filled in, and the tools, food scraps and bones were covered until modern times.

By the beginning of this century, peasants were finding human teeth at this site. Java Man and Heidelberg Man were known at that time, yet the discovery of Peking Man was a surprise for science and considered a great sensation. In 1921, the Swede John Gunnar Andersson had found this rich source of fossils that attracted many other scientists. In 1927, systematic excavations began, and just two years later the complete upper skull of Peking Man was found. It was, unfortunately, lost in the troubled times of World War II and today only copies of this skull exist.

Who found Peking Man? The Chinese say that it was a Chinese palaeonthropologist, Pei Wenzhong. In other countries, however, a Jesuit priest, Teilhard de Chardin, is often claimed to have discovered it. The latter, at any rate, took part in the excavations for several years, when many fossils were discovered. Up until the beginning of the Japanese invasion in 1937, fossil remains of more than 40 individuals of both sexes were found. The men of that age were some 1.5 metres (5 ft) tall, the women slightly smaller. These early humans had skulls about a third smaller than today's people, and could, with their broad shoulders and strong muscles, already walk upright. Their hands could use stone tools, and they understood the use of fire. Altogether, four caves have been discovered in Zhoukoudian. In the Upper Cave, the remains of *Homo sapiens* who settled here some 18,000 years ago were discovered.

There has been a small **museum** on the discovery site since 1949, close to the Peking Man Cave and the Upper Cave. The exhibits, divided into three departments, provide information on evolution, of Peking Man in particular, and about the development of an independent Chinese palaeontology.

Marco Polo Bridge: A visit to the home of Peking Man can comfortably be combined with a trip to see the **Lugouqiao (Marco Polo Bridge)**, which is 15 kilometres (9 mi) away from Beijing, in a southeastern direction. It can also be reached by bus from Guang'anmen. The Italian merchant Marco Polo, who stayed at the court of the Mongol emperor Kublai Khan in the 13th century, admired this bridge. "Ten miles past Cum-

Preceding pages: street snookers; the Marco Polo Bridge. *Left,* stone tablet on the Marco Polo Bridge. *Right,* Zhoukoudian: entrance to the cave of Beijing Man.

baluc (Khanbaliq) the traveller will reach the broad river Pulisanghin. Merchants travel on it with their wares down to the sea. A magnificent stone bridge crosses the river, and it has no equal anywhere in the world. The bridge is three hundred paces long and eight paces broad. Ten riders, flank to flank, could cross it with no difficulty. The twenty-four arches and the twenty-four pillars are of grey, finely dressed and well-placed marble blocks. Marble slabs and pillars form a balustrade on both sides. The first pillar is at the bridge head; it bears a marble lion, and at its base another lion can be seen. The next pillar is one and a half paces away, and it also bears two lions. The space between is closed by a grey marble slab, so that none can fall into the water. It is wonderful to see how the row of pillars and the slabs are so cleverly joined together."

The Chinese name Lugou means Black Ditch, and is an earlier name for the **Yongding River**, which flows under the bridge. The bridge, built in 1189, was seriously damaged in a flood in

1698 and rebuilt in exactly the same form that year. There are 11 bridge arches, each with a total length of 7.5 metres (25 ft) crossing the river. On the balustrade on either side are 140 stone posts crowned with lions, of which not one is identical to another. At each end of the bridge is a 5-metre (15-ft) high stele. One reports on restoration work on the bridge under Emperor Kangxi (1662–1722), the other is inscribed "The moon at daybreak over the Lugou Bridge," which also describes one of the eight wonders of the old city of Yanjing.

The people of Beijing claim that the stone lions are too many to be counted. In fact, there are 485 lion figures altogether to be found on the posts, some measuring only a few inches tall, others dozens. In playful fashion, the smaller lion carvings are added to the big lion statues. As the Yongding River used to be prone to flooding, the bridge was fastened with iron clamps, and has recently been closed to traffic. Upriver a dam has created an artificial lake, so that the river bed is usually dry in summer. Therefore, the place has lost some of its original charm as a river landscape. Until this century, however, there was a landing place here from which travellers embarked on journeys to the south.

The bridge gained world-wide fame mainly because of the "incident" at the Marco Polo Bridge, which marked the start of the Japanese invasion in Asia during World War II. On 7 July 1937, Japanese troops of the Tianjin garrison attacked the Marco Polo Bridge, provoking the Chinese guards to fire. This eventually provided the pretext for further aggression by the Japanese. By August, China and Japan were at war.

Beijing University: The students of **Beijing Daxue (Beijing University)**, or Beida for short, formed the political *avant garde* in the massive anti-Japanese demonstrations two years before the Marco Polo Bridge incident, as they have in many other political movements of the century. From the May Fourth Movement of 1919 through the Cultural Revolution, and then with their demand for more democracy with demonstrations and wall newspapers in 1979, and **Traditional point of view.**

finally with the mass student demonstrations that led to the Tiananmen massacre, Beida students have been at the forefront of causes seeking change. Beida also numbers many famous politicians among its graduates. The university, founded in 1898, used to be in the centre of the city, in the eastern part of the old Imperial City. The present campus, in the western district of Haidian, on bus route No. 332 towards the Summer Palace, was previously the site of the American-founded **Yanjing University**, which joined with Beijing University in 1953.

Today, more than 10,000 students are studying at Beida, many of them foreigners who are mainly from Third World countries. (In early 1989, attacks on African students gained world-wide attention.) The **Shaoyuan Guesthouse** of Beida has long been an international meeting place. The campus has park-like grounds with a quiet lake, on the shores of which students spend their free time, and a classical Chinese pagoda with pavilions and stone figures.

Unfortunately, since the Tiananmen violence of 1989, visitations to the university have been strictly regulated. Unless you have a pass, or are issued one as a guest, you will not be allowed to pass through their well-guarded gates.

However, one can visit the remains of the old Beijing University – the **Honglou (Red Building)** – at the eastern end of Shatan Street. Here, Li Dazhou, one of the founders of the Chinese Communist Party, used to teach, and Mao Zedong used to work in the library. Chen Duxiu, the first General Secretary of the Chinese Communist Party, also taught at the Beida.

Bell and Drum Towers: These two towers, **Zhonggulou**, which date from the rule of Kublai Khan, have survived so many of the twists and turns of history that the wars and revolutions of modern history only form one episode among many. Both the towers at the northern end of Di'anmendajie Street once formed the northernmost point of the city. However, during the period of Mongol rule, they stood in the centre of

Beida students calling for a boycott of Japanese goods after the May Fourth Movement of 1919.

the contemporary capital city of Dadu. Under the Ming emperor Yongle, the towers were rebuilt in 1420, somewhat to the east of their original position.

After the originally-wooden **Bell Tower** was destroyed in a fire, the present tower, 33 metres (108 ft) high, was built in 1747. The **Drum Tower** was last restored in 1800. In earlier years, 24 big drums used to be kept inside – only one has survived – which were struck 13 times every evening at 7 to signal the start of the night hours and also the closing of the city gates. The drums were struck again every two hours, the last time being at 5am. By that hour, the officials to be present at the imperial morning audience were supposed to have taken up their kneeling positions just in front of the Hall of Supreme Harmony; failure to do so brought heavy penalties.

The day officially began at 7 am with the ringing of the huge iron bell of the Bell Tower. When this proved to be not loud enough, an even bigger bronze bell was installed in the tower, which could be heard, so it was said, 20 kilometres (12 mi) away. The bronze bell has now disappeared, but the iron bell is on display behind the tower. The building is so sturdy it supposedly survived the serious earthquake of 1976 without damage; only one stone ornamental figure on the roof is said to have fallen down.

Today, inside the recently refurbished drum tower is the one remaining original drum, damaged during the opium wars of the 19th century, and now flanked by two brightly-painted replicas. In addition, the tower houses an exhibition of black-and-white photos by Xu Yong, a portion of his *101 Photographs of Beijing Hutong*. There is also a scale model of a *siheyuan*, the rectangular shaped dwellings built around courtyards whose walls form the hutong or small alleyways that pervade the older city. The model shows the original layout of the siheyuan before they became cluttered with the additions needed to house the growing population.

But another reward awaits visitors who climb the staircase of 69 steps, so steep and tall it is similar to climbing a ladder. The balcony of the tower provides an unmatched view of an old-style neighbourhood. Looking down upon the grey and often grass-covered tile roofs, separated into various geometric shapes by the walls of the hutong, visitors gain a sense of how each siheyuan is a community in itself. Meanwhile, in the distance, tall, gleaming structures, and an ungodly number of construction cranes, remind visitors of the role progress plays in an ever-changing Beijing.

China Ethnic Culture Park: If Beijing is your only stop in China, as it is for so many, you may want to check out the **China Ethnic Culture Park**. As home to 56 minorities, the homes, lifestyles, crafts, and traditions of the Chinese are as varied as its history. Located next to the National Olympic Centre on the north fourth ring road, the park contains replicas of the buildings found in each minority's home territory. Their songs and dances are performed by the minorities, and crafts are in the traditional manner. Contrived perhaps, but reflective of China's diverse lifestyles.

Left, old city lanes in the shadow of the great palace buildings. **Right**, in front of the ancient Bell Tower.

THE GREAT WALL

When in this large country, one will doubtless hear someone say, "If you haven't climbed the Great Wall, you haven't seen China." You will not be able to argue this point, for who would want to travel to China and miss the opportunity of seeing this most famous sight in Beijing, and which is, in fact, a symbol of China itself?

The greatest fortification in human history, built to prevent invasion by nomadic tribes from the steppes of central Asia, it is now the goal of mass invasions by tourists. It has also been discovered by skilled advertisers eager to use it for commercial purposes. The wall has been used as a background for Japanese children's choirs, American fashion shows, religious services, sporting events, and other advertising campaigns. Illusionist David Copperfield has even walked through the wall.

Recently, tourists have also been asked for contributions to be used towards the restoration of the Great Wall. Contributors can have their names recorded for posterity on the wall, where they are engraved in brick, although countless Chinese visitors have been doing this for some time for free.

Because of the wall's popularity, it can be a little difficult to see it without a horde of other tourists by your side. The main site for visits, especially organized tours that inevitably combine it with a visit to the Ming Tombs, is **Badaling**. Here, a plethora of tacky souvenir and T-shirt vendors compete for sales, not only as you approach the wall, but also on the wall. A brisk walk of an hour and a half might actually lead to an uncrowded portion, if it's a good day.

Not much further from Beijing, and infinitely less crowded, is the Great Wall at **Mutianyu**. A short distance past Huairou – site of the NGO Forum of the United Nations Fourth World Conference on Women in 1995, Mutianyu still has enough vendors to satisfy the tourist, but far fewer groups visit here, making it much easier to escape the crowds. It should be noted that if climbing is not one's forté, both Badaling and Mutianyu have cable cars to whisk visitors to the top. An unrestored section at Huanghuacheng, midway between the Badaling and Mutianyu sections, is growing in popularity.

But if one really wants to see the wall at its most spectacular, then most will agree that the Great Wall at **Simitai** is the place to go. About a two-hour drive from Beijing, Simitai has fewer visitors than Mutianyu and Badaling. It is also the most difficult of the three sites, with portions so steep, and some so thin, good climbing shoes and a little courage are required. Jinshanling, which adjoins Simitai to the west, is a well-restored but relatively quiet section of the wall.

Greatest construction on Earth: One of the greatest tourist attractions in the world, the Great Wall is known to the Chinese as **Wan Li Chang Cheng**, which means Wall of 10,000 *li* (1 *li* = 500 metres), or simply, Chang Cheng (Long Wall). *Wan*, the Chinese character for 10,000, is a synonym for unimag-

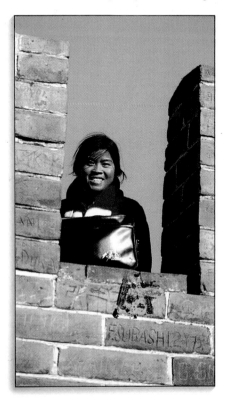

inable hugeness. It is, indeed, almost impossible for the human mind to grasp how people could have built so huge a fortification, the only human construction that astronauts, it has been claimed, could recognise with the naked eye.

Archaeologists have now discovered a great number of walls, some of which date back to the 5th century BC. The farming peoples who had settled in the fruitful plains of the basin of the Huanghe (Yellow River) and its tributaries had to protect themselves against constant attack from the nomadic peoples in the north. Great walls built of beaten earth were intended to keep the nomads, travelling in search of new pastures, from invading the settlements of the Chinese farmers. As a unified China did not exist in those times, but several states existed within the territory of modern China, each state built its own wall. The total length of walls discovered by archaeologists so far comes to some 50,000 kilometres (31,000 mi).

Qin Shi Huangdi, who is described as the first Chinese emperor (221–210 BC), forced all the Chinese states to submit to him, bringing about the unification of China. For the first time, the various walls were put together into one defensive bulwark. Under the leadership of his general, Meng Tian, an army of 300,000 forced labourers is said to have worked on the building of the Great Wall; the actual figure was probably even higher. In those days, the Wall began in the west of Lintao, to the south of the town of Lanzhou, and ran in an easterly direction through Inner Mongolia, the modern provinces of Shaanxi and Hebei, and ended to the east of Liaoning Province.

The construction visible today, most of which was built in the 15th century, is some 6,400 kilometres (4,000 mi) long, on average 8 metres (26 ft) high and 7 metres (21 ft) broad at the base. The upper part is wide enough to allow five or six soldiers to ride side by side. The flights of stairs up to the outer wall are fairly widely spaced. A countless number of inner walls, outer walls, fortified towers, signal beacon towers, fortifications and garrisons complete this

complex, and make up the whole system of the Great Wall.

The victory of the first Ming emperor Zhu Yuanchang (1368–1398), whose imperial title was Taizu, over the Mongols ended a long period of foreign rule in the north of China. For that reason, the fortification of the Great Wall was a matter of life or death for the young Ming dynasty, which continued to defend itself against the attacks from the Mongols. For more than 200 years, work went on to strengthen the wall. The original earth was surrounded by a wall of fired brick, the fortified towers were extended, and the whole logistics were overhauled and improved.

The fort at Badaling: Far to the east of Beijing, at Shanhaiguan on the Bohai Bay, is a great fortress, on the gates of which this inscription can be read: "The First Gate on Earth." This is where the Great Wall begins (or ends). Part of it runs further in an easterly direction, till the wall meets the Yalu River in Liaoning Province.

This part, however, was less well-

The bricks used to build the Great Wall were fired in furnaces like these.

212

built and is thus almost in ruins. To the west, the wall snakes over countless hills and valleys like an endless serpent until it reaches Jiayuguan in Gansu Province, the western end of the Great Wall. Behind the gate with the inscription "First Fortified Gate on Earth," the Gobi desert begins.

From Beijing, travel 60 kilometres (40 mi) by bus in a northwesterly direction to reach the **Juyongguan fortress**, built in a narrow, 20-kilometre (13-mi) long valley north of the Nankou Pass and south of the Badaling Pass. Today, one can still see the old walls climbing the steep slopes. In the middle of the valley is a stone platform of white marble, the **Yuntai (Cloud Terrace)**. Built in 1345, it once served as the foundation for a great gate with three stone pagodas. After the fall of the Yuan dynasty, the pagoda gate was destroyed and replaced years later with a temple, which burned down in 1702. In the vaulted passage of the gate there are splendid reliefs, mostly Buddhist motifs, among them the four Tianwang (Celestial Kings), and inscriptions of Buddhist sutras in six different languages: Sanskrit, Tibetan, Tangut, Uighur, Mongol and Chinese.

At the end of the valley is **Badaling**, where a well-preserved and restored part of the Great Wall can be visited. Badaling can also be reached by a special train that leaves for the Great Wall every morning from the main station in Beijing. The destination of Qinglongqiao lies beyond the great gate through the Great Wall. Within the station precincts, the traveller can see a bronze statue of the Chinese engineer Zhan Tainyou, who made his name as a pioneer builder of Chinese railways. After foreign engineers had dismissed as uneconomic and too difficult the project to build a railway through the hills to the north of Beijing, right up to Baotou in Inner Mongolia, this engineer realised the great plan himself.

To truly experience the splendour of the Great Wall, according to the Chinese, you should not only see the Great Wall, you need to walk on it as well.

Manchu troops overrunning the Great Wall.

Hence the saying: "You cannot be a hero until you walk the Great Wall." The way up on both sides leads to raised towers, from which there is a view of the northern plain and of the wall snaking across the slopes of the hills. The left, western side is steeper and therefore more difficult to climb. On this trip one should, therefore, wear solid and comfortable shoes.

Nowadays, tourists no longer have to stay hungry. There are several restaurants to choose from, but because of the great crowds, the cuisine is not of the finest quality. The variety of souvenirs on offer, displayed so clearly that one cannot miss it, ranges from Great Wall T-shirts to diplomas certifying that you have climbed the Great Wall.

Badaling is also the highest point on the whole stretch of the Great Wall. This strategically-important site was therefore well-fortified by the Ming emperors. The gate facing west bears the inscription "The Bolt of the Northern Gate," while the one facing east states, "The First Line before Juyongguan."

The towers are solidly built, and man-high arrow slits on all sides, together with additional beacon towers, made this fortress almost impregnable. Enemy attacks were signalled to the capital by beacon fires, and by cannon fire. For instance, smoke signals from four different points, augmented by four explosions, were the signal for an enemy troop of 5,000 men. Next to the Great Wall is the rock of Wangjingshi, and the capital can be seen from its peak. On a clear day you can make out the White Dagoba in Beihai Park.

In the Gold Mountains: Another part of the Great Wall has now been restored and opened to tourists. This part of the wall is in the **Jinshanling (Gold Mountains)**, and can be reached by a two-hour bus journey. The Great Wall here is part of an approximately 100-kilometre (60-mi) long stretch of wall between Shanhaiguan and the district of Chanping, which belongs to the metropolitan area of Beijing. Building on this stretch of the wall did not start until the end of the 16th century. Here, in the

A worthwhile investment for a photographer working near the Great Wall.

Gold Mountains near Gubeikou, the 158 fortified towers are particularly remarkable for their variety of shapes: rectangular, round, oval and polygonal.

The myth of impregnability: The Great Wall has not always fulfilled its purpose of keeping enemies out and has been even less successful in preventing contact between peoples. The emperors of the Tang dynasty (618–907) had extended the borders of their empire well beyond the Great Wall and had established trade contacts with many peoples in the north and west. The Khitan, Nüzhen and Mongols, as foreign rulers from the north, had no need of the Great Wall. Since it lay right in the middle of their territory, it had lost its function as a boundary and defence bulwark.

In times of peace, the wall was mostly left to decay. Even the Qing emperors had no further interest in it after the 17th century, and so wind and weather gradually made the wall crumble away. Also, the peasants soon discovered it as an excellent source of building material, and many a farmhouse was built from bricks taken off the Great Wall. During the Cultural Revolution in the 1970s, army units built whole barracks out of bricks taken from the Great Wall.

The Great Wall was not even an obstacle to the Manchu troops when they conquered the Ming empire in 1644. The Ming general, Wu Sangui, who was in command of the Shanhaiguan fortress, collaborated with the Manchu conquerors and surrendered the fort to the enemy without a struggle. By his action, he opened the way to Beijing for the Manchu armies. This treason was, it must be said, not an isolated case, for the failing authority of the Ming emperors led many influential Chinese to consider an early move to the conquerors' side to be more profitable. After all, the learned Confucian officials could be certain that the Manchu conquerors, just as all foreign conquerors had before them, would soon be making use of their knowledge and skills.

Bitter weeping: Much has been written about the Great Wall that is of an uplifting or admiring nature, but many tragic stories are also told. Still very popular today is the legend of Meng Jiangnu. The first emperor, Qin Shi Huangdi, had hundreds of thousands of his subjects forcibly recruited to work on the Great Wall. This fate also befell the husband of Meng Jiangnu, and he was soon considered to be lost forever. Anxious about her husband, Meng Jiangnu set off to look for him. After many months of wandering, she came to Shanhaiguan, the eastern end of the Great Wall, and there she discovered that her husband, as had happened to so many others, had fallen victim to the murderous work and had been dead for some time. On hearing this, she wept so bitterly that part of the wall collapsed, exposing her husband's body. The emperor Qin, who was in Shanhaiguan at the time on a tour of inspection, heard of this story and took a liking to the woman. She gave in to his wooing, but not before getting his permission for a state funeral to be conducted for her husband.

After the funeral ceremony, she flung herself into the sea near Shanhaiguan, in full sight of the emperor.

Souvenir snap.

IMPERIAL TOMBS

Although Beijing has been a capital city of the Middle Kingdom for five dynasties, the tombs of the Ming emperors are the only ones in the vicinity of modern Beijing. The tombs of the Liao dynasty (916–1125) are in northeastern China, and those of the Qing emperors (1644–1911) are 125 kilometres (80 mi) northeast of Beijing. The tombs of the Jin dynasty were destroyed at the end of the Ming era, and as the Mongol rulers of the Yuan dynasty (1271–1368) had no special burial rites, no tombs from this period survive.

The Ming tombs (Shisanlin): The Ming tombs lie in a valley to the south of the Tianshou Mountains in Changping district, 50 kilometres (30 mi) to the northwest of Beijing. The foothills of the Yanshan Mountains form a natural entrance to the 40-square-kilometre (15-sq-mi) basin, "defended" on both sides by the Dragon and Tiger Mountains, which are said to keep harmful winds away from this holy ground.

Thirteen of the 16 Ming emperors are buried here. The **Dagongmen (Great Palace Gate)** marks the beginning of the Avenue of Stone Figures or Avenue of Ghosts, as the 7-kilometre (4-mi) stretch of road to Changling, and the tomb of the emperor Yongle, are called. Right behind the Dagongmen, you will come to a square stele pavilion with a great tortoise bearing a tall stele on its back. Beyond this lies the famous **Avenue of Stone Figures**, flanked by pairs of stone lions, elephants, camels, horses and mythological creatures, followed by 12 military and civil dignitaries representing the imperial court. Just beyond them is the **Longfengmen (Dragon and Phoenix Gate)** with three entrances, which in earlier years were closed off by heavy doors.

Changling, the tomb of Emperor Yongle (1403–24), is the biggest and best preserved of the 13 surviving Ming tombs. Built on a south-facing slope, its three courtyards are surrounded by a wall. The first courtyard stretches from the massive three-arched entrance gate to the **Ling'enmen (Gate of Eminent Favours)**. In the east of this courtyard is a pavilion with a stone tablet, a stone camel and a stone dragon. The **Ling'endian (Hall of Eminent Favours)** is in the second courtyard. The central section of the stone steps leading up to the hall is adorned with sea monsters and dragons. In the east and the west parts of the hall there are fire basins, in which balls of silk and inscriptions were burned as offerings to the imperial ancestors. Four mighty wooden pillars, each one made out of a single trunk of the nanmu tree, *phoebe nanmu*, along with 28 smaller posts, support the construction.

In the third and last courtyard, a stele tower can be found, with an incense basin and other ritual objects in front of it – the so-called "nine stone utensils." On the stele is the inscription "Tomb of the Emperor Chengzu of the great Ming dynasty" (Chengzu was the temple name of Emperor Yongle). A wall with a circumference of about 1 kilometre, known as Precious City, was built to enclose the burial mound, 31 metres (102 ft) long and 38 metres (125 ft) broad. To the east and west are the tombs of the 16 imperial concubines, who were buried alive to serve their emperor in the underworld.

The **Dingling (Tomb of Emperor Wanli)** (1573–1619), with its subterranean palace, lies to the southwest of Changling. The emperor Wanli was buried here in 1620, together with his two wives, Xiaoduan and Xiaojing. About 30,000 workers took a total of six years (1584–90) to complete the tomb, which cost 8 million taels of silver (equivalent to the total land tax for two years). A tunnel leads down to a depth of more than 7 metres (23 ft), to the first massive gate of the **subterranean palace**. The palace consists of five rooms with mighty marble vaulting and a floor of highly polished stones, known as golden stones. The 50,000 stones were specially prepared in Suzhou over a period of three years and were then transported 1,400 kilometres (900 mi) to the north.

An empty hall adjoins the central hall,

in which the marble thrones of the emperor and his wives stand. An "eternal lamp" (an oil lamp with a floating wick that was believed to burn forever) and five sacrificial offerings (an incense bowl, two candelabra, and two vases of yellow-glazed earthenware) can be seen in the room.

Next to the central hall lie two side chambers that contain pedestals for coffins. These platforms, which are covered with the "golden stones" and filled with yellow earth, are known as the Golden Fountains. No coffins have been found in this chamber.

The rear hall is the largest (9.5 metres [30 ft] high, 30 metres [100 ft] long and 9 metres [30 ft] wide) and the most imposing in the subterranean palace. On pedestals in the middle of the hall are the coffins of the emperor Wanli and his empresses. Around the coffins are 26 lacquered chests filled with crowns, gold and jade pitchers, cups, bowls, earrings, and wine containers. There are also sacred objects of jade, and blue-and-white Ming porcelain. Among the more than 3,000 objects is an extraordinarily fine filigree crown of gold adorned with two dragons playing with a pearl. This crown, together with a valuable embroidery showing 100 playing children, and other exhibits of historical interest, can be viewed in the two exhibition halls within the Dingling complex.

The tombs of the other Ming emperors are at present not open to the public, but you can wander around the grounds for several miles discovering the ruins of other tomb structures. Because the crowds do not generally do so, this may prove to be the more interesting and rewarding portion of a visit.

Eastern Qing Tombs: Approximately 125 kilometres (80 mi) to the northeast of Beijing are the **Qingdongling (Eastern Qing tombs)**, among the most beautiful and largest tombs in China. To the west of the village of Malanyu, in the Zunhua district of Hebei Province, lies this tomb complex of more than 2,500 square kilometres (965 sq mi). The following emperors were buried here: Shunzi (1644–1661), Kangxi (1662–

The Hall of Eminent Favours in the Changling tomb of Emperor Yongle.

220

1722), Qianlong (1736–1796), Xiang-feng (1851–1861), Tongzhi (1862–1875) and the Empress Dowager Cixi (died 1908). In addition, there are four smaller tomb complexes that contain 14 tombs of empresses; five other tomb complexes contain the mortal remains of 136 imperial concubines, and another single complex contains various princesses.

The Jingxing mountain range, which looks like an upturned bell, borders the area to the south. The main entrance to the Eastern Qing Tombs is a great white marble gate. As with wooden memorial gates, its rectangular surfaces are covered with inscriptions and geometric ornamentation. Pairs of lions and dragons form the base of the pillars.

Beyond this is the **Dagongmen (Great Palace Gate)**, which served as the official entrance to the actual mausoleum complex. There is a tower here, in which a *bixi* (a tortoise-like animal) bears a tall stone tablet on its shell. Engraved on the tablet are the "sacred virtues and worthiness" of the emperor Shunzi. Passing a small hill to the north, you come to a road with 18 pairs of stone figures, similar to the Avenue of Stone Figures in the Ming tombs, but a little smaller. This road leads through the **Longfeng-men (Dragon and Phoenix Gate)**, crossing a marble bridge with seven arches. This is the longest and most beautiful of the almost 100 bridges in the complex, and is known as the **Five Notes Bridge**. If you step on one of the 110 stone slabs, you will, it is said, hear the five notes of the pentatonic scale.

At the other end of the bridge is the **Ling'enmen (Gate of Eminent Favours)**, the entrance to the **Xiaoling (Tomb of Emperor Shunzi)**. The distance from here back to the main entrance is 5 kilometres (3 mi). Beyond the Gate of Eminent Favours is the **Ling'endian (Hall of Eminent Favours)**. This was where the ancestor tablets and the offerings to the ancestors were kept. A stele tower lies right behind the hall. The stele within is covered with red lacquer and bears the following inscription in Chinese, Manchu and Mongol: "Tomb of the emperor Shunzi." The underground tomb of this em-

peror, the first of the Qing dynasty, has yet to be excavated.

However, the **Yuling (Tomb of the Emperor Qianlong)**, and the **Ding-dongling (Tomb of the Empress Dowager Cixi)** have been restored and can now be visited by the public.

The Qing dynasty blossomed during the rule of Emperor Qianlong. He reigned for 60 years, longer than any of the other nine Qing rulers. In 1743, after eight years of rule, he began to plan his mausoleum, which was to cost a total of 1.8 million taels of silver. The **subterranean palace** covers an area of 327 square metres (126 sq ft) and consists of three vaulted chambers. A relief of the goddess of mercy, Guanyin, adorns the eight wings of the four double doors. Behind the doors are finely-worked sculptures of the Tianwang, the four Celestial Kings, each seated with their characteristic Buddhist insignia: pipe, sword, banner and pagoda. Other reliefs cover the vaulting and the walls of the tomb: the Buddhas of the five points of the compass, and 24 more Buddhas as

Stele at entrance to Dingling tomb.

well as Buddhist inscriptions in both Sanskrit and Tibetan.

The Dingdongling tomb lies about one kilometre to the west of Yuling. Here, the two wives of Emperor Xianfeng lie buried: the eastern Empress Dowager Ci'an, and the infamous western Empress Dowager Cixi. The two tombs were originally symmetrical and built in the same style. But Cixi was not satisfied and had Ling'endian, the Hall of Eminent Favours, pulled down in 1895. The tomb that she then had built for 4,590 taels of gold is more splendid and extravagant than that of the eastern Empress Dowager and even the Yuling.

As Cixi died before the work on her tomb was completed, the underground part of her tomb is relatively plain, and is outshone by the fine craftsmanship of the stone slabs between the steps in front of the tomb, and the balustrades in front of the hall. These show complicated carvings of dragons in the waves and phoenixes in the clouds – traditional symbols that represent the emperor and empress. Today, one can see an exhibition in the Hall of Eminent Favours of Cixi's clothes, articles for daily use, and a number of other tomb offerings. Also on display is the Dharani, or robe of sacred verses, woven in pure silk and embroidered with more than 25,000 Chinese characters in gold thread.

In this tomb complex there are 38 burial mounds of the concubines of Emperor Qianlong. The first mound in the second row of tombs to the east of the stele tower contains the body of Rongfei, who was buried here in 1788. Better known as the **Fragrant Concubine**, **Xiangfei**, she was the legendary daughter of a prince of the Uighur kingdom in Central Asia, as is indicated by the grave offerings and the remains of coloured satin inscribed in an indecipherable language.

Other small tombs worth seeing in the complex are the **Xiaodongling** (the tomb of the wife of Emperor Shunzi), the **Changxiling** and the **Mudongling**. These tombs, excavated in the last few years, were discovered to have been ravaged and plundered.

Taking break on a marble bridge in the Western Qing tombs.

The **Zhaoxiling** stands alone outside the Great Palace Gate. Although Zhaoxi, who was buried here in 1687, was a simple concubine, she was given the title of Empress Dowager because she had given birth to the future emperor Shunzi. According to the dynastic history of the Qing, Zhaoxi's political influence was a result of her choosing her eight-year-old grandson, some 20 years later, to be the heir to the throne. In 1662, this youth ascended to the Dragon Throne as the Emperor Kangxi, and Zhaoxi's title was raised to Great Empress Dowager.

Western Qing Tombs: These tombs lie in a hilly district of more than 100 square kilometres (40 sq mi). They are located on the southern slopes of the Yongning Mountains in Yixian, Hebei Province, 125 kilometres (80 mi) southwest of Beijing. They are bordered by the Zijing Pass to the west, the River Yi to the south and the area of the former second capital of the kingdom, Yan, in the east. The Qing emperors Yongzheng, Jiaqing, Daoguang and Guangxu, along with three empresses, seven princes and many imperial concubines, are buried here in this tomb complex.

The main tomb in this imperial burial ground is the **Tailing (Tomb of Emperor Yongzheng)**. It is said that he was afraid of being buried close to his father, Kangxi, in the Eastern Qing Tombs, because he, Yongzheng, had gained the throne in an illegal manner. In order to consolidate his 13-year rule, he did not hesitate to have his brothers and ministers imprisoned and executed. He was extremely suspicious and developed a network of spies who were supposed to observe the activities of his ministers. He rarely left his palace for any length of time, and only six years after ascending the throne, he began to seek a suitable site for his tomb.

In 1790, his 13th younger brother and a respected geomancer, whom he trusted the most, chose a favourable site to the east of Taipingyu. According to a decree of Emperor Qianlong, the emperors of subsequent reigns were to find their last resting places alternately ei-

Western Qing Tombs.

ther in the Eastern or the Western Qing Tombs. The emperors Jiaqing and Daoguang were therefore buried in the Western Tombs, and Xianfeng and Tongzhi in the Eastern Tombs.

The Tailing, the biggest tomb in the whole complex, was built between 1730 and 1737. Next to the **Way of Souls**, which leads to the mausoleums, is a series of carefully placed buildings. To the right, just beyond the **Great Palace Gate** – the main entrance to the grounds – is the **Hall of Robes**, where the priest presiding over the imperial funeral rites changed his robes before leading the rites. To the north of this is a hall, 30 metres (100 ft) high, with two tablets in memory of the "sacred virtues and worthiness." The Way of Souls leads north across a bridge of seven arches, and is bordered by stone sculptures consisting of six animals, and two civil and two military dignitaries.

Passing a natural protective wall, the so-called **Spider Hill**, you reach the **Longfengmen (Dragon and Phoenix Gate.** Continuing north, pass a small

stele pavilion and three stone bridges, each comprising three arches, before coming to a large square, where the sacred kitchen and a well pavilion are to be found. The eastern and western waiting halls and guard houses are laid out in terraced form.

The **Gate of Eminent Favours** serves as the main entrance to the Tailing. Within the gate there are furnaces for burning the offerings of silk, and the former storehouses for paper offerings, which now serve as exhibition halls. Offerings were made in the **Hall of Eminent Favours**, the main building of the Tailing complex. The hall contains the thrones of the emperor and the empress, together with an altar for offerings and gifts.

Beyond the hall there are two gates, several stone receptacles for offerings, and a stele tower, below which lies the underground palace of the emperor. Yongzheng died unexpectedly in 1735, but was not buried here until 1737, when he was buried together with his empress, Xiaojingxian, and his concu-

Tomb of Emperor Guangxu.

bine, Dunsuhuang, both of whom had died before him.

Not far away to the west is the **Changling (Tomb of Emperor Jiaqing)**. The number of buildings and the their style are almost identical to that of the Tailing. The Changling was completed in 1803, but Jiaqing was not buried here until March, 1821. According to the customs of the Qing dynasty, the Empress Xiaosurui, who had died before Jiaqing, was buried in the Changling, but her successor, who died after the emperor, was laid in a tomb to the west of the Changling.

Five kilometres (3 mi) to the west of the Changling tomb is the **Muling (Mausoleum of Emperor Daoguang)**, built between 1832 and 1836.

After he had ascended the throne, Daoguang immediately began to have a mausoleum built in the Eastern Qing Tombs. One year after its completion, it was discovered that the subterranean palace was full of water. The enraged Daoguang blamed the builders of the tomb, and in 1832, he personally went to the Western Qing Tombs to chose a new site for his mausoleum. It is said that Daoguang considered the flooding of the eastern tomb to have been due to the fact that building work had driven several dragons out of their homes.

Therefore, when the new subterranean palace of the western tomb was being built, new homes had to be found for as many dragons as possible. Hence, the unique work of art of the **Hall of Eminent Favours**: on its coffered ceiling of nanmu wood, every panel bears a writhing dragon and the unpainted beams are carved in dragon forms.

The **Chongling (Tomb of Emperor Guangxu)** lies 5 kilometres (3 mi) to the east of the Tailing. It was built in 1909, and is the last of the imperial tombs, although Guangxu was not to be the last emperor of the Qing dynasty. That place was held by Xuantong (Aisin-gioro Puyi), who was made emperor at the age of six in 1909, and who, in 1967, was an ordinary mortal when he died. Thus he was not buried beside his imperial ancestors.

The mausoleum of Emperor Guangxu was begun after his death and left incomplete after the fall of the Qing dynasty. In 1915, the republican government had it finished off with money from treasury funds of the former Qing imperial household.

To the east of the Chongling is the mausoleum for the concubines of Emperor Guangxu. The tombs hold the remains of the famous concubines, Zhen Fei and her sister, Jinfei. Zhen Fei was Guangxu's favourite and actively supported him in his attempts at reform. This brought her the enmity of the Dowager Empress Cixi, who had her placed under arrest and tortured. All contact with the emperor was forbidden to her. When Cixi fled Beijing in 1900 to escape the invasion of the Europeans, she ordered her chief eunuch to get rid of Zhen Fei. He is supposed to have drowned her in a well.

Her body was found in 1901 and buried in Taincun, a small village outside Xizhimen. In 1915, her mortal remains were transferred to the Western Qing Tombs.

Emperor Guangxu.

CHENGDE – THE SUMMER RESIDENCE

If staying in Beijing for several days, consider taking a trip to Chengde. You can get to the town, which lies 250 kilometres (150 mi) to the north of Beijing, beyond the Great Wall, by train. The journey takes four to five hours, so plan for at least a one- or, if possible, two-night stay.

The name Chengde means to inherit virtue; Chengde used to be better known by the old name, Jehol, which is derived from the name of the river, Rehe (Warm River). The throaty northern Chinese dialect makes *rehe* sound like *jehol*, as the "R" sounds more like the "J" in the French *jour*. Jehol or Rehe was, during the 18th and 19th centuries, the summer residence of the Manchu emperors of the Qing dynasty.

The Manchu were originally the Jurjen (Nüzhen in Chinese transliteration), who had ruled the north of China in the 12th and 13th centuries and founded the Jin dynasty. Nurhaci, the Great Khan of the Jurjen, had established another dynasty in the north, also named Jin, and a few years later his son, Abahai, brought the whole of northern China under his control. In 1635, he replaced the name Jurjen with Manchu, and changed the name of the dynasty to Daqing, which means Great Qing Dynasty.

The successors of Nurhaci and Abahai were the great emperors Kangxi (1662–1722) and Qianlong (1736–1796), whose names are closely linked with Chengde. Once the first Qing emperor had settled in Beijing, the search was on for a summer residence which would offer protection from the dusty heat of Beijing. The scouts that were sent out looked to the north, in the direction of the original Manchu home, and eventually found what they were looking for along the Rehe river.

In the year 1703, Emperor Kangxi ordered the building of the summer palace **Bishushanzhuang (Hill Palace that Protects from Heat)**. Building went on for 87 years, and the residence finally covered 560 hectares (1,400 acres) surrounded by a wall 10 kilometres (6 mi) long. This makes it the biggest imperial residence in China that has survived in its original condition. The average temperature in the mountainous area remains 20 degrees Celsius, even in the hottest months. Outside the palace walls, to the north and west, a total of 11 temples – mostly in the Tibetan style – were built. Seven of them have survived to this day. The temple complex was divided into eight groups and hence was named **Eight Outer Temples**.

Emperor Kangxi wrote: "Several times I have travelled to the shores of the Yangzi and have seen the lush beauty of the south. Twice my way then led me on to Gansu and Shaanxi, and therefore I know the land in the west well. In the north I have crossed the Dragon Sands, and in the east I have wandered in the region of the White Mountains, where the peaks and the rivers are mighty, but the people and their lives have remained true to the simplicity of nature. I cannot count all the places I have seen, but I have chosen none of them, and here, in the valley of Rehe, is the only place in which I desire to live."

Apart from the palaces in Jehol, there were 18 additional small palaces, all along the route that led to a 400-square-kilometre (150-sq-mi) hunting reserve to the northeast of Beijing. This was where the emperors Kangxi and Qianlong and their court met with Mongol princes for hunting excursions, equestrian games and other diversions. There was, of course, a political purpose underlying the entertainment: in this way, relationships with the peoples on the border were maintained. For nearly 150 years, the Qing emperors resided in Chengde for several months every summer and conducted state business from there. Before the court set off on its long annual journey, a flurry of building activity took place. The roads were improved, and the many little palaces on the route, which served as rest stations for the court, had to be prepared for the emperor and his entourage. Chengde was set up as the second political centre of the Qing dynasty after Beijing.

Preceding pages: view of the Temple of Happiness.

From 1820 onwards, the palace was allowed to fall into ruin. The emperor Jiaqing had been killed by lightning in Chengde in that year, and the court avoided the place in the decades following, so as not to tempt fate a second time. Emperor Xianfeng was the only one to reside here again for a short time, when he had fled in 1860 during the Second Opium War from the allied troops of Britain and France. It was in this old summer palace that he was forced to sign the Treaty of Peking with its many concessions to the foreigners, before dying only a year later.

The palaces: The palaces are in the south of the grounds, and border one of the northern suburbs of Chengde. The palaces and grounds of Chengde consist of three great complexes, which are reached by passing through the **Lizhengmen**, a gate that has a tablet bearing inscriptions in Chinese, Mongol, Manchu, Tibetan and Uighur. The **Neiwumen** bears the inscription, in Kangxi's hand, *Bishushanzhuang*, the residence's official name.

Just as with the Imperial Palace in Beijing, the first halls entered are those in which state business was conducted and various ceremonies were held, with the private imperial apartments taking up the rear of the palace. The main hall of **Zhenggong (Main Palace)** is built of precious *nanmu* wood from southwest China, and is therefore sometimes simply called Nanmu Hall. This was the hall in which, in 1860, Emperor Xianfeng signed the treaty dictated by the British and the French, curtailing Chinese sovereignty.

Songhezhai (The Hall of Pines and Cranes), on the east of the Zhenggong main palace, was the private residence of the emperor's mother. Beyond this hall is **Wanhesongfeng** (Ten Thousand Pine Valleys in the Wind Hall), from which one can get a marvellous view of the magnificent scenery of the northern grounds. Here, the 12-year-old Qianlong was instructed by his grandfather, Kangxi, in the proper form of answering petitions, and in classical literature. In memory of Kangxi, Qianlong later

The Qing emperors Qianlong and Kangxi had the Summer Residence built and extended.

named the hall **Ji'entang (Hall for Remembering Kindness)**.

The **Donggong (Eastern Palace)** lies in the southeastern part of the residence. Almost none of it exists today, although it was not until 1948 that the three-storey theatre burned completely.

The park adjoining the palaces to the north can be divided topographically into three areas. Directly bordering the palaces to the north is the lake area, which is reminiscent of southern Chinese scenery. In the northwestern part is a plain, which could represent the Mongolian steppes; to the west is a forested, hilly landscape with many ravines and valleys. In earlier years, there were countless imperial buildings here, but none of them have survived.

About 55 hectares (135 acres) of the park area are covered with water. **Chengdu Lake** (Lake of Pure Water) is divided by a number of dams into eight smaller lakes. Everywhere are little pavilions, tea houses and resting places, very reminiscent of the southern Chinese lakes, such as the area around the West Lake near Hangzhou. Chengdu Lake is fed from the **Requan (Warm Spring)**, so that it never freezes, not even in the cold north Chinese winters.

The artificial **Jinshan (Golden Hill)** acts as a belvedere. The hilltop **Jinshan Pavilion** is a replica the Jinshan Tower near Zhenjian, in Jiangsu Province. Here, the Qing emperors made offerings to Daoist gods such as the Jade Emperor.

Further north lies a broad plain, which the emperor Qianlong named **Wanshu-yuan (Park of Ten Thousand Trees)**. Pines, acacias, willows and old cypresses grow in abundance here. Qianlong is supposed to have delighted in the many birds and in the plentiful red deer of the park. Mongol-style banquets were often held in Wanshuyuan. Here, the court met in Mongol yurts, feasting and watching horse-riding displays or wrestling bouts, enjoying displays of the minority peoples' folk customs and arts. To the west of the gardens was a great riding arena, where the emperors chose their horses and then had them broken in and trained for equestrian performances.

Dragon figure on a bell.

In the southwest of this plain is one of the seven famous libraries of the Qing dynasty period, the **Siku Quanshu (Collected Writings of the Four Categories of Literature)**. Working from 1772 to 1782, a team of 360 scholars collected all available works and manuscripts. They are said to have thus collected more than 80,000 volumes, which were then copied by 15,000 scribes. This collection, housed in the Beijing Library since 1915, is the most valuable library collection of old Chinese works.

In the northwestern part of the summer residence, the hilly and forested landscape forms a dramatic background to the scenery of the lakes. The hills, rising above the plain to 180 metres (590 ft), were originally dotted with many little pavilions and halls. Of the four pavilions on the summits, only the **Nanshanjiuxe (Snowscape at Southern Hill Pavilion)** remains. Some 44 gardens were laid out here during the reigns of Kangxi and Qianlong. In the Zhuyuan temple grounds there used to be a pavilion cast from 200 tonnes of

Putuozong-shengmiao is modelled after the Dalai Lama's Lhasa palace.

copper, but it was demolished and removed by the Japanese towards the end of World War II. A copper tablet and two copper plaques in the **Museum of the Summer Residence** are reminders of the magnificent temple grounds. The mountainous landscape is crossed by five deep valleys: the Songyunxia (Pine Cloud Valley), the Lishiyu (Pear Tree Valley), the Song'linyu (Pine Forest Valley), the Zhenziyu (Hazel Valley), and the Xiyu (West Valley).

Eight Outer Temples: The sight of the many temples at Chengde may confuse visitors, as some of these buildings are in the Tibetan style. To explain this curious phenomenon, one needs to look briefly at Chinese history.

For the Manchu, the path to victory lay through the steppes. The first important victory was won when the East Mongols from the eastern part of the Gobi desert allied themselves with the Manchu. However, this expansion also upset the many nomadic peoples of the western steppes and in Central Asia. Conflict was brewing, made more ex-

treme by the religious differences of the peoples involved. The Qing rulers had accepted Chinese culture even before their conquest of China and had surrounded themselves with Confucian Chinese advisers. But the peoples of the steppe were, almost without exception, followers of Tibetan Buddhism, also known as Lamaism.

When the Mongols first conquered Tibet in the 13th century, they were strongly influenced by the Tibetan religion and culture, and eventually converted to the faith. During the subsequent centuries, the Tibetan form of Buddhism spread among nearly all the peoples of the steppe. The Qing rulers may have embraced the Buddhist faith and declared themselves to be protectors of the Yellow Sect, the Tibetan Gelugpa sect, but their motives were probably very mixed. Without a doubt, this course of action had many political advantages. Under the emperors Kangxi and Qianlong, at any rate, diplomatic ties between China and Tibet were closer than they had ever been.

As early as 1652, the fifth Dalai Lama came on a visit, following an invitation made by the Chinese emperor. The White Dagoba in Beihai Park in Beijing was built in his honour. As a consequence, many Buddhist writings were translated and printed in Beijing. Ties with Tibet were strengthened by these signs of favour of the Chinese emperors, and after an army of Dsungars was driven out of Tibet in 1751, the country finally came under the control of Beijing. These same Dsungars were defeated again in the northwest, which was conquered in 1758 and 1759 and renamed Xinjiang (New Territories). Afterwards, the Chinese empire's territory covered about 11.5 million square kilometres (4.5 million sq mi), an area that it was never to match again.

The Tibetan temples in Chengde were another sign of favour to the Tibetan religion. Eleven such temples were built to the west and northwest of the palace during the rule of Kangxi and Qianlong. They were divided into eight groups and therefore were known as the **Eight**

Xumitushou-miao is based on Tibetan monastery in Xigaze.

Outer Temples. The main gates of these buildings all pointed towards the palace and symbolised the unity of the various peoples under the central rule of the Qing emperors. Seven temples remain, all modelled on famous Tibetan buildings. One can find replicas of the Potala Palace, the Tashi Lhunpo monastery, and the Samye monastery in Tibet, and of the Gu'erzha temple in Xinjiang, the Shuxiang temple in the Wutaishan Mountains and also that of the Anguo temple in Zhejiang Province.

The furthest northeastern temple is the **Shuxiangsi (Temple of the Majusri Statue)**, dating from 1774. A replica of the Shuxiang temple in the Wutaishan Mountains, it holds a precious treasure: a Manchu translation of the Buddhist scriptures, the Kanjur.

Further west, directly to the north of the summer residence, lies the **Putuozongshengmiao Temple**, which bears the name of a sacred Buddhist mountain on an island in the East China Sea, Putuo Shan. It is modelled on the **Potala Palace**, the residence of the Dalai Lama in Tibet, and is also known as the Little Potala. Building started in 1767, and the temple was completed a mere four years later. It served as a residence for high Tibetan dignitaries when they stayed at the Chinese Imperial Court.

Behind the entrance gate is a stele pavilion with three stone pillars. These bear historical inscriptions that tell of the inclusion of many different peoples into the Qing empire. Beyond this, pass through the **Five Pagoda Gate**, which is in the Tibetan style and bears five Tibetan stupas. Beyond this, go through another Chinese gate of honour with glazed tiles before seeing the **Little Potala**. It consists of a 17-metre (56-ft) high white fundament upon which the **Red Palace** is built. From the outside, the palace appears to have seven floors, but actually only has three. Above the Red Palace is another hall, **Wanfaguiyidian**, also known as the **Golden Temple** because of its gilded roof. The hall contains many Bodhisattva figures.

The **Xumifushoumiao (Temple of Happiness and Longevity)** was built

in 1780, on the occasion of Qianlong's 70th birthday. The sixth Panchen Lama had announced his intention to travel from Tibet to attend the festivities, and as a special honour, Qianlong had a replica of the Panchen Lama's residence (the Tashi Lhunpo monastery in Xigaze) built. The roof of the main hall is covered with scale-like, gilded copper plates and there are eight gilded dragons adorning the roof beams. The bodies of the mythical animals are bent and their tails raised, so that they look as if they are to launch themselves into the air. The main part of this temple is also a Red Palace. A building to the east of it houses a throne in which Emperor Qianlong listened to sermons preached by the Panchen Lama. Completing the temple buildings is a pagoda of glazed bricks.

A little out of the way to the northwest, on the banks of the Wulie River, lies the **Puningsi (Temple of Universal Peace)**, built in 1755. The model for the rear buildings of the temple was the Samye monastery in Tibet, and the buildings in the front part are in the Han Chinese style. The **Mahavira Hall** is the main building in the front part of the temple. Three Buddha statues and 18 Lohan figures can be seen here.

The Mahayana Pavilion symbolises the Meru Mountain – the cosmic centre of the Buddhist world. The pavilion is flanked by a **Moon Hall** and a **Sun Hall**, while Tibetan stupas surround the building. The Mahayana Pavilion, at 37 metres (120 ft) high, is China's tallest wooden pavilion. Inside is a statue of the Boddhisattva Avalokiteshvara, 22 metres (73 ft) tall, measuring 15 metres (49 ft) about the hips, and weighing more than 120 tonnes. His 42 arms and countless eyes symbolise the inexhaustible powers of salvation possessed by this Boddhisattva. On its head, the figure bears a statue of the Buddha Amitabha.

To the south of Puningsi is the **Anyuanmiao (Temple of Pacifying Distant Regions)**, built in 1764 as a replica of the Gu'erzha temple in Ili, in Xinjiang Province. Only the **Pududian (Hall of Universal Conversion)** survives, with its statue of the Boddhisattva Ksitigarbha, the King of Hell, whom the Chinese know as Ludumu. Further south lies the **Pulesi (Temple of Universal Joy)**. Also known as the Round Pavilion, it was built in 1766 in honour of Kazhak, Kirghiz and other nobles from the distant northwest of China. The building, a typical Han Chinese temple, has an entrance gate, beyond which lie bell and drum towers on either side, and a hierarchical arrangement of various halls with their side buildings. The main building is the **Xuguangge (Round Pavilion)**. The Chinese name translates literally as the Pavilion of Morning Light. It rests on a square terrace, the combination symbolising Heaven and Earth according to the Chinese conception of the cosmos. Adjoining the temple grounds to the south is the **Pushansi (Temple of All-Encompassing Goodness)**, which has, unfortunately, fallen into ruin. And finally, adjoining the Pushansi temple to the south is the **Purensi (Temple of All-Encompassing Charity)**. The southernmost of the Eight Outer Temples, it was built in 1713 for Emperor Kangxi's 60th birthday.

Left, the Mahayana Hall, Puningsi. **Right**, the Summer Residence of the emperors in Chengde.

INSIGHT GUIDES
TRAVEL TIPS

Simply travelling safely

American Express Travellers Cheques

- are recognised as one of the safest and most convenient ways to protect your money when travelling abroad

- are more widely accepted than any other travellers cheque brand

- are available in eleven currencies

- are supported by a 24 hour worldwide refund service and

- a 24 hour Express Helpline service provides assistance and information when travelling abroad

- are accepted in millions of shops, hotels and restaurants throughout the world

Travellers Cheques

Getting Acquainted

The Place

Beijing covers an area of 16,807 square kilometres (10,443 sq. mi). The city is divided into 10 districts: Dongcheng, Xicheng, Xianwu and Chongwen in the city centre, surrounded by Chaoyang, Fengtai, Haidian, Shijingshan, Mentougou and Yanshan. In addition, there are nine areas outside the city: Daxing, Tongxian, Shunyi, Changping, Pinggu, Fangshan, Miyun, Huairou and Yanqing.

Beijing's geographic location on the northern edge of the North Chinese Plain is at approximately the same latitude as Ankara, Madrid and New York: 39° 56' north, longitude 116° 20'.

The city centre, Qianmen, is 43.71 metres (143.4 ft) above sea level. The land is hilly to the north and northwest and opens out into a wide level plain to the southeast. About 60 percent of the area of Beijing is hilly, but the city centre is quite flat. The Western Mountains (1,000–1,500 metres; 3,281–4,921 feet) lie to the northwest, with the Jundu Range (highest peak rises to 2,000 metres or 6,562 feet) to the north. Two fairly large rivers flow north to south: the Yongding to the west of the city, and the Chaobai to the east.

Time Zones

The time difference between Beijing time and Greenwich Mean Time is eight hours, i.e. when it's noon in London, it is 8pm in Beijing. Beijing time applies to the whole of China.

Climate

The ideal time for travelling to Beijing is late spring (May to mid-June) and autumn (end of August to mid-October). Beijing has a continental climate, and the four seasons are clearly distinguishable in the Chinese capital.

Winter is dry and cold with little snow, for it is almost always sunny. Sharp winds blow frequently from the northern and desert regions. Spring, which begins in April, is the shortest season. In early spring, there are sand storms (from Central Asia) which cease by mid-May at the latest. The average temperature rises quickly.

Spring in Beijing is warm, dry and often windy. Summer begins around mid-June and reaches its height in July and August. Both the temperature and the rainfall are highest in these two months. About 75 percent of the annual rainfall occurs in June, July and August. There are often thunderstorms in the late afternoon; temperatures climb to over 30°C, and to 35°C or more on some days. It is often muggy in summer.

Autumn is the best season in Beijing: the sky is blue most of the time, and the air is cleaner (a noticeable cloud of smog hangs over Beijing). It is sunny and warm during the day and pleasantly cool in the evening. Autumn, which in Beijing lasts from early September to early November, is definitely the best season for a visit to Beijing and is considered as the golden season for tourists. However, Beijing is very crowded with visitors during these months, and the hotels are often fully booked. But the town has its special charm in each season.

The People

The population of Beijing has risen as follows:
1949: c. 1.20 million
1980: c. 9.23 million
1995: 13 million (but this figure doesn't include an estimated 2 million immigrants from the rural areas.)

About 73 percent of the population live in the city districts, the rest in the country areas.

Culture and Customs

One thing you need in China is a lot of patience. If something doesn't quite happen as you imagined, stay calm and relaxed. As a rule, complaining, shouting and loud criticism only result in mutual loss of face and a deterioration of the situation. This doesn't mean that one shouldn't openly and honestly give one's view or criticise. As everywhere, it is the way it's done that counts.

In general, Chinese people are very polite to foreigners, but it is one of the numerous myths about the Chinese that politeness is deeply rooted in China. Once you've witnessed the rush hour on the public buses, you will experience how ruthless Chinese people can be. Some of the government's campaigns in fact urge people to be polite and considerate. A foreigner will be most successful by remaining polite and calm. And if you really encounter trouble, it may be best to try and explain this privately to the person concerned. In the service sector – in hotels or restaurants – the service is sometimes bad or the food is indifferent; don't feel inhibited from giving your view and, if necessary, asking to see the manager. If you are travelling in a group, you can always talk to the group leader.

A short handshake is usual when being introduced to someone in China. Chinese people quite happily talk about such things as age, weight, and other personal matters. This is not considered rude, and direct questions about the family or income are part of a normal conversation after quite a short acquaintance. You will probably only make close friends after quite a long stay.

Despite the greater openness of China towards the West, it is best, as a foreigner, to show a minimum of public demonstrative affection such as kissing, embracing, and holding hands. In private company, and on tourist trips, it is not necessary to dress formally, though people on a business trip should wear formal clothes for receptions and meetings. You don't need to wear an evening dress to go to the theatre or the Beijing opera.

Chinese women are not very happy if someone puts their arm around their shoulder for a photograph. One important rule: Never arrive late. If you are invited to a private function, it's best not to bring flowers but rather a good bottle of spirits. Chinese women rarely drink alcohol, practically not at all in public. Smoking for women is also not done.

More colour
for the world.

HDCplus. New perspectives in colour photography.

AGFA

Probably the <u>most</u> <u>important</u> TRAVEL TIP you will ever receive

Before you travel abroad, make sure that you and your family are protected from diseases that can cause serious health problems.

For instance, you can pick up *hepatitis A* which infects 10 million people worldwide every year (it's not just a disease of poorer countries) simply through consuming contaminated food or water!

What's more, in many countries if you have an accident needing medical treatment, or even dental treatment, you could also be at risk of infection from *hepatitis B* which is 100 times more infectious than AIDS, and can lead to liver cancer.

The good news is, you can be protected by vaccination against these and other serious diseases, such as *typhoid, meningitis* and *yellow fever.*

Travel safely! Check with your doctor at least 8 weeks before you go, to discover whether or not you need protection.

Consult your doctor before you go... not when you return!

SB

SmithKline Beecham
VACCINES

Produced as a service to public health

Planning The Trip

What to Bring

There is a limit of 20 kg for baggage on international and internal flights. It is advisable to take strong suitcases which are lockable.

The following items could be useful to take, depending on the type of accommodation you have planned: an adaptor, light raincoat, disinfectants, cream or lotion against mosquitoes, medicine for digestive problems and colds, films for transparencies, and batteries.

Electricity

The modern and luxury hotels all have 220-volt sockets; cheaper hotels still have the old British three-pin plugs or quite narrow pin sockets. The hotel reception will usually have adaptors. For a longer stay, it is worth buying one, or to use battery-driven implements.

Entry Regulations

Visas and Passports

A tourist visa is necessary for entering China. This can be applied for at the various embassies of the People's Republic of China.

On entry, a health declaration, entry card and customs declaration have to be filled in. These forms are given out on the airplane or at the airport. A duplicate of the customs declaration must be shown on departure. A fine may be imposed if it is lost. All jewellery, equipment and the amount of foreign exchange in one's possession should be declared, and the rule is that all imported items must be taken out again. There are likely to be spot checks at the departure point. Items which have been imported but are not taken out again are subject to customs payments. It is advisable to keep receipts of items bought. There are export restrictions on antiques. Those antiques which can be exported carry a special customs sticker.

For passengers leaving China by plane, there is a departure tax.

Health

No vaccinations are required for China. It may be advisable to strengthen the body's resistance by having a gamma-globulin injection just before travelling. A malaria jab, recommended by the World Health Organisation for parts of China, is not necessary for Beijing.

If anyone planning to spend more than a year in the country needs a health certificate which includes an AIDS test. Travellers with active tuberculosis and carriers of the AIDS virus are banned from the country.

Toilets

All hotels have acceptable or good toilets in Western style. The public toilets are not recommended, since they mostly consist of a pit with several holes over which you have to perch without a rail, and you'll find large numbers of interested spectators.

Currency

The standard Chinese currency is called *renminbi* (RMB); the basic unit is the yuan, often called "kuai". One yuan is worth 10 jiao – also called "mao". Jiao come in both coin and paper form, as does 1 yuan.

Foreign currency and travellers' cheques can be changed in most hotel lobbies, and at most branches of the Bank of China. Money exchange booths may also be found in most areas frequented by foreign shoppers. For credit card cash advances there are automatic teller machines scattered throughout the city, the handiest for most people being in the Friendship Store on Jianguomenwai. Banks will also issue cash advances, but charge 4 percent. Credit cards can now be used in most larger places or heavy shopping areas

When you change money, you'll get a receipt that allows you to change RMB back to foreign currency if you leave within 6 months, but you can only do so for 50 percent of the original amount.

There are always money changers roaming the streets willing to give you a better rate than the banks, but beware; like dealing on street corners anywhere, there is the chance of getting ripped off.

If you must change your money on the street, use people in stalls. They have to be there the next day. In any case, with the Chinese government promising fully exchangeable RMB by the year 2000, there will soon be no need for a black market.

If you are having any problems, the main branch of the Bank of China is at 410 Fuchingmennei Dajie (at Second Ring Road), Tel: 6601-6688.

China is still suffering from high inflation, which runs anywhere from 18 to 25 percent.

Public Holidays

The following are official, non-working holidays in Beijing – and the rest of China:

1 January: New Year's Day
Jan/February: Spring festival (varies) (4 days)
8 March: International Women's Day
1 May: International Workers Day
1 October: National Day (2 days)

Apart from the spring festival – the New Year's festival according to the traditional Chinese calendar – the other holidays listed above are observed according to the Gregorian calendar. They reflect the political changes since 1949 in the People's Republic of China. Other important political celebrations which are not public holidays are 1 July, the day of the foundation of the Chinese Communist Party, and 1 August, the founding day of the People's Liberation Army. There are also traditional festivals which – while mostly restricted during the Cultural Revolution – have been revived and indeed have experienced a renaissance in recent years. This is more evident in Beijing's rural areas. For example, stilt walkers and dragon dancers can still be seen during the spring festival.

The traditional festivals are fixed by the Chinese lunar calendar (which, however, is not purely a lunar calender, but relates to the lunar/solar year). In the Chinese calender, there is after a 30-month period (29 or 30 days each) a leap month at changeable intervals, which results in the date differences compared to the Gregorian calendar.

The origins of these traditional festivals go back a long way, some to the Shang dynasty (16th to 11th century BC). Some lost their original meaning over time, changed in contents or gained a religious meaning; others represented a sort of memorial day for specific persons or historic events, others were for the worship of ancestors or gods. Of the three former "Festivals of the Living" (New Year, Dragon Boat Festival and Moon Festival), and the three "Festivals of the Dead" (Qingming Festival, All Souls Day and the Songhanyi Festival, the festival of sending winter clothes to the ancestors) from the past, what has remained in the People's Republic of China in a more or less changed form is the Spring Festival (*Chunjie*, Chinese or the New Year Festival), the Lantern Festival, the Qingming Festival (Remembrance Day for the Dead), the Dragon Boat Festival and the Moon Festival.

The most important traditional festival is the **New Year Festival**, which is the only public holiday. If you are travelling in China during that time you should expect somewhat restricted services, because many Chinese travel to their homes for this festival. The New Year Festival is traditionally a family gathering, similar to our Christmas celebrations. In the past, it was customary that all debts had to be paid before the Spring Festival. This is because the earth god leaves the earth a few days before the festival to report to the Jade Emperor about the behaviour of a family. During the festival, which lasted several days, all work had to stop in the house, which had been prepared and renovated. Today, people still tidy and clean thoroughly before festivals. The evening before New Year's Eve, the entire family gathers, a feast is prepared and fireworks are burned. Only the sacrifices for the gods and ancestors made in the past are missing. The first day is taken up with meals and family visits, the second and third day are for friends and acquaintances. People visit each other and bring their good wishes for the Spring Festival. If you travel to China during this time, you should expect all train services to be fully booked before the Spring Festival.

The **Lantern Festival** used to signify the official end of the New Year celebrations. Today, people work normally on that day. Only the meal of little round rice dumplings with sweet filling has remained from the old customs. In recent years, processions of banners have been promoted again by the Department of Culture of Beijing. This custom goes back to the Ming period. The processions include banners with pictures of deities, musicians, lion dancers and Yangge-groups; the banners are from groups which perform peasant dances.

The **Qingming Festival** (the Festival of Light) was originally a day of renewal of life around springtime; only later did it become a festival to remember the dead. In the past, those who could afford it would go on a pilgrimage to the graves of their ancestors and bring cooked chicken, pork, vegetables, fruit, incense and candles, they would burn paper money, sometimes clothes, furniture and houses made of paper (constructed by using bamboo and coloured paper) as sacrifices. After the sacrifice, the cleaning of the graves would begin. People in the country areas are again going to the graves, sweeping them and burning paper money. In Beijing, school classes lay wreaths of flowers in the Square of Heavenly Peace in memory of revolutionaries who died.

While the **Dragon Boat Festival** is not celebrated in Beijing but mostly in southern China, the **Moon Festival** is still popular in Beijing. On this day, people eat moon cakes, filled with pieces of meat, spices, melon kernels, almonds, orange peel, sugar, etc. They are to remind people of the revolt against the Mongolian emperors of the 14th century. According to ancient Chinese myth, the hare and the toad live on the moon. Stories about the moon hare and Chang'e, the "woman in the moon" are still popular. If the weather is good, people sit together outside on the day of the Moon Festival (which today is a normal working day), chat, look at the moon and eat moon cakes.

Traditional Western holidays like Christmas are not celebrated in the People's Republic of China and are not usually observed. Concessions are made to foreigners in Beijing, however, for instance with American-style Christmas parties. Christmas is of course celebrated by the Christian community in Beijing, just as Moslems and Buddhists celebrate their own festivals.

Late summer is the time for the Cricket Championships. During the Moon Festival, which, according to the Chinese peasant calendar, is celebrated on the 15th day of the eighth month, the male crickets – just like their owners – are in a fighting mood. Hundreds of cricket fanciers, many of them members of clubs, now prepare for the annual contests. If you own a white jade-tailed or a double-toothed cricket, you have a good chance of winning. The crickets are put into elaborate cricket containers, or into simpler ones made out of pumpkin shells, and taken for walks under the coat of their owners.

During the competition, owners put their crickets into a container and wait for one to send the other packing. The professionals, however, first weigh the little creatures on special scales and then divide them – just like boxers or wrestlers – into heavyweight, middleweight or featherweight fighters. Such precisely prepared fights usually promise to be full of suspense, especially if a bit of money's been put on the participants. Betting is strictly prohibited in China, but it is part of the fun on these occasions.

Getting There

By Air

All visitors need a Chinese visa before embarking on a flight.

Airports: The Capital International Airport is about 30 kilometres (18 mi) from the city centre, approximately 30 to 40 minutes by taxi but at peak hours can take one hour or more. Depending on the category of taxi, the fare will be from 65 to 100 yuan. Beware of drivers who approach you before you reach the taxi rank; agree on a price before setting off, or ensure the driver uses a meter.

Air China offers coach services from the airport to several downtown destinations for 16 yuan. Destinations include the main Air China booking office on Chang'an Avenue, close to Xidan; the Lufthansa Centre; and the Beijing International Hotel, close to Beijing Railway Station. Taxis are available at all stops.

Most of the major hotels offer limousine pick-ups and free bus transfers.

Beijing's Capital Airport has connections to more than 50 other cities in China. Hotels usually have flight-booking services, and most major airlines have offices in Beijing. You must check in at least 30 minutes before departure for domestic flights, although delays are common on many domestic routes, and at least one hour before departure on an international flight. (For shorter journeys within China, the train is generally more enjoyable.) International airport departure tax is 90 yuan, domestic is 50 yuan.

AIRLINES

Aeroflot, Jinglun Hotel (Beijing-Ioronto). Tel: 6500-2412.
Air China, 15 Xi Chang'an Avenue, Xicheng district. Tel: 6601-7755 (general information), 6601-3336 (domestic), 6601-6667 (international).
Air France, Rm 2716, China World Trade Centre. Tel: 6588-1388.
Alitalia, Rm 139/140 Jianguo Hotel. Tel: 6561-0375.
All Nippon Airways, 1st Floor, China World Trade Centre. Tel: 6505-3311.
Asiana Airlines, Rm 134, Jianguo Hotel. Tel: 6468-1118.
British Airways, Rm 210, Scitech Tower. Tel: 6512-4070.
Canadian Airlines, Lufthansa Centre. Tel: 6468-2001.
China Eastern Airlines. Tel: 6522-8627.
China Northern Airlines, Air China building. Tel: 6602-4078.
China Northwest Airlines, Air China building. Tel: 6601-7755, ext 2200.
China Sichuan Airlines, Air China building. Tel: 6601-7755 ext 2265.
China Southern Airlines, 227 Chaoyangmenwai Dajie. Tel: 6595-3622.
Dragonair, Rm L107, China World Trade Centre. Tel: 6518-2533.
Fesco Air Services (domestic flights), 1st Floor, China World Trade Centre. Tel: 6505-3330.
Finnair, Rm 102, Scitech Tower. Tel: 6512-7180.
Garuda Indonesia, Rm 116A, West Wing, China World Trade Centre. Tel: 6505-2901.
Japan Airlines, Hotel New Otani, Changfugong. Tel: 6513-0888.
KLM, Rm 104, China World Trade Centre. Tel: 6505-3505.
Korean Air, Rm L115C, West Wing, China World Trade Centre. Tel: 6505-0088.
Lufthansa, Beijing Lufthansa Centre. Tel: 6465-4488.
Malaysian Airlines, Rm 115A, West Wing, China World Trade Centre. Tel: 6505-2681.
MIAT (Mongolian), 1st Floor, Golden Bridge Plaza. Tel: 6507-9297.
Northwest Airlines, Rm 104, China World Trade Centre. Tel: 6505-3505.
PIA, 1st Floor, China World Trade Centre. Tel: 6505-1681.
Qantas, Rm 102, Lufthansa Centre. Tel: 6467-4794.
SAS, 1st Floor, Scitech Tower. Tel: 6518-3738.
Singapore Airlines, Rm L109, China World Trade Centre. Tel: 6505-2233.
Swissair, 2nd Floor, Scitech Tower. Tel: 6512-3555.
Thai International, Rm 207-209, Scitech Tower. Tel: 6460-8899.
United Airlines, 1st Floor, Office Building, Lufthansa Centre. Tel: 6463-1111.

By Train

Beijing has two main railway stations: Beijing Station (Beijing-zhan) and Beijing West (Xi-zhan). Some trains to other parts of China run from the city's three smaller stations. Trans-Siberian trains leave from Beijing Station in a fascinating five-day (via Mongolia) or six-day (via northeast China) journey to Moscow. Tickets and visas are easier to obtain for Beijing–Moscow than for Moscow–Beijing. The Chongwenmen and Beijing International hotels both have international train ticket-booking offices. Allow at least a week to obtain Russian and, if necessary, Mongolian and Polish visas in Beijing. Don't forget to bring plenty of passport photos; otherwise there is a photo booth inside the main entrance to the Friendship Store, on Jianguomenwai, and another in the CITIC building next to the Friendship Store.

For travel within China, the best place to buy tickets is the foreigners' booking office to the left of the main concourse inside Beijing Station. One can also buy tickets here for trains leaving from Beijing West. Beijing West also has a foreigners' booking office. If you want a sleeper berth, especially in summer, it is best to buy the ticket two or three days in advance. Return tickets can be purchased for Hong Kong–Beijing but not for other routes.

Individual Travel

Most individual travellers to Beijing are either people on business, who are generally looked after by Chinese partners, or the "backpackers" who arrive in China with just an air ticket and visa.

Independent travel in China can prove difficult if you have no bookings and don't speak Chinese. Problems with booking transport and accommodation can spoil your visit, particularly during the summer peak period and if on a tight schedule.

If you do want to organise your own trip, here are some tips:
- Avoid the peak tourist season (May–September).
- Get detailed information. When you arrive in Beijing, first head for a travel agency such as CITS, which, for a small fee, will help book rooms and tickets. Using agencies or hotel travel services can save a lot of hassle.

Besides the main travel agencies, Beijing has many small-scale, sometimes-unlicensed tour operators. On some of the organized tours, as in many countries, the operators take tourists to shops and restaurants that pay the guides a commission. Others charge double for entrance tickets you can buy yourself. But most tour companies are reasonably trustworthy, and usually cheap.

Another possibility for independent travel to Beijing is to book a mini package or full "tailor made" package through a company that organises trips to China. They will book rooms, transfers and sightseeing including an interpreter, if you want one.

Booking by mail or fax is no problem for major hotels, but is unlikely to succeed with cheaper hotels because of the lack of English speakers. Ensure you have received confirmation of your booking before you arrive in Beijing.

Trade Organizations

There are now many foreign banks and company representatives in Beijing. Since the main ministries and important foreign trade organisations are based in Beijing, China's capital is often the first point of contact for foreign business people. Many trade fairs are held here, and the following organisations can give more detailed information about business trips and arranging business connections:

UK: Department of Trade and Industry, Overseas Trade Division Branch 2 (China), Kingsgate House, 66-74 Victoria Street, London SW1E 6SW. Tel: (071) 6215-5357.

USA: National Council for US-China Trade, 1050 17th Street, N.W., Washington D.C. 20036. Tel: (202) 6429-0340.

Chambers of Commerce:
American Chamber of Commerce (Amcham), Rm 352, Great Wall Sheraton Hotel, 8 Dongsanhuan Beilu. Tel: 6500-5566 ext 2378/2379, Fax: 6501-8273.
British Chamber of Commerce, 2nd floor, 31 Technical Club, 15 Guanghuali, Jianguomenwai Dajie. Tel: 6593-6610, Fax: 6501-8281.

Practical Tips

Emergencies

Security and Crime

Visitors, including women, don't need to take any special precautions in Beijing, though you should never leave money and valuables unguarded. Crime in China is low, but rising. Always keep luggage locked.
Emergency calls:
Police: 110
Ambulance: 120
Fire: 119

Public Emergency Services: Getting used to a different climate and foreign food can affect one's health. It is worth taking medicines for colds, diarrhoea, and constipation in your medical kit, as well as a stock of any regular medication you need. While traditional Chinese remedies are often excellent, language difficulties may make it hard to buy the right ones. If you need medical help, most tourist hotels offer this. The **Swissotel** has its own pharmacy. In case of serious illness, foreigners can get treatment in special sections for foreigners at major

local hospitals, but partly because of language problems, the service is not always Western-style.

The best hospitals with foreigner sections are the **Sino-Japanese Friendship Hospital**, Heping Donglu, Chaoyang District. Tel: 6422-1122; and **Capital Hospital**, 53 Dongdanbei Dajie. Tel: 6529-5269, emergency: 6529-5284.

More expensive, but the best place for treatment of serious illness, is the private **Beijing United Family Health Centre**, 2 Jiangtai Lu (close to Lido Hotel). Tel: 6433-3960, Fax: 6433-3963. Staff speak excellent English.

You will generally be given Western medicine in the foreign sections of hospitals, and antibiotics are readily available. You have to specifically request traditional Chinese medicine treatment, whether herbs or acupuncture. Chinese hospitals are divided into those using Western medicine and those using traditional medicine though some use both.

For non-emergency treatment, there are a few other foreign clinics, including the **International Medical Clinic**, Rm 106, Regus Office Bldg, Lufthansa Centre. Tel: 6465-1561, Fax: 6465-1984; and the **Hong Kong International Medical Clinic**, 3rd floor, Swissotel, Hong Kong Macau Centre, Dongsishitiao. Tel: 6501-2288 ext 2346, Fax: 6500-4660. Many hotels have in-house doctors who are trained in both traditional Chinese and Western methods. The larger embassies have doctors who are willing to see patients in serious cases. They can also help arrange medical evacuation.

Some people take their own chopsticks when eating at streetside or other small restaurants, but these days most restaurants use disposable chopsticks, except for some of the upmarket places, where chopsticks should be properly cleaned.

Tipping/Gifts

It is useful to bring a small stock of items such as lighters, pens, calculators, penknives and the like to give to Chinese friends you may make. Other good gifts are cassettes, photo albums or typical souvenirs from your hometown. Foreign cigarettes, which are expensive in China, are also in demand.

Tips are not usually expected and are often refused, but waiters in large hotels and restaurants, as well as a few taxi drivers, do court tips. Before you tip, remember that the average wage is relatively low – less than 1,000 yuan a month.

Religious Services

Greater Beijing has more than 30 Christian churches with regular services on weekdays and Sundays. Catholic mass (including Sunday mass in English) is said in **Nantang Cathedral**, 141 Qianmen Dajie (right outside Xuanwumen underground station), Tel: 6602-5221, and **Beitang Cathedral**, 33 Xishiku Dajie, near Beihai Park, Tel: 6617-5098. Protestant services are held at **Gangwashi Church**, 57 Xisinan Dajie, Xicheng District, Tel: 6617-6181; and **Chongwen District Church**, Hougou Hutong, Chongwenmen, Tel: 6524-2193. Muslims can attend several mosques, including **Niujie Mosque** in Niujie Street, Southwest Beijing. Buddhists have countless places of choice among Beijing's restored temples.

Media

Newspapers and Magazines

Beijing has several Chinese daily papers, including the official party newspaper *Renmin Ribao* (*People's Daily*), *Guangming Daily*, which is mainly for intellectuals, as well as local *Beijing Daily* and *Beijing Evening Post*. For foreign visitors, *China Daily*, which is published daily except on Sundays, is the only nationally distributed English daily. As well as some propaganda, it includes daily listings of cultural events in Beijing, international news, and good sports coverage. Several foreign daily papers can be bought in Beijing (a day late) from the big hotels and the Friendship Store. These include the *South China Morning Post* and *Hong Kong Standard*, which have the best coverage of China, the *International Herald Tribune* and *Financial Times*. Magazines available include *Newsweek*, *Time*, *The Economist*, *Asiaweek*, and the German publications *Der Spiegel* and *Die Zeit*.

Beijing listing magazines *City Edition*, *Metro Weekly* and *Beijing Beat*, and the *China Daily* publication *Beijing*

When you're

bitten by the travel bug,

make sure you're protected.

Check into a British Airways Travel Clinic.

British Airways Travel Clinics provide travellers with:

- A complete vaccination service and essential travel health-care items
- Up-dated travel health information and advice

Call **01276 685040** for details of your nearest Travel Clinic.

BRITISH AIRWAYS
TRAVEL CLINICS

Insight Guides portray destinations in depth, providing the complete picture and the top photography

Insight Pocket Guides focus on the best choices for places to see and things to do and include large fold-out maps

Insight Compact Guides' portability makes them the perfect books to carry with you for on-the-spot reference

Three types of guide for all types of travel

INSIGHT GUIDES Different people need different kinds of information. Some want *background information* to help them prepare for the trip. Others seek *personal recommendations* from someone who knows the destination well. And others look for *compactly presented data* for on-the-spot reference. With three carefully designed series, Insight Guides offer readers the perfect choice. Insight Guides will turn your visit into an experience.

The world's largest collection of visual travel guides

Weekend all have useful weekly guides to entertainment, the arts and expat events. Xianzai is a weekly e-mail listing for Beijing, with a website at www.xianzai.com.

Television

Chinese TV shows many foreign films, usually dubbed into Chinese but sometimes left in the original language and subtitled. CCTV broadcasts a daily English news programme at 10.30pm. Many large hotels carry CNN and satellite broadcasts from Hong Kong-based Star TV. *China Daily* prints a daily television programme schedule.

Postal Services

You will find postal facilities in most hotels. Letters and postcards to and from China take around six days. Postage rates are still cheap but sending parcels by air is more expensive. Parcels must be packed and sealed at the post office to allow customs inspection. The main **International Post Office** for poste restante mail and for posting abroad is on the Second Ring Road, just north of Jianguomen intersection.

International express courier services, normally with free pick-up, are offered by: **DHL-Sinotrans**, Rm 11, China World Trade Centre. Tel: 6505-2173; **Federal Express**, Golden Land Building, Liangmaqiao Road. Tel: 6468-5566; **UPS**, Kelun Building, Tower 2, 12A Guanghua Road. Tel: 6593-2932.

Telecoms

Calls within Beijing from your hotel room are generally free. In most hotels you can telephone direct abroad, though in some you still need to ask the operator to call for you. In the leading hotels, you can use credit cards and international telephone cards but, be warned, that China's IDD rates are among the highest in the world.

Many hotels, shopping centres and other public places now have card phones, which allow one to see just how fast your money is disappearing on an IDD call. Cards (30-, 50- or 100-yuan) can usually be bought from nearby reception desks.

Other options are the International Post Office on the Second Ring Road

(open 8am–7pm). Besides long distance calls, it handles remittances, money orders and telegraphic money transfers. The Long-Distance Telephone Building at Fuxingmen Dajie (7am–midnight) handles long-distance, conference and per-booked calls. The Telephone Building on West Chang'an Avenue (24 hours) has a complete range of telephone and fax services.

Local calls can be made from the many streetside booths manned by attendants. They generally cost one jiao. These booths can also be used for long-distance calls but charges can be high.

Telex and fax: Almost all hotels have telex and fax services.

Telegrams: Telegrams are relatively expensive. Express dispatches, which take four hours, cost double.

E-mail: For e-mail and internet users, many hotels have facilities in their business centres. Some, such as the **Twenty-First Century Hotel**, have separate internet centres. Beijing also has several internet cafes, including the **Unicom Sparkice Internet Cafe** at the China World Trade Centre, Tel: 6505-2288 (www.sparkice.com.cn).

Tourist Offices

Tourist Information

You can obtain information about China from the various tour operators; it is best to approach the one specialising in China. While you can get tour brochures in travel agencies, you won't get much information about China. In the UK, you can approach China National Tourist Office, 4 Glentworth Street, London NW1, Tel: (0171) 6935-9427, Fax: (0171) 6487-5842 In the US try China National Tourist Office at Lincoln Building, 60 E 42nd Street, Suite 3126, New York NY 10165, Tel: (212) 6867-0271, Fax: (212) 6599-2892; or 333 West Broadway, Suite 201 Glendale CA 92104, Tel: (818) 6545-7504, Fax: (818) 6545-7506, though you may not always get satisfactory and detailed answers. More information can be obtained from the Society for Anglo-Chinese Understanding, 152 Camden High Street, London NW1, or from the National Committee for US-China Relations, 777 UN Plaza, New York, NY 10017.

Travel Agencies

China Civil International Tourist Corporation, Jingdu Hotel, Worker's Stadium, Beijing 100027. Tel: 6501-8869, Fax: 6501-8870, Tlx: 210673 CCT.

China Comfort Travel, Head Office, 57 Di'anmenxi Dajie, Beijing 100009. Tel: 6603-5423, 6601-6288, Fax: 6601-6336, Tlx: 222862 KHT.

China Everbright Travel, 9/F East Bldg, Beijing Hotel, 33 Chang'an Avenue East, Beijing 100004. Tel: 6513-7766/9022, Fax: 6512-0545, Tlx: 222285 CETI.

China Golden Bridge Travel, Head Office, 171A Tiananmen Street West, Beijing 100035. Tel: 6601-5933, Fax: 6603-2628, Tlx: 222367 CGBT.

China International Sports Travel, 4 Tiyuguan Road, Beijing 100061. Tel: 6701-7364, Fax: 6701-7370, Tlx: 222283 CIST.

China International Travel Service, Head Office, 103 Fuxingmen'nei Street, Beijing 100800. Tel: 6601-2055, Fax: 6512-2068, 6601-2013, Tlx: 22350 CITSH.

China M&R Special Tours, A7 Beisanhuan Road West, Beijing 100088. Tel: 6202-6611/4166, Fax: 6201-0865, 6201-0802, Tlx: 222880.

China Merchants International Travel, Tiandi Building, 14 Dongzhimennan Street, Beijing 100027. Tel: 6501-9198, 6506-2228, Fax: 6501-1308, Tlx: 210390 CMITC.

China Rail Express Travel, Blk 3, Multiple Service Bldg, Beifengwo Road, Beijing 100038. Tel: 6324-6645, Fax: 6326-1824, Tlx: 222224 YTSRB.

China Rainbow Travel, 5A Agricultural Exhibition Road North, Beijing 100026. Tel: 6501-7901, Fax: 6501-7901, Tlx: 211177 YAAH.

China Supreme Harmony Travel, Rm 944, Media Hotel, B11 Fuxing Road, Beijing 100859. Tel: 6801-4422/3944, Fax: 6801-6218.

China Swan International Tours, Rm 2018-2020 East Building, Beijing Hotel, Beijing 100004. Tel: 6513-7766/2020, Fax: 6513-8487, Tlx: 222517 CSIT.

China Travel Service, Head Office, 8 Dongjiaominxiang, Beijing 100005. Tel: 6512-9933, Fax: 6512-9008, Tlx: 22487 CTSHO.

China Women's Travel Service, Head Office, 103 Dongsinan Street, Beijing

100010. Tel: 6655-3307, 6513-6311, Fax: 6512-9021, Tlx: 21160 CWTS.

China Workers' Travel Service, Head Office, 1 Ritan Road, Beijing 100020. Tel: 6512-8657, 6512-8379, Fax: 6512-8680, Tlx: 211129 RTH.

China Youth Travel Service, Head Office, 23B Dongjiaominxiang, Beijing 100006. Tel: 6512-7770, Fax: 6512-0571, 6513-8691, Tlx: 20024 CYTS.

CITIC Travel, 19 Jianguomenwai Dajie, Beijing 100004. Tel: 6500-5920, Fax: 6512-7514, Tlx: 22967 CTI.

Mongolia Juulchin Travel (for tours to Mongolia), Rm 4015, Beijing International Hotel, 9 Jianguomen'nei Dajie, Beijing 100005. Tel: 6525-4339, 6512-6688, Fax: 6525-4339, Tlx: 79318 JULN MH.

CATEGORY A TRAVEL AGENCIES IN BEIJING

Beijing CITIC Guo'an International Travel Service, Rm 304, Guo'an Hotel, 1 Guangdongdian Beijie. Tel: 6501-0885, Fax: 6500-3263.

Beijing Divine Land Travel, 19 Xinyuan'nan Road, Dongzhimenwai. Tel: 6467-7619, 6466-6887, Fax: 6467-7307, Tlx: 210347 DLTS.

Beijing Youth Travel Service, Building 3, 96 Andingmen'nei Street. Tel: 6403-3521, Fax: 6403-3560, Tlx: 210098 BYTS.

China Air International Travel Service, 8 Dongsanhuan Beilu. Tel: 6508-2163, Fax: 6508-2163.

China International Travel Service (CITS), Beijing Tourism Building, 28 Jianguomenwai Dajie. Tel: 6515-8562, 6515-0515, Fax: 6515-8602, Tlx: 22047 CITSB.

China Peace International Tourism, 14 Chaoyangmen'nan Dajie. Tel: 6512-2504, Fax: 6512-5860, Tlx: 222354 CLTI.

China Travel Service, Beijing Tourism Bldg, 28 Jianguomenwai Dajie. Tel: 6515-8844, 6515-2802, Fax: 6515-8557, Tlx: 22032 BCTS.

Huayuan International Travel Service, Holiday Inn Crowne Plaza, 48 Wangfujing Dajie. Tel: 6513-3388 ext 1212/13, Fax: 6513-2513, Tlx: 222872 HYITS.

New Ark Travel, 3 Zhaoying Road. Tel: 6500-4385, Fax: 6500-4118, Tlx: 211229 BNATS.

North Star International, No. 10, Blk 3, Anhuili. Tel: 6491-0682, 6491-0683, Fax: 6491-0684, 6491-0691, Tlx: 210303 NSITC.

Sunshine Express, A101 Jingding Commercial Bldg, North Langjiayuan. Tel: 6586-8069, 6586-8075, Fax: 6586-8077, E-mail: sunpress@public.bta.net.cn.

Embassies and Consulates

Overseas Representations

UK, 24-51 Portland Place, London W1N 3AH. Tel: (visas) (0171) 6636-5637, (0171) 6636-5726.

USA, 2300 Connecticut Avenue, Washington, DC 20008. Tel: (202) 6328-2515.

Beijing

Australia, 21 Dongzhimenwai Dajie. Tel: 6532-2331, Tlx: 22263 AUSTM CN.

Austria, 5 Xiushui Nanjie, Jianguomenwai. Tel: 6532-2061, Tlx: 22258 OEBPK CN.

Canada, 19 Dongzhimenwai Dajie. Tel: 6532-3536, Tlx: 222445 CANAD CN.

France, 3 Dongsan Jie, Sanlitun. Tel: 6531-1331.

Germany, 5 Dongzhimenwai Dajie, Sanlitun. Tel: 6532-2161, Tlx: 22259 AAPEK CN. Visa and Trade Section, Dongsijie, Sanlitun. Tel: 6532-5556, Tlx: DDPEK CN.

India, 1 Ritan Donglu. Tel: 6532-1856.

Ireland, 3 Ritan Donglu. Tel: 6532-2691.

Israel, 405 China World Trade Centre. Tel: 6505-2970.

Italy, Dong'er Jie, Sanlitun. Tel: 6532-2131.

Japan, 7 Ritan Lu, Jianguomenwai. Tel: 6532-2361.

Malaysia, 13 Dongzhimenwai Dajie. Tel: 6532-2531.

Mongolia, 2 Xiushui Beijie, Jianguomenwai. Tel: 6532-1203.

Nepal, Xilujie, Sanlitun. Tel: 6532-1795.

Netherlands, 4 Linagmahe Nanlu. Tel: 6532-1131.

New Zealand, Dong'er Jie, Ritanlu. Tel: 6532-2731, Tlx: 22124 RATA CN.

Norway, 1 Dongyi Jie, Sanlitun. Tel: 6532-2261.

Pakistan, 1 Dongzhimenwai Dajie. Tel: 6532-2660/2021, Tlx: 22673 CMREP CN.

Philippines, 23 Xiushui Jie, Jianguomenwai. Tel: 6532-1872.

Poland, 1 Ritan Lu, Jianguomenwai. Tel: 6532-1235.

Russia, Dongzhimen Beizhongjie. Tel: 6532-2051, visas: 6532-1267, Tlx: 22247 SOVEN CN.

Singapore, 1 Xiushui Beijie, Jianguomenwai. Tel: 6532-3926.

South Africa, C801 Lufthansa Centre, 50 Liangmaqiao Lu. Tel: 6465-1941.

South Korea, 4/F China World Trade Centre. Tel: 6505-3171.

Spain, 9 Sanlitun Lu. Tel: 6532-1986.

Sweden, 3 Dongzhimenwai Dajie. Tel: 6532-3331.

Switzerland, 3 Dongwu Jie, Sanlitun. Tel: 6532-2736.

Thailand, 40 Guanghua Li. Tel: 6532-1903.

United Kingdom, 11 Guanghua Lu. Tel: 6532-1961, Fax: 6532-1939 ext 239, Tlx: 22191 PRDRM CN.

United States, 3 Xiushui Beijie, Jianguomenwai. Tel: 6532-3831, Fax: 6532-3178, Tlx: 22701 AMEMB CN.

Vietnam, 32 Guanghua Lu. Tel: 6532-1155.

Getting Around

Orientation

Beijing has two main ring roads (the Second and Third), plus a partially completed fourth ring road. Most of the other main roads run north-south or east-west, making it relatively easy to navigate through the city. Main streets are commonly divided in terms of *bei* (north), *nan* (south), *xi* (west) and *dong* (east); and in terms of *nei* (inside) and *wai* (outside the Second Ring Road). On the other hand, many housing estates are full of indistinguishable (unless one can read Chinese) high-rise buildings, making it easy to get lost, especially at night. The words *jie, dajie, lu* and *men*, which you'll find on all maps, mean street, avenue, road and gate respectively.

City Maps: Reasonably accurate maps in English are available from most hotels. Bookshops and kiosks mainly sell Chinese maps, which usually include bus and underground routes. The most useful maps are those which have street and building names in both Chinese characters and English. Similarly, Chinese name cards for hotels, restaurants, shops or other destinations are useful for showing taxi drivers or bus conductors.

Underground

The city's underground system is limited to just two lines but provides a useful link between Beijing Railway Station and some major tourist areas, like Tiananmen Square, Yonghegong and Kongmiao, and the Drum and Bell towers. All journeys cost 2 yuan, irrespective of distance. One route runs parallel to the Second Ring Road, more or less following the demolished city wall around the north of the city, and the other follows the western extension of Chang'an Avenue from Fuxingmen to the Capital Steelworks.

Work has started on extending this latter route eastwards to China World Trade Centre. A northern suburban light railway is also planned, to run from Xizhimen in the northwest to Dongzhimen in the northeast. Other routes are on the drawing board, such as a link from the Fragrant Hills to the airport, but it is likely to take the city many years to find the funds it needs to complete all these projects.

The first stretch of the Beijing underground was opened in 1971. It shares the advantages and disadvantages of most city underground routes all over the world. It may be missing the baroque splendours of the Moscow underground and the gleaming chrome of many Western systems, but it is efficient and quick, and outside the rush-hours, not quite as crowded as the buses. It is easy to find your way around, especially as signs and announcements are in both Chinese and English.

The system urgently needs extending and you will see nothing of the city except tired faces if you rely on the underground. Trains can also skip stations if they are behind schedule. This viewed as a normal inconvenience by other passengers, who simply get off and catch the next train going back.

Buses

The network of red, yellow and blue buses is excellent, as you can see on any good street map. Buses force their way through the streets from 5am to 11pm. Rides only cost a few jiao, depending on the distance. A few routes have been improved, with air-conditioned, double-decker buses. But Beijing's buses are generally slow and crowded, and the gaps between stops are sometimes long. They are extremely crowded during the rush-hours, and you will need to use your elbows, pushing and shoving like the locals do, just to get on the bus. Once on board, you will rarely get a seat and will probably be wedged securely against other passengers. Remember to secure money and other valuables before you board.

The conductors, mainly women, usually sit at tall metal desks close to the doors. The issue regular cries requesting passengers to pay their fares. Give the conductor a few jiao bills and rely on her help or on that of your fellow passengers, to whom you can perhaps show your destination on map or name card. You will find people who just struggled violently to get on the bus in front of you will now be extremely helpful if you speak to them.

According to the bus company, only about 20 percent of passengers use single tickets, while the rest use monthly season tickets. But these figures ignore the fact that at least one-third of passengers don't buy tickets at all, taking advantage of the chaotic tide to get a free ride. When one of the fare-dodgers is confronted by the conductor, you get an idea of the explosive powers of the Beijing dialect. Buses are worth taking on at least one short journey, for that alone.

Taxis

Taxi journeys are among the favourite conversation topics – and the source of much annoyance – for foreigners who have lived in Beijing for some time. For most Chinese, taxis are too expensive. Yet Beijing is now oversupplied with taxis, which are very cheap by Western standards (1.0, 1.2 or 1.6 yuan per kilometre) and convenient. It is true that their drivers often refuse to take passengers to destinations they consider inconvenient, and that they sometimes use the ignorance of foreign visitors as an extra source of income. Always make sure the meter is switched on before setting off.

There are several types of taxis available, from the yellow "breadbox" *miandi* (sadly for many, most were phased out in 1999), which has a minimum fare of 10 yuan for the first 10 kilometres, to larger vehicles charging 3 yuan per kilometre. Any waiting time is charged extra. At night, the basic fare and the cost per kilometre are higher. All taxis have a meter. If you don't know your way around, ask your hotel receptionist how much your journey should cost, and roughly how many kilometres it is.

Many drivers will try to quote a flat rate to your destination. Do not accept this as it will never be cheaper than the meter charge. The price per kilometre is indicated on a red sticker displayed in the taxi window, and they all have a minimum charge of 10 to 12 yuan. Once you've used up the minimum fare, the price jumps to 50 percent per kilometre, unless you're using the taxi for a return trip before 11pm. The backlash from foreigners and locals has prompted the city to list an address where you can lodge a complaint if a taxi driver refuses to take you where you want to go or uses a different route from the one you instructed.

Most taxi drivers speak little or no English. If travelling with other people, make sure the driver doesn't try to charge the meter price for each passenger. Always carry enough change, since taxi drivers are often unable, or unwilling, to change a 100-yuan bill.

Taxis can also be hired for longer trips, such as whole-day tours or visits to the Great Wall or Ming Tombs. If you plan to do this, make sure you agree the total fare and the precise itinerary in advance. Here are some of the city's major taxi firms:

Beijing Car and Limousine Service, Bldg 14, Shuyunuanli. Tel: 6848-3312. **Beijing Taxi Corp**, 26 Fuchengmenwai Dajie. Tel: 6831-2288 (24 hours). **Capital Taxi Co**, 10 Yuetan Beijie. Tel: 6852-7084.

Car Rental

You can hire a car with driver via most travel agencies and hotels, or from taxi companies; minibuses are also available. Try **Beijing Minibus Co**, Tel: 6721-1558; or **Beijing Transport Co Service for Foreigners**, Tel: 6502-2616. Alternatively, try negotiating a whole-day or half-day price direct with a driver. If you ask at the front desk of your hotel, most will arrange a car for the day for you, giving the driver clear instructions where you want to go and what time you want to return, do not pay in advance.

Minibuses

Minibuses ply the same routes as the larger buses but offer a faster, more comfortable service at several times the bus fare, though they are still cheap by Western standards (1 yuan to 10 yuan, depending on distance). They generally seat 16 people. For example, they run between the Summer Palace and the zoo, between the zoo and Qian gate (behind it is a main stop for minibuses), from the zoo to the Beijing railway station via Wangfujing shopping street, from Qianmen to the station, and from the Summer Palace to Xiangshan Park (and of course return the same way). They have official stops, but if they have space will usually stop wherever they are flagged down.

Tourist Buses

If travelling in a group, you will rarely need taxis, public transport or bicycles. Most tourist groups travel in comfortable, air-conditioned buses. There are bus companies in several places, for instance opposite Chongwenmen Hotel, which organise regular excursions to the most important sights. There is another such company at 2 Qianmen Lu (northeast of Qianmen Gate).

Private Transport

Bicycles

The vehicle most used by the inhabitants of Beijing is the bicycle; some 8.5 million steeds move day in, day out through the streets of Beijing. Foreign visitors can rent a bicycle in Beijing, and several hotels offer this service; there is a cycle hiring place across the street from the Friendship Store on Jianguomenwai. If you have the time and leisure, it is worth exploring Beijing by bicycle, because you will get a completely different view of life in the city. You can and must park the bicycles on one of the numerous parking places reserved for bicycles in Beijing, which are guarded. Parking costs a few fen. Beijing bicycles don't have lights (they do have rear reflec-

tors) or pumps. You can pump up the tires, or have repairs done almost anywhere in the city, as there are repair people on every street corner and in every alleyway.

Of course, this is still the best way to explore Beijing, especially the old city. You should remember the long distances though. As an alternative, exploration on foot can be quite comfortably combined with a trip by taxi, public transport or on a bicycle.

Bicycle Rental

Dongdan bicycle repair service, Dongdan Beidajie. Tel: 655-2752.
Xidan Zixingche Xiulibu, Xidan bicycle repair shop, Xuanwumennei Dajie. Tel: 633-2472.
Xidan Beidajie. Tel: 666-7928.
Shatan bicycle repair service, Shatan Beidajie. Tel: 644-2498.
Superior Speedy Bicycle Repair Service, 247 Dongsi Nan Dajie. Tel: 655-3612.

Domestic Travel

As China's capital, Beijing is the main traffic centre for the country. All traffic routes come together here: Beijing has international flight connections to all parts of the world, and internal flights and railways to other parts of the country. In addition, it connects with Europe through the Trans-Mongolian and Trans-Siberian railway.

By Air

China's national tourist offices and various travel agencies have the current flight schedules of the state airlines. The number of domestic airlines has mushroomed recently; there are 35 airlines now. All are, effectively, under the umbrella of the Civil Aviation Administration of China (CAAC). Accompanying this growth in the aviation business, there have been improvements in service. But because budgets have been tight – especially in the smaller airlines – and the business has grown so rapidly, there have also been accidents resulting from lax safety standards. Partly in an effort to improve safety, the government has sought to slow the growth of the aviation business.

You can buy tickets from travel agencies or airline booking offices; travel agencies may be more conven-

ient as, although they charge a fee, they are more likely to have English speaking staff. Or, try **China Civil Aviation Passenger and Cargo Sales Corp** (**CASA**), 9 Dongxing Jie, Chaoyangqu, Tel: 6466-5380. Since all flights are usually booked up, it is advisable to buy your tickets well beforehand.

By Rail

You can buy your rail ticket through a travel agency, or at the foreigners' booking office – accessed via the international waiting room on the ground floor – at Beijing railway station. Tickets for foreigners are up to 75 percent more expensive than for Chinese people and must be paid for in Foreign Exchange Certificates. Please remember that you have to expect a long wait. There are four different classes on Chinese trains: soft couchette (*ruanwo*), soft seats (*ruanzuo*) hard seats (*yingzuo*) and hard couchettes (*yingwo*). The soft class has comfortable compartments with four beds; in the hard class, three couchettes are usually stacked one above the other.

Beijing Huochezhan (Central Station)
Information: 655-4866, 6557-6851
Luggage: 6558-2372.
Customs Export: 655-1619.
Customs Import: 655-6242.
Lost & Found: 6558-2042.

Where to Stay

Hotels

In recent years there has been a veritable boom in hotel construction in Beijing. Today, many of the big palatial hotels, some with huge glass fronts and a rotating roof restaurant, contribute to the city's skyline. Some of these hotels of international standard are either joint ventures or are entirely owned by a foreign hotel chain. Top management positions are often occupied by foreigners (mostly from Hong Kong). These hotels, of course, charge international prices. There are more than 4,000 hotels in Beijing, but only a little over one hundred are open to forcigncrs. Since mostly luxury and top hotels have been built in recent years, there is a shortage of good hotels at medium and low prices.

The top hotels are situated like enclaves in the Chinese capital and give the impression of small, independent towns which have no connection with their surroundings. This is probably also because business people often live there for longer periods, and foreign firms have their offices there. All top hotels have telex and fax, post and banking facilities, restaurants, shopping arcades, swimming pools and other sports facilities, doctors, massage parlours, night clubs and discos. Some include supermarkets and special shops where one can buy foreign sausage, cheese etc. In the top hotels you can telephone directly abroad; in other hotels you have to go through the exchange, though this usually takes little time.

All hotels now have air conditioning. Rooms frequently have a television; some hotels stock their own videos. In general, all hotels have bathrooms and shower facilities, and the rooms have drinkable running water (hot and cold). The top hotels also have a small bar; they often provide a 24-hour service. There are taxis in front of most hotels, though sometimes one may have to wait. Remember that in the main tourist season (especially between July and October) many hotels are fully booked. At less popular times, hotels may offer discounted room rates and special packages. Some hotels will take reservations from abroad.

The following list gives a choice of hotels of different standards. We have chiefly listed star-rated hotels. Prices for 5-star hotels are around US$80–180 and upwards; for 4-star hotels US$60–100; and for 3-star US$35–70. Several of the hotels listed here without star ratings were recently built. Since hotel prices in China are constantly changing, and since the People's Republic also suffers from inflation and the prices in most hotels are adjusted to the state of the dollar, it is worth finding out in advance what the exact cost will be.

5-Star

Beijing Hotel, 33 East Chang'an Avenue. Tel: 6513-7766, Fax: 6513-7703, 6513-7307, Tlx: 222755 BHCRD. Opened in 1917, still considered one of the best hotels in Beijing. Centrally located, on the corner of the main shopping street Wanfujing, near Tiananmen Square.

China World Hotel, 1 Jianguomenwai Avenue. Tel: 6505-2266, Fax: 6505-3167/9, Tlx: 211206 CWH. Top of the line service and accommodation, well located for business.

Daioyutai Star Guest House, Sanlihe Road, Haidian District. Tel: 6859-1188, Fax: 6851-3362, Tlx: 22798 DYTSG. Formerly reserved for high-ranking Chinese functionaries and foreign state guests, this hotel is very expensive since it is still used to accommodate VIPs, and one can expect special security measures. Reportedly has rooms at US$20,000 per night.

Grand Hotel Beijing, 35 East Chang'an Avenue. Tel: 6513-7788, Fax: 6513-0049, Tlx: 210454 BHPTW. Hong Kong joint venture attached to the Beijing Hotel, just one block from Tiananmen Square.

Great Wall Sheraton Hotel, North Donghuan Road. Tel: 6500-5566, Fax: 6500-1919, Tlx: 22002. Immediately recognisable by its reflecting mirror facade, this pleasant, American joint venture hotel lies only five minutes by taxi from Jianguomenwai, where the embassies and many companies are located. Offers well-organised day tours of main Beijing sites.

Hilton Hotel Beijing, 1 Dongfanglu, Dongsanhuan Beilu. Tel: 6466-2288, Fax: 6465-3052. Handy to both downtown and the airport, it has, like all Hiltons, everything needed for comfort.

Holiday Inn Crown Plaza, 48 Wangfujing Dajie. Tel: 6513-3388, Fax: 6513-2513, Tlx: 210676 HICPB. Located in a busy shopping street in central Beijing, close to the Forbidden City.

Jing Guang New World Hotel, Hu Jia Lou, Chaoyang District. Tel: 6501-8888, Fax: 6501-3333, Tlx: 210489 BYJGC.

Kempinski Hotel (Beijing Lufthansa Centre), Xiao Liangmaqiao, Chaouyang District. Tel: 6465-3388, Fax: 6465-3366, Tlx: 21062 KIRV. Shiny new hotel with complete facilities. Attached to Youyi Shopping City.

Kun Lun Hotel, 2 Xinyuannan Road, Chaoyang District. Tel: 6500-3388, Fax: 6500-3228, Tlx: 210327 BJKLH. Looks like a replica of the Great Wall Sheraton directly opposite. Has a well-known and much-frequented disco.

New Century Hotel, 6 Shoutinanlu. Tel: 6849-2001, Fax: 6849-1103. Located on the west side of town, not far from the zoo.

New Otani Chang Fu Gong Hotel, 26 Jiangoumenwai St. Tel: 6512-5711, Fax: 6513-9811, Tlx: 210465 BCFGH. Japanese joint venture, well located for business in the eastern part of the city.

Palace Hotel, 8 Goldfish Lane, Wongfujing. Tel: 6512-8899, Fax: 6512-9050, Tlx: 2222696 PALBJ. The building combines, for the first time, functional construction with the traditional palace architecture of China. Centrally located for shopping and imperial sites on a lively downtown alleyway.

Shangri-La Hotel, 29 Zizhuyuan Road. Tel: 6841-2211, Fax: 6841-8006, Tlx: 222231 SHABJ. Located on the western edge of town, but shuttle buses are available.

Swissotel Beijing (Hong Kong Macau Centre), Dong Si Shi Tiao, Li Jiao Qiao. Tel: 6501-2288, Fax: 6501-2501, Tlx: 222527 HMC. New high rise hotel just west of the main business area.

4-Star

Beijing Continental Grand Hotel, 8 Bei Chen Dong Street, North Sihuan Road, Anding Men Wai. Tel: 6491-5588, Fax: 6491-0106, Tlx: 210564 ICH.

Beijing International Hotel, 9 Jianguomennei Avenue. Tel: 6512-6688, Fax: 6512-9961, Tlx: 211121 BIH. Near Beijing railway station, well situated for sight-seeing and business.

Beijing Mandarin Hotel, 21 Che Gong Zhuang Road. Tel: 6831-9988, Fax: 6832-2135, 6831-1818, Tlx: 221042 XDDH.

Beijing Movenpick Hotel, Xiaotianzhu Village, Shunyi County, PO Box 6913. Tel: 6456-5588, Fax: 6456-5678, Tlx: 222986.

Beijing-Toronto Hotel, 3 Jianguomenwai St. Tel: 6500-2266, Fax: 6500-2022, Tlx: 210012 JLH. One of the most popular hotels for foreign business people because of its convenient location and its excellent service. Cuisine is one of the best among the hotels in Beijing.

Capital Hotel, 3 Qian Men Dong Avenue. Tel: 6512-9988, Fax: 6512-0309, 6512-0323, Tlx: 222650 CHB.

Central Plaza Hotel, 18 Gaoliang Qiao Lu, Xizhimenwai. Tel: 6831-8888, Fax: 6831-9887, Tlx: 222988 ZYH.

China Resources Hotel, 35 Jianguo Road, Chaoyang District. Tel: 6501-2233, Fax: 6501-2311.

CVIK Hotel, 22 Jianguomenwai. Tel: 6512-3388, Fax: 6512-3542.

Fragrant Hills Hotel, Fragrant Hill Park, Haidian District. Tel: 6256-5544, Fax: 6256-6794, Tlx: 222202 FHH. Lying 20km (approximately 45 minutes by car) northwest of the city centre, this hotel is near the Summer Palace, and set in lovely surroundings.

Friendship Hotel, Grand Tower, 3 Baishiqiao Road. Tel: 6849-8888, Fax: 6849-8866, Tlx: 222362 GHBJ. Old style state-run hotel in the peaceful northwest corner of town, near the universities and the Summer Palace.

Garden View Garden Hotel, Nancaiyuen, Xuanwu District. Tel: 6326-8899, Fax: 6326-3139.

Gloria Plaza Hotel Beijing, 2 Jianguomenan Avenue. Tel: 6515-8855, Fax: 6515-8533.

Grace Hotel, 8 Jiangtai Road West. Tel: 6436-2288, Fax: 6436-1818, Tlx: 210599 BJGH.

Guang Dong Regency Hotel, 2 Wangfujing. Tel: 6513-6666, Fax: 6513-4248.

Holiday Inn Lido, Jiang Tai Road, Jichang Road. Tel: 6437-6688, Fax: 6437-6237, Tlx: 22618 LIDOH. Like an enclave in the capital, with shops, supermarket, offices and apartments for foreign businessmen. Lies about 20 minutes from the airport; a drive to the city centre takes 20–30 minutes.

Jianguo Hotel, 5 Jianguomenwai Avenue. Tel: 6500-2233, Fax: 6500-2871, 6501-0539, Tlx: 22439 JGHBJ. A favourite for longtime business travellers to the city. Experienced staff and a comfortable atmosphere, located in eastern Beijing.

Landmark Towers, 8 North Dongsanhuan Road. Tel: 6501-6688, Fax: 6501-3513.

New Century Hotel, 6 Southern Road, Capital Gym. Tel: 6849-2001, Fax: 6849-1107, Tlx: 222375 NCH.

Peace Hotel, 3 Jinyu Hutong, Wangfujing. Tel: 6512-8833, Fax: 6512-6863, Tlx: 222855 PHB. Unremarkable rooms, centrally located in a neighbourhood with lively nightlife.

SAS Royal Hotel, 6A East Beisanhuan Road. Tel: 6466-3388, Fax: 6465-3186.

Tianlun Dynasty Hotel, 50 Wangfujing Avenue. Tel: 6513-8888, Fax: 6513-7866, Tlx: 210574 TLX.

Traders Hotel, 1 Jianguomenwai Avenue. Tel: 6505-2277, Fax: 6505-0818, Tlx: 222981 THBBC. Good solid service, food and accommodation, well located for business in the east section of the city.

Xi Yuan Hotel, 1 Sanlihe Road. Tel: 6831-3388, Fax: 6831-4577, Tlx: 22834 XYH.

Yuyang Hotel, Xinyuan Xili, Chaoyang District. Tel: 6466-6610, Fax: 6408-1101, Tlx: 4666601.

Zhaolong Hotel, 2 Worker's Stadium Road North, Chaoyang District. Tel: 6500-2299, Fax: 6500-3319, Tlx: 210079 ZLH.

3-Star

Beijing Asia Hotel, 8 Xinzhong Xijie, Gongti, Beilu. Tel: 6500-7788, Fax: 6500-8091, Tlx: 210597 AHR.

Chains City Hotel, 4 Gongti East Road. Tel: 6500-7799, 6500-7668, Tlx: 210530 NWTBJ.

Chongwenmen Hotel, 2 Chongwenmenxi Dajie. Tel: 6512-2211. Fax: 6512-2222.

Dongfang Hotel, 11 Wanming Road, Xuanwu District. Tel: 6301-4466, Fax: 6304-4801, Tlx: 222385 DFH.

Dragon Spring Hotel, North Shuizha Road, Mentougou. Tel: 6984-3366, 6984-3362, Fax: 6984-4377, Tlx: 222292 DSHBJ. Beijing's first international hotel built in classic Chinese architectural style. Located about an hour's drive from Tiananmen Square, near the Western Mountains.

Exhibition Hall Hotel, 135 Xizhimenwai. Tel: 6831-6633, Fax: 6832-7450, Tlx: 222395.

Grand Hotel, 20 Yumin East Region, Deshengmenwai, West City District. Tel: 6201-0033, Fax: 6202-9893, Tlx: 222227 YSH.

Guangming Hotel, Liangmaqiao Road, Chaoyang District. Tel: 6467-8888, Fax: 6467-7682, Tlx: 210383 BGC.

Holiday Inn Downtown,98, Beilishilu, Xichengqu. Tel: 6832-2288, Fax: 6534-0696.

Huadu Hotel, 8 South Xin Yuan Road. Tel: 6500-1166, Fax: 6500-1615, Tlx: 22028 HUADU. Comparatively centrally located in the diplomatic quarter; used predominantly by travel companies.

Huilongguan Hotel, Huilongguan, Deshengmenwai. Tel: 6291-3931, Fax: 6291-3376, Tlx: 210083 BHLGH.

Jin Lang Hotel, 75 Chongnei Street, Dong Cheng District. Tel: 6513-2288, Fax: 6512-5839.

Media Hotel, 11B Fuxing Road. Tel: 6801-4422, Fax: 6801-6288, Tlx: 22836 MEDIA.

Minzu Hotel, 51 Fuxingmennei Street. Tel: 6601-4466, Fax: 6601-4849, Tlx: 22990 MZHTL. Lies about 3km to the west of Tiananmen Square; business people who are staying for longer periods in Beijing tend to stay here.

Novotel Beijing, 88 Deng Shi Kou, Dong Cheng. Tel: 6513-8822, Fax: 6513-9088. Clean, no frills, centrally located. A bargain for Beijing.

Olympic Hotel, 52 Baishiqiao Road, Haidian. Tel: 6831-6688, Fax: 6831-5985, Tlx: 222859 OLHTL.

Park Hotel, 36 Huang Yu Road South. Tel: 6721-2233, Fax: 6721-1615, Tlx: 22968.

Parkview Tian Tan Hotel, 1 Tiyuguan Road, Chongwen District. Tel: 6701-2277, Fax: 6701-6833.

Poly Plaza Hotel, 14 Dongzhimen Nandajie. Tel: 6500-1188, Fax: 6501-0288.

Qianmen Hotel, 175 Yongan Road. Tel: 6301-6688, Fax: 6301-3883, Tlx: 222382 QMHTL. Standard accommodation in old outer city, near the Temple of Heaven. Peking opera performances nightly.

Rainbow Hotel, 11 Xijinglu, Xuanwu District. Tel: 6301-2266, Fax: 6301-1366, Tlx: 222772 RBH.

Taiwan Hotel, 5 Jinyu Wutong, Wangfujing North. Tel: 6513-6688, Fax: 6513-6896, Tlx: 210543 TWHTL.

Twenty-First Century Hotel, 40 Liang Ma Qiao Lu. Tel: 6466-3311, Fax: 6466-4809, Tlx: 210615 SJYEC.

Xinqiao Hotel, 2 Dongjiaomin Xiang, Chongwenmen. Tel: 6513-3366, Fax: 6512-5126, Tlx: 222514 XQH. Elegant old-style hotel located in the former Legation Quarter, close to Tiananmen Square.

Yanjing Hotel, 19 Fuxingmenwai Avenue. Tel: 6832-6611/7, Fax: 6832-6130, Tlx: 20028 YJHTL.

Yan Shan Hotel, 138A Haidian Road. Tel: 6256-3388, Fax: 6256-8640, Tlx: 211203 YSHBJ.

Yanxiang Hotel, A2 Jiang Tai Road, Dongzhimenwai. Tel: 6437-6666, Fax: 6437-6231, Tlx: 210014 YXH. Located in the northeast of the city; mostly used by travel agencies.

2-Star

Beiwei Hotel, Xijing Lu 13, Xuanwu District. Tel: 6301-2266, Fax: 6301-1366. Located in the southern part of the city near the Temple of Heaven; one of the cheapest places for foreigners in Beijing.

Dadu Hotel, 21 Chegongzhuang St. Tel: 6831-9988, Fax: 6832-2136.

Guanghua Hotel, 38 Dongzhuan Zhonglu. One of the most popular hotels for individual travellers with limited money.

Guoan Hotel, Dongdaqiao, Chaoyang District. Tel: 6500-7700, Fax: 6500-4568.

Guotai Hotel, 12 Yonganxili, Jianguomenwai. Tel: 6501-3366, Fax: 6501-3926.

Ritan Guest House, 1 Ritan Park, Jianguomenwai. Tel: 6512-5588, Fax: 6512-8671. Intimate little hotel inside Ritan Park. Peaceful and reasonably priced for basic accomodation.

1-Star

Jingtai Hotel, 65 Yongwai Jingtaixi. Tel: 6721-2476. A favourite with backpackers. Cheap and clean, its location, with a market and lots of small restaurants around the corner, allows you to feel you're really in China.

Eating Out

Beijing Cuisine

There are two styles of cooking in Beijing cuisine, the imperial cuisine, which is based on Qing dynasty recipes, and the Tan cuisine from the Tan family, which is based on a synthesis of salty northern dishes with the rather sweeter dishes of the south. But apart from its local specialities, Beijing also offers delicacies from the different regions of China in its many restaurants.

While you are in Beijing, certain dishes must be tried. Peking Duck is the most famous culinary speciality of the Chinese capital. There are also steamed or fried dough rolls stuffed with mincemeat; a sour-sharp soup known as *suanlantang*; an endless choice of *jiaozi*, or meat-and-vegetable-filled pasta parcels; and Mongolian Hotpot. The most common speciality after Peking Duck, Mongolian Hotpot combines fondue-style cooking with unlimited meat and vegetables. It is usually eaten from a communal hotpot, though in some restaurants each diner gets his or her own pot.

The latest trend to sweep the capital is a return to the "Old Beijing" food and lively dining style common before 1949. Dressed in traditional clothes, waiters shout across the restaurant to announce those coming and going. Diners usually order a range of snacks and fried dishes, which are whisked through the restaurant and clattered down. At **Tangenyuan** restaurant you can take a rickshaw ride to the door of a courtyard-style building. Inside is a re-creation of old Beijing streets (though the TV sets look out of place). Acrobats, opera singers and magicians entertain, though sometimes the Peking opera is a little too loud.

To accompany your meals, all restaurants serve beer, mineral water, tea and soft drinks. The best known local beers (*pijiu*) are Qingdao, Yanjing, Beijing and Five-Star (Wu Xing). Most restaurants, even the smaller ones, now offer at least one imported beer, usually Beck's, Carlsberg, Budweiser or Heineken. Draft beer is still relatively new in China and sometimes not well-kept, so in smaller restaurants it is best to drink bottled beer.

Local grain liquors (*baijiu*) are all very strong, with a taste that, for most, takes some getting used to. The best known brands are Erguotou, Maotai, Wiliangye and Fenjiu. You can pay anything from five yuan to a couple of hundred yuan per bottle. Most foreigners say they can't tell the difference.

If you like rice wine, avoid traditional Chinese rice wine, as this rather like a very sweet, weak sherry. But it is cheap enough to try without having to finish the bottle.

A couple of Sino-French joint ventures produce reasonable grape wines, including Dragon Seal, which produces a cabernet sauvignon. Dynasty and Great Wall wines also sell well in the capital's upmarket restaurants. Imported wines are generally overpriced, although the range available is growing rapidly and prices are slowly falling.

Beijing is a city teeming with restaurants, from streetside noodle vendors and full meals served at sidewalk tables, to the famous Peking Duck served in five-star hotels. Sichuan restaurants stand between Korean and Xinjiang Muslim restaurants, surrounded by numerous four-table outlets where the toilet is "out the door, down the alleyway, and turn left." After shopping, eating is Beijing's most popular pastime.

In recent years, Korean, Japanese and Western restaurants have mushroomed, though the quality and authenticity of some is disappointing. McDonald's and Kentucky Fried Chicken have outlets all over the city. Gone are the days when Western food could be found only in the large hotels. As Western culture continues to infiltrate the city, so does its food. In the Sanlitun embassy area, and to a lesser extent the Jianguomenwai area, new Western-style bars and restaurants open almost weekly. These places, some of which are hard to distinguish, cater to expats and affluent young locals. But some Beijing entrepreneurs have opened bars with their own special characters. You can now find bars specializing in punk rock, sportscasts, film and other forms of entertainment.

Eating out is definitely better value in local spots. At most Chinese restaurants you can eat a full meal, with beer or soft drinks, for 25-50 yuan per person. At the more expensive restaurants, where you might have Peking Duck or better-quality Western food, one might expect to pay around 100 yuan per person.

The major hotels are expensive, charging Western prices for all food. The alternative is to hit the smaller, independent restaurants that are giving the hotel restaurants a run for their money.

The main meal times are 11am–2pm for lunch and 5–9pm for dinner, but Beijing also has several 24-hour restaurants. Listed below are some of the better known Beijing restaurants. They are not classified, but experience indicates you should get good food and service in them. Some restaurants, including most of those listed below and those in the large hotels, take telephone reservations. For Peking Duck, you normally have to make a reservation because of the preparation time involved. Outside the hotels, even some of the larger restaurants have no English menus, so be prepared to point.

Peking Duck Restaurants

Bianyifang Roast Duck Restaurant, 2A Chongwenmenwai Dajie. Tel: 6712-0505.

Jingxin Quanjude Roast Duck Restaurant, 2A Dongsanhuan Beilu. Tel: 6466-0895.

Quanjude Roast Duck Restaurant, 32 Qianmen Dajie. Tel: 6511-2418.

Old Beijing Cuisine

Jinghua Shiyuan, 8A Longtan Xilu. Tel: 6711-5331. Look for a giant copper teapot, 200 yards south of the northwest gate to Longtan Park. Set around a large courtyard perfect for summer dining. English menu.

Old Beijing Noodle King, Chongwenmen 6705-6705. Handy for the Temple of Heaven. Look for the rickshaws outside.

Tangenyuan, East Gate, Ditan (Temple of the Earth) Park. Tel: 6428-3358. Easily combined with trips to the park, Lama Temple or Confucius Temple, this is the ideal place for a lively group dinner. Reservation essential.

Yiwanju Old Beijing Noodles, Fangzhuang branch, 6 Pufang Lu. Tel: 6766-6667. Southeast of the Temple of Heaven.

Yiwanju Old Beijing Noodles, Yayuncun (Asian Games Village) branch, Building 6, Anhuili District 4. Tel: 6765-4321 Both branches of Yiwanju have talking mynah birds.

Mongolian Hotpot

Donglaishun, 198 Wangfujing Dajie. Tel: 6525-3562. Also serves Peking duck.

Hongbinlou, 82 Chang'an Avenue (near the main post office). Tel: 6601-4832.

Nengrenju, 5 Taipingqiao, Baitasi. Tel: 6601-2560.

Minzu Wenhua Gong (Minorities' Cultural Palace), Fuxingmen Dajie, next to Minzu Hotel. Tel: 6666-0544.

Other Restaurants

Afanti, 2 Houguaibang Hutong, Chaoyangmen Nei Dajie. Tel: 6525-1071. This lively Xinjiang Muslim restaurant has belly dancers and other shows. Afanti encourages you to join him on the tables. The roast mutton and nans are good, too. Reservation advised.

Beijing Sucai Fanguan, 74 Xuanwumen Dajie, south of the Xidan crossing. Tel: 6605-6130. Vegetarian cuisine.

Fangshan, inside Beihai Park. Tel: 6401-1889. Idyllic setting, popular imperial cuisine; reservations essential.

Fengzeyuan, 11 Beili. Tel: 6721-1332. Shandong cuisine in one of the city's most praised restaurants.

Gongdelin, 158 Qianmen Nan Dajie. Tel: 6702-0867. Vegetarian, specialising in mock meat dishes.

Jinyang, 241 Zhushikou Xidajie. Tel: 6303-1669.

Kangle, 259 Andingmen Nei Dajie. Tel: 6404-2223. Fujian and Yunnan cuisine.

Sichuan Restaurant, 51 Xirongxian Hutong. Tel: 6603-3291.

Tingliguan (Pavilion for Listening to the Orioles Singing), inside the Summer Palace. Tel: 6258-1608. Imperial cuisine in imperial setting.

Attractions

Culture

Museums

Beijing has a wealth of museums and permanent exhibitions. There are often smaller exhibitions in various temples. The most important museums and galleries are:

Ancient Observatory, 2 Dongbiaobei Hutong, Jiangguomenwai Dajie. Tel: 6524-2202.

Beijing Lu Xun Museum, Fuchengmennei Dajie. Tel: 6602-1604.

China National Art Gallery, 1 Wusi Dajie, Chaoyangmennei. Tel: 6401-2252.

Military Museum, 9 Fuxingmenwai Dajie. Tel: 6851-4441.

Museum of Chinese History, Tiananmen Square, east side. Tel: 6512-8321.

Museum of the Chinese Revolution, Tiananmen Square, east side. Tel: 6526-3355.

Museum of Natural History, 126 Tianqiao Nandajie. Tel: 6702-4431.

National Agricultural Exhibition Centre, 16 Dongsanhuan Beilu, Sanlitun. Tel: 6501-8877.

Palace Museum, inside the Imperial Palace. Tel: 6513-2255.

Xu Beihong Memorial Hall (Xu Beihong Jinianguan), 53 Xinjiekou Beidajie. Tel: 6225-2265.

Theatre

If you are lucky, you may be able to see one of the foreign artists or conductors on tour in Beijing – they come in increasing numbers. But most visitors will surely want to see a typical Chinese production, and one possibility is Peking opera. Some of the best-known opera venues are:

Chang'an Theatre, Jianguomen Nei Dajie (next to the International Hotel). Tel: 6512-1856.

Guanghe Theatre, 46 Qianmenroushi Jie, Qianmen Dajie. Tel: 6702-8216.

Lao She Teahouse, 3rd Floor, 3 Qianmenxi Dajie. Tel: 6303-6830.

Liyuan Theatre, Qianmen Hotel, 175 Yongan Lu. Tel: 6301-6688 ext 8860.

Some of the traditional Peking opera theatres have adapted to modern trends and stage pop concerts, performances of *Xiangsheng* (crosstake, or comic dialogues) or similar pieces. Young people in particular no longer like the often complex plays and style of Peking opera, and they prefer disco, karaoke or TV.

Beijing has many cinemas, costing 10 to 20 yuan. Most cinemas have morning, matinee and evening showings. The latter usually start at 6.30pm. Cinemas showing foreign films are especially popular (*Titanic* is as well known in China as anywhere), but more expensive.

Theatre attract larger audiences than Peking opera venues. Local plays, including many avant garde pieces, as well as foreign plays are performed. The main theatres are:

Capital Theatre, 22 Wangfujing Dajie. Tel: 6655-0978.

Beijing Drama Theatre, 11 Hufanglu. Tel: 6303-8149.
Beijing Exhibition Centre Theatre, Xizhimenwai Dajie. Tel: 6835-1383.

Dance and song ensembles and other performances are also shown in the following places:

Chaoyang Theatre (acrobatics), 36 Dongsanhuan Beilu, Hujialou. Tel: 6507-2421.
China Puppet Theatre, 1 Anhuaxili. Tel: 6424-3698.
Beijing Concert Hall, 1 Beixinhua Jie. Tel: 6605-5812. Beijing's main venue for Chinese and Western classical music concerts.
Universal Theatre (acrobatics), Dongsishi Qiao. Tel: 6502-3984.

Concerts often also take place in the sports halls of the Chinese capital, for instance, at Capital Gymnasium near the zoo, not far from Xiyuan Hotel.

Cinema

Movies popular with locals include Hong Kong comedies and action flicks. Some Chinese-made films are more easily seen abroad. Western films are shown, but these may be dubbed into Chinese. You can find the current cinema programme and theatre performances in *China Daily*, though the weekly listings magazines *City Edition*, *Metro Weekly* and *Beijing Beat* provide more detailed and reliable information. For those who read Chinese, *Beijing Daily* and *Beijing Evening Post* are recommended. You can buy tickets at each venue; it is often difficult to book in advance by telephone. If you are travelling with a group or on a package tour, you can ask your tour guide.

In addition, each Sunday at 2.30pm and Tuesday at 7.30pm, the Holiday Inn Crowne Plaza (48 Wangfujing Dajie. Tel: 6513-3388) shows English films. Also on Tuesday evenings, you can catch a French film, usually with English subtitles, at the French Embassy (Sanlitun Office Bldg 1-12. Tel: 6532-1422). Finally, every second Friday, at the Sino-Japanese Youth Exchange Centre, a film, usually Chinese with English subtitles, is shown by Cherry Lane Movies. Tel: 6522-4046.

Many Chinese people still make a big event of taking their family to one of the parks in Beijing on their day off. In summer, one can go boating in the parks; in winter, ice skating. The Summer Palace, Temple of Heaven Park, Beihai Park and Purple Bamboo Park (Zizhuyuan) are all popular and well frequented. In the summer months, it is worth visiting the parks early to see people practice taijiquan, wushu, Peking opera, kite flying and other hobbies. There is also Beijing version of Disneyland in Shijingshan, and a bungee-jumping centre in the picturesque valley near Shidu, southwest of the city.

Group Travel

The best way of getting to know Beijing and all its sights without having to worry about organisation is to travel in a group. Group trips to Beijing and other parts of China are organised by many travel agents and China's national tourist offices.

Nightlife

Many people will tell you that Beijing is not China. The quality and quantity of entertainment available, for both locals and foreigners, supports that claim. Since the early 1990s, as the expat community has grown, so have the facilities to serve it. Once you could only find bands, dancing, foreign beer and mixed drinks in the large hotels, but now they are readily available in any area frequented by expats or affluent locals.

Pubs, Bars and Discos

As mentioned earlier, the Sanlitun and Jianguomenwai embassy districts are magnets for Western style bars and restaurants. In some, you can find live rock music or jazz; in others, DJs spin dance tunes.

Because new places appear so quickly, it is sometimes best to aim for one of the two main bar areas, Sanlitun and Jianguomenwai, rather than a specific place. To the northeast of Sanlitun, one of the trendiest bars in Beijing, opened in 1998, is **Half Dream**, 5 Xingbu Yicun Xili (near the Leyou Hotel). Tel: 6415-8083. In contrast, **Mexican Wave** (Dongdaqiao Lu,

Tel: 6506-3961) is an old favourite with expats. A few other places worth visiting are:
Arcadia, Building 3, Jindu Apartments, Fangchengyuan. Tel: 6764-8271.
CD Cafe, Dongsanhuan Lu. Tel: 6501-6655 ext 5127.
Goose and Duck, Ritandongyi Jie. Tel: 6509-3777.
Henry J Bean's, China World Trade Centre. Tel: 6505-2266.
Minder Cafe, Dongdaqiao Xiejie. Tel: 6599-6066.
Mushroom Bar, Xiushui Dinglu. Tel: 6592-1446.
Sanwei Bookstore, 60 Fuxingmenwai Dajie. Tel: 6601-3204.
Sentiment Bar, Sanlitun Lu. Tel: 6415-3691.
Schller's, Liangmaqiao Lu. Tel: 6461-9276.

Two of the best known discos, normally open until 4am, are:
Hotspot, Sanhuan Donglu. Tel: 6531-2277.
Nightman, 2 Xibahe Nanli. Tel: 6466-2562.

Shopping

Below are the main shopping centres and some important shops and markets. But first some tips: examine everything you buy carefully, especially at streetside stalls; goods are often defective, and there is no right to exchange goods in China; bargain hard at all markets and private shops. If you like something buy it, otherwise you may later regret a lost opportunity because what you see today in one shop will probably be gone tomorrow. And don't miss a shopping spree in one of the big shopping centres; at the same time, you will get a chance to see the old part of Beijing. Especially in the free markets, it is advisable to compare prices and watch how much the Chinese pay. All too often, free market traders will happily fleece unwary customers.

WANGFUJING STREET

The former Morrison Street is one of the biggest shopping street in Beijing. It runs north from Chang'an Avenue at the Beijing Hotel. Here you will find Xinhua bookshop (No. 214), a fur and leather shop (Zhongguo Pihua Fuzhuangdian, No. 142), the New China children's shop (No. 172), the Baihuo department store (No. 255), and, diagonally opposite, Dongfeng Market. At the northwest corner, close to a crossroad, is the Foreign Languages Bookstore, a good place to buy English books about China. Other interesting shops are: Capital Medical Shop, a musical instruments shop (on corner with Dong'an Street), and an art shop with scroll paintings and stone rubbings (No. 265). At No. 289, the Beijing Huadian, a gallery, sells paintings by modern artists in both contemporary and traditional styles.

XIDAN

Xidan Street is an old commercial quarter. It is to the east of Minzu Fandian (Minzu Hotel), and can be reached by taxi in about five minutes from Beijing Hotel in a westerly direction along Chang'an Boulevard (or from there with bus No. 1). Xidan Dajie forks off from that boulevard in a northerly direction at the Xidan crossing; in addition to department stores (the largest is Xidan Baihuo Shanchang) and restaurants, there is also a good shoe shop (No. 178), and a few houses further on one can buy ballet shoes. In No. 160 is the Xidan chopstick shop (Xidan Kuaizi Shangdian) which also sells porcelain.

QIANMEN STREET

Qianmen Street runs south direct from Qianmen Gate, the southerly end of Tiananmen Square. Qianmen Street and the roads going off it are a century old commercial quarter; during the imperial period it was the Chinese quarter. A walk around this quarter is also an exploration of the old part of Beijing. In Qianmen Street you will find the Beijing silk shop (Beijing Sichou Shangdian, No. 5), the music shop (Xinsheng Yueqidian No. 18), which specialises in traditional musical instruments, and the Hall of Eternal Youth (Chang Chun Tang, No. 28), a traditional Chinese chemist; there is also the Hunan pottery shop (Hunan Taoci Shangdian, No. 99) and the porcelain shop (Jingdezhen Yishu Cipi Fuwubu, No. 119).

Qianmen Street also boasts of having one of the best known Peking duck restaurants. It is diagonally across from a bicycle parking space from which the Dazhalan (Great Gate Street) forks off in a westerly direction. (It is the third side street to the right when coming from Qianmen Gate and walking in a southerly direction.)

DAZHALAN STREET

Dazhalan Street, which is only 300-metres long, is one of the biggest shopping streets in Beijing; it has one of the most important silk shops called Ruifengxian, an old shop with a marble gate and an unusual interior as well as a fountain surrounded by balustrades. There is also the best known pharmacist for traditional Chinese medicine, the Tongrentan pharmacy. It also has a big theatre and a cinema. This street and the streets around it have a long history as an entertainment centre; five of the biggest Beijing opera houses used to be here. If one walks from Dazhalan Street southwestwards towards Hufangqiao, one finds the Qianmen Hotel only a few houses down (just over a mile from Dazhalan Street). Towards the west through the hutong, the alleys of Beijing's old quarter, one can get to Liulichang Street, which is full of antique shops, in ten minutes.

You may have problems going by taxi into Qianmen Street as far as the crossing of Dazhalan Street, because taxis are not permitted to stop here. It is best to stop at Qianmen Gate and walk, or take a taxi to Liulichang and walk from there to Dazhalan Street and Qianmen Street. Qianmen Hotel is not far from there. If you are taking the underground, get off at Qianmen stop.

Finally, you can find the theatre shop which used to be on Qianmen Street near Xinqiao Hotel and Chongwenmen Hotel. Here you can get both antiques and old theatre costumes and relics.

LIULICHANG

This is known as antique street because one can buy good antiques here, paintings and woodblock print reproductions, utensils for traditional Chinese painting, and old (and new) books. The street has been completely renovated in recent years and has a new splendour with even more shops than before. Even if one doesn't necessarily want to buy something, the concentration of so many shops in one street makes it fun to wander around and window shop. Liulichang Street runs in a westerly and easterly direction from Nanxinhua Jie; the most famous shop is the Rongbaozhai Studio in the eastern part of the street, which is famous for its paintings, pictures and its brilliant woodblock prints; you can find expensive as well as many cheap souvenirs and gifts in the shops in Liulichang Street, including nice stone rubbings. Unfortunately, there are very few real antiques and many of the pictures on sale are surely not the best in China.

If you are seeking antiques, there are three other markets you won't want to miss. The Chaowai Market, at the north end of Ritan Lu, has two large warehouses that are well worth perusing: one warehouse is devoted to furniture, the other to small antiquities. Prices are generally good, and as with all the antique markets, bargaining is the norm.

Another is Hongqiao market, housed in a department-style building at the northeast corner of Tiantan Park. Here you will not only find antiques, but a pearl market and furs. Once again, bargaining is expected. The third market worth visiting is directly across the street from the front door of the Kempinski Hotel. There are about 40 stalls, set in short laneways, who make the collective claim that everything there is genuine.

FRIENDSHIP STORE (YOUYI SHANGDIAN)

A visit to the Friendship Store is definitely one of the most comfortable ways of shopping in Beijing. It is located in Jianguomen Way, the continuation of Chang'an Boulevard in an easterly direction, next to the International Club and the CITIC skyscraper. Its opening hours are 9am–9pm. You can buy practically anything in the Friendship Store: from dried mushrooms to cloisonne; there is a big carpet department and a stock of good silk. The Friendship Store will arrange to send any goods abroad and deal with the necessary customs formalities. It also has a dressmaking department, a watch repair shop and a dry cleaners. the basement is a supermarket, which is mostly used by the foreigners from the nearby diplomatic quarter.

JOINT VENTURE SHOPPING CENTRES

Directly across from the Friendship Store is Yaohan, a Japanese department store full of luxury imports.

The Youyi Shopping City, at the Beijing Lufthansa Centre, takes in a broader price range. Its five floors cover everything from ginseng to roller blades. There are plenty of restaurants and snack bars, and in the basement is a Western-style grocery.

FREE MARKETS

Once the shops and offices have closed, the housewives and mothers of Beijing hurry to the free markets to find eggs or a cabbage for supper. In the free markets, vegetables are usually a few jiao per jin (half a kilogram or about one pound) less expensive than in the state shops, you rarely have to queue, and the goods are fresh. Sometimes, you can even bargain. Be aware though, that as a foreigner you might be a target for higher prices, especially if you don't speak Chinese. Watch what others pay for the goods you desire.

Since the reforms in agriculture and trade, these markets have been an indispensable source of goods for the local people, supplementing those offered by the "people's co-operatives" and the scarce, rationed, staple foodstuffs such as rice, flour, oil, eggs, pork and sugar. Now these markets can now be found in virtually every neighbourhood

One such market that has especially flourished is the **Hongqiao-shichang**. Located across the street from the east gate of the Temple of Heaven, in a building that looks more suited to housing a department store than a market, it has grown so large it now contains almost any type of fresh food, as well as household items, toys, pearls, gold, and antiques.

The basement floor is devoted to the food stalls. Here, grain and dried fruit are sold beside fresh fruits and vegetables. The smells of fresh coriander, ginger and leeks, aniseed and fennel seed, dried prawns and pepper, the basic ingredients of Chinese cuisine, mingle with the fascinating sights of dragons' eyes (dried fruit, similar to lychees), trees' ears (a type of fungus), melon seeds and steaming sweet potatoes to form a confusing and intense assault upon the senses.

Walk a few steps down to the next section and you'll find a huge seafood market, where barrels of live fish, turtle, and shrimp stand beside cages of crabs, frogs and snakes. The following area contains the fresh meats. Occasionally, one might even see dog on a table beside goats' heads and sides of beef and pork.

Once purchase decisions are made, prices are added on an abacus, the age-old calculator of the Chinese, consisting of a wooden frame with vertical rods and six beads on each rod. The traders push the beads up and down calculating bill totals faster than the average person can using a calculator.

But Hongqiao market is no longer just for food. On the first floor are stalls with bird cages, earthenware tubs for pot plants, bamboo bicycle seats for children, red plastic bowls and other household items. Watches, radios, walkmans and beepers may all be found here. At the east end there's an entire section devoted to toys. On the second floor you'll find jeans, leather clothing, fur coats, and furniture, all being sold by individual stalls.

But the third floor is the one floor you truly don't want to miss. Here you'll find strings of pearls by the hundreds, at a fraction of their cost in the western world. There are also about 50 small stalls dealing in antiques. Consisting mostly of small items, you can find everything from small brass containers, turned an "ancient" green that belies their youth, to ceramic buddhas and wooden masks. If you shop carefully, you can find some great deals. Take your time and look around before you buy; sometimes the price of an item in one stall can be many times its price in another.

The markets of Beijing sell services as well as goods. Children who are not in line for perms or other extravagances can be seen sitting in the open air under hairdressers' capes, having their hair professionally cut. Next to them will be people offering you a stool for a quick massage. In neighbouring stalls, members of the tailor's trade are offering their skills. You'll also find rows of elderly men perched atop tiny stools before ancient sewing machines ready to repair your shoes. Beside them, of course, will be several shoe shine men waiting to give your shoes that final touch before you leave.

In the last few years, as reforms have take place and state companies no longer profitable have closed, more and more independent service people have appeared. No longer just in the markets they can be found on most street corners, and in any park. One of the best places in the city to see some of them work is next to the antique market across from the north gate of Beihai Park.

One market which still offers something quite unique is the **Guanyuan** market. Specializing in wildlife, the curious visitor is attracted by the little colourful birds in the long rows of cages, either piled on top of each other or hanging from poles and tree branches. On the western side of the market there are brilliantly coloured ornamental fish, swimming in huge glass containers or in small enamel bowls.

But perhaps the most interesting of the Beijing markets is the **bird market**, in the southeast of the city. Hundreds of people come to buy or look, particularly on Sunday mornings. The traders set up their stalls in the open air, along the banks of a former lake in Longtan Park. Orioles, thrushes and budgerigars twitter and hop about in a cheerful, mixed crowd, competing for the favour of the passers-by with their songs. The "bird with a hundred souls", as the Chinese call Mongolian larks, is among the most popular and expensive of birds. Some birds may be frightened if someone wearing bright red appears, and the traders react angrily too; frightened birds don't sing and can't be sold, or only for a meagre profit. Next to its appearance, a bird's singing is what makes it desirable, and therefore, expensive.

Bamboo cages are available from 10 yuan upwards. However, if you want a special, skilfully carved antique cage with fancy brass fastenings, you'll have to dig much deeper into your pocket or wallet.

In late summer, the bird market is the place where the cricket fanciers meet. The insects are pitted against each other in an annual fighting competition, and anyone who has neither the time, nor the inclination, to hunt these chirping insects by night in the fields outside the city can buy crickets in the market.

The peasant market is another big market, near Beitaipingzhuang on the Third Ring Road, five minutes by car from the Friendship Hotel. Silk Alley, or Xiushijie, near the diplomatic area, has all types of silk. Just a few blocks away on the west side is the growing Ritan Park clothing market, with cotton clothes, wool sweaters and down coats. A few blocks north of Ritan Park, up an alley, is the Chaoyang Antique Market.

BOOKSTORES

The state owned Xinhua bookshop has over 100 branches in Beijing. The biggest bookshop for Chinese books is the Xinhua Shudian in Wangfujing Dajie. Another shop for foreign books is the Foreign Languages Bookstore, on Wangfujing Dajie and north of Baihuo Dalou, in a northerly direction from the Beijing Hotel on the left side. It stocks mostly foreign books published in China, language teaching books and music tapes. Unfortunately you can't order books in Chinese bookstores.

If you are looking for English language books, the lobbies of most hotels will have a selection of the latest thrillers and pulp fiction. There are also several foreign language book stores in town. Two are on the west side of Wangfujing Street, north of the Beijing Hotel, and another is on the west side of Xidan Street, just north of Fuxingmennei Dajie (Chang'an Boulevard). These not only have a good selection of classics, but also have numerous books and tapes for learning Chinese. Both the hotels and the foreign language bookstore will have a good selection of photo books on China.

Beijing offers the foreign visitor a rich choice for shopping, ranging from simple shops in the streets, via free markets, big stores in the main shopping streets to the luxurious shopping arcades in the top hotels. Popular and cheap gifts from Beijing include silk, jade jewellery, cloisonne goods, lacquer carvings, filigree and inlay work, jewellery, carpets, watércolour woodblock prints. Prices vary considerably, and good items will cost a lot of money in Beijing today. Although many utensils for daily use seem cheap to us (and are often also of poor quality), artifacts and antiques often fetch surprisingly high prices.

Objects dating from before 1840 are not permitted for export. Most antiques date from the last period of the imperial dynasty or from the time of the republic. In recent years, souvenirs have tended to become tourist oriented, and it has become rarer to find really beautiful pieces such as good woodblock prints of traditional pictures. All hotels have shops, and the top hotels often have elegant shopping arcades with exquisite articles. But the most interesting and charming, and by far the most inexpensive way, is still wandering around one of the main shopping areas in the capital, along Wangfujing Street or Qianmen Street. Here you will find a typical Chinese shopping atmosphere and you'll get a vivid impression of the large number of people in China. Often the people you see in the shopping centres are not necessarily Beijing residents but visitors from other regions, business people, relatives on a visit, or people on holiday. Shops generally open from 9am–8pm every day. Prices in the shop are fixed by the government, and as a rule you can't bargain; this is different in the free markets, where prices depend on supply and demand, and bargaining is definitely expected.

Sports and Leisure

The Chinese people are generally very keen on sport, and there are regular competitions and tournaments in the various halls and stadiums in the Chinese capital. You can find notices about these in the *China Daily*. Shadow boxing or *taiji* is often practiced in the parks in the morning. Chinese television shows, local and international sporting events, and names such as Beckenbauer or Gullit are almost as well known in China as Marx and Engels. Many top hotels have sports facilities (and of course a swimming pool). A permit is necessary to visit the swimming pool in the **International Club**, next to the Friendship Store, Tel: 6532-2046. This can be obtained at the City Hospital after a checkup. The International Club also has open-air tennis courts. The courts (Tel: 6532-2046) are open from 9am–7pm (with a break between noon and 3pm). Rackets and balls must be brought along. There are also indoor courts. Badminton, table tennis and bowling facilities are also available at the International Club. **Dongdan Sports Centre** (Dongdan Dajie, Tel: 6512-9377, 6522-6210) has a swimming pool, tennis courts, and other facilities right in the centre of the city. China World Hotel also has good indoor tennis courts from 6am to 10pm, Tel: 6505-2266, ext. 33.

You can take photos of basically everything in Beijing, though some military installations are prohibited. In some places a fee has to be paid for taking photographs, or it is prohibited in order to encourage people to buy the expensive slides on offer. In many historic places (palaces and temples), taking photos inside buildings is not permitted. It would be polite to ask permission if one is taking photos of people. You can buy foreign film materials in Beijing – in most medium and top class hotels for instance – without difficulty. Photo transparencies by Kodak and Fuji are usually available. Some Beijing hotels will develop transparencies and photos. You should take flashes and good batteries in sufficient quantities (Chinese batteries are not very good). If something is wrong with your camera, ask your hotel for a photography shop (there are some in Wangfujing). Authorisation is needed for 16mm cameras. This does not apply to video and 8mm films.

Language

In Beijing, people obviously speak Chinese; but in most hotels you will always find someone who can speak (more or less) English; in the top and first-class hotels good English is usually spoken. You can generally also manage in English in the streets, because Chinese people seem to be learning English. However, taxi drivers often speak poor or no English at all.

Language and Writing

For 93 percent of the population in the People's Republic of China, Chinese is their mother tongue. Many national minorities – such as the Tibetans and Mongolians – have their own script and language. Today, modern Chinese (*putonghua*, meaning "common language" is also called Mandarin) is taught throughout the country. It is based on the northern Chinese dialect – one of eight dialects in China. In Beijing, a slightly different dialect is spoken, the Beijing dialect. Although the pronunciation in Beijing is probably very close to standard Chinese, it can be recognised by specific characteristics. The dialect is particularly recognisable because an "er" sound is added to many syllables, and is pro-

nounced with a tilted-back tongue. There is considerable difference in the pronunciation of the different dialects; though the written symbols are the same everywhere. In Chinese writing, which consists of pictures and symbols, each symbol represents a word or a meaning. Some symbols still used today go back more than 3,000 years. There are strict rules in the method of writing and it is not flexible. While in the past the script was written from the top down and from the right to the left, today it is mostly written from left to right. Some 6,000 symbols are in regular use; 3,000 symbols are sufficient for reading a daily newspaper. Nowadays, simplified symbols (there have been several reforms of writing since 1949) are being used, but in Hongkong and Taiwan the old symbols are still common.

Since 1958, Hanyu Pinyin has been used as a script in the People's Republic of China, i.e. the symbols represent syllables on the basis of the Latin alphabet. This system has become internationally accepted, so that "Peking" is today written as Beijing (pronounced Bayjing), Canton is Guangzhou, Mao Tsetung is now written as Mao Zedong. At first this seems confusing to us, but it is a good, practical system which is increasingly being used in China. You will for instance find many shop names written in Pinyin above the entrance, the names at railway stations are in Pinyin, and it is useful to learn the basic rules of the Pinyin system.

Pronunciation

The pronunciation of the consonants is similar to those in English. b, p, d, t, g, k are all voiceless. p, t, k are aspirated, b, d, g are not aspirated. The i after the consonants ch, c, r, sh, s, z, zh is not pronounced, it indicates that the preceding sound is lengthened.

It is often said that the Chinese language is monosyllabic. At first sight this may seem the case since, generally, each symbol is one word. However, in modern Chinese, most words are made up of two or three syllable symbols, sometimes more. Chinese generally lacks syllables, there are only 420 in Mandarin to represent all symbols in sounds. The sounds are used to differentiate – a specifically

Chinese practice which often makes it very difficult for foreigners when first learning the Chinese language. Each syllable has a specific sound. These sounds often represent different meanings. For instance, if one pronounces the syllable *mai* with a falling fourth sound *mài* it means to sell; if it is pronounced with a falling-rising third sound, *mǎi*, it means: to buy. When one reads the symbols carefully this is always clearly shown. To show this again with the simple syllable *ma*:

First sound *mā* mother
Second sound *má* hemp
Third sound *mǎ* horse
Fourth sound *mà* to complain

The Chinese language has four sounds and a fifth, 'soundless' sound: The first sound is spoken high pitched and even, the second rising, the third falling and then rising, and the fourth sound falling. The individual sounds are marked above the vowel in the syllable in the following way: First sound ¯, second sound ´, third sound ˇ, fourth sound `.

The Chinese sentence structure is simple: subject, predicate, object. The most simple way of forming a question is to add the question particle mǎ to a sentence in ordinary word sequence. It is usually not possible to note from a Chinese word whether it is a noun, adjective or another form, singular or plural. This depends on the context.

Names and Forms of Address

Chinese names usually consist of three parts, sometimes of two syllables. The first syllable is the family name, the second or the two others are personal names. For instance, in Deng Xiaoping, Deng is the family name, Xiaoping the personal name. The same is true for Fu Hao, where Fu is the family name, and Hao the personal name. While a few years ago the address "Comrade" (*tongzhi*) was common amongst Chinese people, this has changed fundamentally in recent years. Today, the Chinese equivalent for Mr – *Xiansheng* – is much more common, and for Mrs, *Furen*. A young woman can be addressed with *Xiaojie* (Miss), as well as female service personnel in hotels or restaurants. Address male colleagues with *Xiansheng* (Mr) or *Shifu* (Master).

Index

A
B
C
D
E
F
G
H
I

a

c
d
e
f
g
h
i
j
k
l

The World of Insight Guides

400 books in three complementary series cover every major destination in every continent.

Insight Guides

Alaska
Alsace
Amazon Wildlife
American Southwest
Amsterdam
Argentina
Atlanta
Athens
Australia
Austria
Bahamas
Bali
Baltic States
Bangkok
Barbados
Barcelona
Bay of Naples
Beijing
Belgium
Belize
Berlin
Bermuda
Boston
Brazil
Brittany
Brussels
Budapest
Buenos Aires
Burgundy
Burma (Myanmar)
Cairo
Calcutta
California
Canada
Caribbean
Catalonia
Channel Islands
Chicago
Chile
China
Cologne
Continental Europe
Corsica
Costa Rica
Crete
Crossing America
Cuba
Cyprus
Czech & Slovak Republics
Delhi, Jaipur, Agra
Denmark
Dresden
Dublin
Düsseldorf
East African Wildlife
East Asia
Eastern Europe
Ecuador
Edinburgh
Egypt
Finland
Florence
Florida
France
Frankfurt
French Riviera
Gambia & Senegal
Germany
Glasgow

Gran Canaria
Great Barrier Reef
Great Britain
Greece
Greek Islands
Hamburg
Hawaii
Hong Kong
Hungary
Iceland
India
India's Western Himalaya
Indian Wildlife
Indonesia
Ireland
Israel
Istanbul
Italy
Jamaica
Japan
Java
Jerusalem
Jordan
Kathmandu
Kenya
Korea
Lisbon
Loire Valley
London
Los Angeles
Madeira
Madrid
Malaysia
Mallorca & Ibiza
Malta
Marine Life in the South China Sea
Melbourne
Mexico
Mexico City
Miami
Montreal
Morocco
Moscow
Munich
Namibia
Native America
Nepal
Netherlands
New England
New Orleans
New York City
New York State
New Zealand
Nile
Normandy
Northern California
Northern Spain
Norway
Oman & the UAE
Oxford
Old South
Pacific Northwest
Pakistan
Paris
Peru
Philadelphia
Philippines
Poland
Portugal
Prague

Provence
Puerto Rico
Rajasthan
Rhine
Rio de Janeiro
Rockies
Rome
Russia
St Petersburg
San Francisco
Sardinia
Scotland
Seattle
Sicily
Singapore
South Africa
South America
South Asia
South India
South Tyrol
Southeast Asia
Southeast Asia Wildlife
Southern California
Southern Spain
Spain
Sri Lanka
Sweden
Switzerland
Sydney
Taiwan
Tenerife
Texas
Thailand
Tokyo
Trinidad & Tobago
Tunisia
Turkey
Turkish Coast
Tuscany
Umbria
US National Parks East
US National Parks West
Vancouver
Venezuela
Venice
Vienna
Vietnam
Wales
Washington DC
Waterways of Europe
Wild West
Yemen

Insight Pocket Guides

Aegean Islands★
Algarve★
Alsace
Amsterdam★
Athens★
Atlanta★
Bahamas★
Baja Peninsula★
Bali★
Bali *Bird Walks*
Bangkok★
Barbados★
Barcelona★
Bavaria★
Beijing★
Berlin★

Bermuda★
Bhutan★
Boston★
British Columbia★
Brittany★
Brussels★
Budapest & Surroundings★
Canton★
Chiang Mai★
Chicago★
Corsica★
Costa Blanca★
Costa Brava★
Costa del Sol/Marbella★
Costa Rica★
Crete★
Denmark★
Fiji★
Florence★
Florida★
Florida Keys★
French Riviera★
Gran Canaria★
Hawaii★
Hong Kong★
Hungary
Ibiza★
Ireland★
Ireland's Southwest★
Israel★
Istanbul★
Jakarta★
Jamaica★
Kathmandu *Bikes & Hikes*★
Kenya★
Kuala Lumpur★
Lisbon★
Loire Valley★
London★
Macau★
Madrid★
Malacca
Maldives
Mallorca★
Malta★
Mexico City★
Miami★
Milan★
Montreal★
Morocco★
Moscow
Munich★
Nepal★
New Delhi
New Orleans★
New York City★
New Zealand★
Northern California★
Oslo/Bergen★
Paris★
Penang★
Phuket★
Prague★
Provence★
Puerto Rico★
Quebec★
Rhodes★
Rome★
Sabah★

St Petersburg★
San Francisco★
Sardinia
Scotland★
Seville★
Seychelles★
Sicily★
Sikkim
Singapore★
Southeast England
Southern California★
Southern Spain★
Sri Lanka★
Sydney★
Tenerife★
Thailand★
Tibet★
Toronto★
Tunisia★
Turkish Coast★
Tuscany★
Venice★
Vienna★
Vietnam★
Yogyakarta★
Yucatan Peninsula★

★ = **Insight Pocket Guides**
with Pull out Maps

Insight Compact Guides

Algarve
Amsterdam
Bahamas
Bali
Bangkok
Barbados
Barcelona
Beijing
Belgium
Berlin
Brittany
Brussels
Budapest
Burgundy
Copenhagen
Costa Brava
Costa Rica
Crete
Cyprus
Czech Republic
Denmark
Dominican Republic
Dublin
Egypt
Finland
Florence
Gran Canaria
Greece
Holland
Hong Kong
Ireland
Israel
Italian Lakes
Italian Riviera
Jamaica
Jerusalem
Lisbon
Madeira
Mallorca
Malta

Milan
Moscow
Munich
Normandy
Norway
Paris
Poland
Portugal
Prague
Provence
Rhodes
Rome
St Petersburg
Salzburg
Singapore
Switzerland
Sydney
Tenerife
Thailand
Turkey
Turkish Coast
Tuscany
UK regional titles:
    Bath & Surroundings
    Cambridge & East Anglia
    Cornwall
    Cotswolds
    Devon & Exmoor
    Edinburgh
    Lake District
    London
    New Forest
    North York Moors
    Northumbria
    Oxford
    Peak District
    Scotland
    Scottish Highlands
    Shakespeare Country
    Snowdonia
    South Downs
    York
    Yorkshire Dales
USA regional titles:
    Boston
    Cape Cod
    Chicago
    Florida
    Florida Keys
    Hawaii: Maui
    Hawaii: Oahu
    Las Vegas
    Los Angeles
    Martha's Vineyard & Nantucket
    New York
    San Francisco
    Washington D.C.
    Venice
    Vienna
    West of Ireland